FOUNDERS OF THOUGHT

R. M. Hare is White's Professor of Moral
Philosophy Emeritus at Oxford University,
and Research Professor at the University of
Florida. His other books include *The
Language of Morals, Freedom and Reason*, and
Moral Thinking, all published by Oxford
University Press.

Jonathan Barnes is Professor of Ancient
Philosophy and a Fellow of Balliol College,
Oxford. He has published extensively on
topics of Ancient Philosophy. His most
recent book is *The Toils of Scepticism*.

Henry Chadwick is Master of Peterhouse,
and Regius Professor Emeritus of Divinity
at the University of Cambridge. Among his
other books are *Early Christian Thought and
the Classical Tradition*, and *Boethius: The
Consolations of Music, Logic, Theology, and
Philosophy* (both published by OUP in
paperback). He, with his brother Owen, is
General Editor of the Oxford History of the
Christian Church.

Founders of Thought

Plato
R. M. Hare

Aristotle
Jonathan Barnes

Augustine
Henry Chadwick

Oxford   New York
OXFORD UNIVERSITY PRESS
1991

Oxford University Press, Walton Street, Oxford OX2 6DP

Oxford New York Toronto
Delhi Bombay Calcutta Madras Karachi
Petaling Jaya Singapore Hong Kong Tokyo
Nairobi Dar es Salaam Cape Town
Melbourne Auckland

and associated companies in
Berlin Ibadan

Oxford is a trade mark of Oxford University Press

British Library Cataloguing in Publication Data
Data available
ISBN 0–19–287684–8

Library of Congress Cataloging in Publication Data
Founders of thought.
p. cm.
Includes bibliographical references and index.
Contents: Plato / R. M. Hare—Aristotle / Jonathan Barnes—
Augustine / Henry Chadwick.
1. Plato. 2. Aristotle. 3. Augustine, Saint, Bishop of Hippo.
I. Hare, R. M. (Richard Mervyn). Plato. 1991. II.Barnes,
Jonathan. Aristotle. 1991. III. Chadwick,Henry, 1920–
Augustine. 1991.
B395.F72 1991 180—dc20 91–11869
ISBN 0–19–287684–8

Typeset by Cambridge Composing (UK) Ltd
Printed in Great Britain by
Biddles Ltd.
Guildford and Kings Lynn

Foreword

Plato, Aristotle, and Augustine were the three most influential thinkers of classical antiquity. Between them, they shaped the whole character of subsequent Western philosophy, science, and religion. Their writings were so prolific, their intellectual power so immense and their range of preoccupations so wide that it was impossible for subsequent generations not to be dwarfed by their heroic stature, just as it is impossible for us today.

Plato has a greater claim than anyone else to be regarded as the founder of philosophy as we know it. His dialogues remain the starting-point for the study of logic, metaphysics, morals, and politics. With his master Socrates, he believed it important to distinguish knowledge from mere opinion; and he held that true knowledge would enable men to live well, for morality could be objective. He also believed that the soul was distinct from the body, and that there was a world of Ideas separate from things in this world. His thought has a mystical dimension, but it also relates to highly practical issues in education and politics of a kind which continue to trouble us.

Aristotle was both philosopher and scientist. He was a polymath who provided organizing categories for the whole of human knowledge. He founded biology, reshaped logic and metaphysics, and determined the subsequent character of thinking about ethics, politics, psychology, and literary criticism. In the Middle Ages his status was such that he was known simply as '*the* philosopher'; for Dante he was 'the master of those who know'.

Augustine effected a synthesis between classical philosophy and Christianity. He did more than anyone to shape the way in which the West would subsequently think about the nature of man and God. He wrote one of the world's greatest autobiographies, and his thought was characterized by exceptional psychological penetration. His reflections upon original sin contributed to an enduring strain of Christian pessimism.

Since they wrote, there has never been a time when the ideas of these three men were of no influence or importance. But each of them has had periods of especial intellectual dominance. Plato's greatest influence was upon the Neoplatonists of late antiquity (including Augustine) and of the Italian Renaissance, the Cambridge Platonists of the seventeenth century and the Romantics, whether philosophers like Hegel, or poets like Blake and Shelley. Aristotle was rediscovered in the twelfth and thirteenth centuries, and his thought dominated intellectual life thereafter until dethroned by the scientific revolution of the seventeenth century. His *Ethics*, *Politics*, and *Poetics* remained deeply influential long after that. Augustine shaped the character of early medieval theology and was invoked again by both sides in the era of the Reformation. His later admirers ranged from Pascal to Wittgenstein. Today no Christian theologian can ignore him, any more than a philosopher can avoid engaging with the thought of Plato and Aristotle.

Of the three, Plato was perhaps the most poetic and imaginative, Aristotle the most orderly and sensible, Augustine the most acutely aware of the limitations of the flesh. But it would be absurd to attempt to label thinkers whose work was so vast and so complex. What can be said is that they were united in seeking to elevate the life of the mind above the other pleasures of the world. Whether in Plato's search for moral excellence or Aristotle's overwhelming desire for knowledge or Augustine's lacerating asceticism, they impress posterity not just by their mental genius but also by their undeviating moral and intellectual seriousness.

The three self-contained studies which make up this volume were originally written for the Past Masters series, which sets out to expound the ideas of notable thinkers of the past in a lucid, accessible, and authoritative manner. Jonathan Barnes and Henry Chadwick bring outstanding scholarly authority to their discussions of Aristotle and Augustine, while R. M. Hare's account of Plato has the special interest of being the work of one who is himself a distinguished moral philosopher. By reprinting their books together, Oxford University Press has provided an indispensable introduction to the work of three thinkers whose arguments and insights continue to engage the liveliest minds of our time.

Corpus Christi College,   KEITH THOMAS
Oxford.   *General Editor*
                                                 Past Masters

Contents

PLATO

R. M. HARE

Preface

This book is not intended as an addition to the already enormous and growing literature of Platonic scholarship, but as an encouragement and help to ordinary people who wish to make Plato's acquaintance. For this reason I have on the whole concentrated on the easier, which means the earlier and middle, dialogues, though the later ones are not entirely neglected. It is safe to say that no single statement can be made in interpretation of Plato which some scholars will not dispute. I have tried to bring out what I think he is up to, in a way that will be comprehensible; but the limits of a popular book do not allow me to defend my views beyond giving a few references to the text. I do not think that they are all that unorthodox, and where there is a lot of dispute I have tried not to conceal it. Above all, I have aimed to show how relevant Plato's dialogues are to questions which trouble us, or should trouble us, today, including some very practical issues about education and politics. To bring this out I have occasionally mentioned the names of thinkers of the modern period; but nothing of importance in my account of Plato will be missed by a reader to whom these names mean nothing.

In concentrating on what I think is the nucleus of Plato's philosophy, I have had to neglect many interesting and important topics. I should have liked in particular to say more on his views about love and about the arts. I have not thought it necessary to dwell on the superb quality of his dialogues as literature and drama; they are still as fresh and delightful as ever, and need no salesman.

A number of colleagues have been kind enough at my request to look at and criticize my typescript, among them Sir Kenneth Dover, Professors Ackrill and Moravcsik, Jonathan Barnes, Russell Meiggs, Christopher Taylor and Julius Tomin. Although all of these know incomparably more about Plato than I do, I have been stubborn enough not always to agree with them; but all the same my debt to them is very great. I should never have undertaken, let alone completed, this book if I had not been privileged to spend the whole of 1980 at the Center of Advanced Study in the Behavioral Sciences at Stanford, where I was made so happy and free from worries that this and another larger book flowed from my typewriter without any of the usual interruptions and frustrations. I am enormously grateful to the Director and staff at the Center, and to Oxford University for letting me go there.

To avoid footnotes, the few references have been consigned to the end of the book, except for those to Plato, which are in brackets in the text, giving the pages of Stephanus' edition as used in the margin of nearly all modern editions and translations. References in brackets preceded by 'p.' are to pages in this book. In the very few Greek words I had to quote, and in proper names in the Index, I have indicated the quantity of vowels by putting a bar over all the long ones, and have used a system of transliteration which relates the Greek words closely to modern English words derived from them (for example, *psȳchē*').

R. M. HARE

Contents

1 *Life and times*

Although this is not a work of biography, it is necessary to say something about the environment in which Plato grew up; for without some grasp of this, we cannot understand how he became a philsopher, and became the kind of philosopher that he was. Of the biographical information that has survived much is unreliable, and very little is of relevance to his philosophical development. There are some letters ascribed to him, some of them explicitly autobiographical. Their genuineness is disputed; but even if spurious they are probably close enough in time to their subject to be of use as evidence. The anecdotes of later writers are mostly either doubtful or trivial or both. So we do not need to go into the question of whether, for example, having been named by his parents Aristocles, he got called Platon because of his broad shoulders or his broad forehead, and other such details. But we do know about at least three episodes in his life which must have made a profound impression on him, and which place him in his historical setting.

Plato was born in 427 BC into an upper class Athenian family, and lived to be eighty. He would have been old enough to witness with young and impressionable eyes the last scenes of a tragedy, the decline and fall of the Athenian Empire. And he lived long enough to see the first beginnings of an empire of a very different sort, that of Philip of Macedon, whose son Alexander conquered a large part of the known world. The intervening period was one of constant and inconclusive warfare between the little Greek city states, with first one and then another achieving a brief hegemony, but none managing to bring any unity to Greece. That was left to the Macedonians after Plato's day.

The Athenian Empire started with a moral basis as a league to secure the freedom of the Greek cities, after their wonderful victories which had delivered them from the threat of conquest by Persia at the beginning of the fifth century. Thucydides, whose history of the period should be read by anybody who wants to understand Plato, puts into the mouth of Pericles, the chief architect of the Empire, a speech in honour of the Athenians who had died in the war with Sparta; and it has become famous as an expression of the ideals which excited Athens in the generation before Plato. Plato parodies this speech in his *Menexenus*. The ideals are high, but not exclusively moral according to our way of thinking. Naked imperialism plays a large part in them, and Pericles is more concerned with the fine figure that Athens is cutting than with justice to the allies whom she was turning into subjects. She ruled them in an ever more grasping and tyrannical fashion, and used their tribute to build the temples on the Acropolis which still amaze us, as well as for the navy which was the basis of her power. Recalcitrant cities were punished with increasing severity as the fear of successful rebellion began to bite: Mytilene was threatened with massacre but reprieved at the eleventh hour; Melos actually suffered total extinction.

Reading dialogues like the *Gorgias* with the history of the Athenian Empire in mind, we can see that Plato was reacting with moral revulsion to an attitude of mind current in Greece at the national as well as the personal level: an attitude which valued honour and glory above the virtues which enable people to 'dwell together in unity'. Of the founders of the Empire he says 'Not moderation and uprightness, but harbours, and dockyards, and walls, and tribute-money, and such nonsense, were what they filled the city with' (519a).

For nearly all the last third of the fifth century, until her defeat in 405 BC, Athens was almost constantly at war with Sparta, which with her allies resisted and in the end brought down the Athenian power. Plato was old enough to have fought in the last part of the war, as all citizens were required to, but we have no reliable record of his military service. A man of his class would naturally have served in the cavalry; and his brothers are said in the *Republic* to have fought well (368a).

The mention of Plato's social position may remind us that there was another dimension to the struggles of the Greek cities during this and the next century. The warfare was not merely between but within the cities. Almost every city was divided politically between the upper class and the rest of the free citizens (the numerous slaves can be left out of this political reckoning). This must not be taken as implying that there were no well-born democrats; indeed patrician Whigs like Pericles played the greatest part in the development of the democracy, and while it prospered, the imperial ideal enjoyed general support from all classes. But increasingly these well-born leaders gave place to self-made men of the people and their sons, who could make themselves congenial to the mass meeting which was their parliament. Plato's class looked on these demagogues with contempt, tinged with fear. The political feelings amid which he would have grown up are those expressed at the beginning of a political pamphlet of the day, the so-called *Polity of the Athenians*: 'The kind of polity the Athenians have chosen is one I do not commend; for by choosing it they have chosen that bad men should come off better than good men.'

Sparta, Athens' enemy, was from inclination and self-interest a supporter of aristocracy or oligarchy; the populist Athenian leaders were always the most violent advocates of the war against her, and the rich, whose wealth and way of life were at risk, showed less enthusiasm for it, as for the Empire. The ambitions that turned young upper-class Englishmen and other Europeans into imperialists in the nineteenth century were indeed there but the prospects were far less attractive; and so, contrary to our way of thinking, it was the poor who were the main beneficiaries and supporters of empire. In most cities the democrats favoured alliance with, or submission to, Athens, and the 'few' sought the support of Sparta.

As the war went on, the internal divisions in the cities became more bitter and more savage; and even after the defeat of Athens the same sort of thing went on throughout the fourth century. Unrestrained personal ambition was a main motive in politicians. In the *Meno* that not untypical young man, asked by Socrates to define 'virtue' or 'excellence', answers that the excellence of a *man* is to be able, while engaging in politics, to do good to one's friends and harm to one's enemies, while taking care not to come to any harm oneself (71e). And in the *Gorgias* another young man holds out as an object of envy Archelaus of Macedon, who by a series of murders of his nearest relatives made himself king (471b).

Athens herself was relatively free of the political murders and massacres which happened elsewhere in Greece; but all the same, if we were to read of events in fifth- and fourth-century Greece in a modern newspaper, we should be glad we did not live there, especially if we had not heard about its cultural achievements—did not know, for example, that the Parthenon was built during this time, or that year by year some of the world's greatest poets and dramatists were bringing out their plays in the festivals. We may note in passing that two moderately sanguinary political leaders, Critias, Plato's cousin, and Dionysius I of Syracuse (both of whom will feature in our story shortly), wrote tragedies which were performed in the Athenian competitions.

Of these two evils in Greece, strife between and strife within cities, Plato says little by way of a remedy for the former (on which his literary rival Isocrates has a better record), and in the *Laws* and elsewhere treats the latter as the principal problem needing solution (628a, b). He thought that civil strife could be ended by a good system of government, and to describe and justify such a system was one of his main aims.

Another more general cause contributed to the moral unsettlement of the Greek cities. This was their increasing intellectual sophistication, the effect, perhaps, of widening cultural horizons. There is a story told in Herodotus' history of the Persian Wars: a Persian ruler confronted some Greeks, who by custom burnt their dead relations, with some Indians, whose practice was to eat them, and concluded from the shocked reactions of both to the others' ways that

> Custom, the king of all,
> Gods and men alike,
> Is their guide.

Plato quotes the same lines of Pindar in the *Gorgias* (484b); they go on

> It justifies the greatest violence;
> Its hand is over all.

The word translated 'custom' also meant 'law'. We can see how the idea got around that law and morality were alike based on mere convention. There was not even a stable religious backing for them. Plato points out in the *Euthyphro* that the gods themselves are, according to tradition, at variance with one another; in heaven as on earth moral differences lead to civil war (7e).

Protagoras, who with Socrates was one of the great thinkers of the preceding generation, articulated this relativism in his doctrine that 'A man is a measure of all things: of what is, that it is, and of what is not, that it is not.' As Plato implies in the *Theaetetus* (152a), where he discusses the doctrine, Protagoras meant 'each man for himself'. We shall come back later to Socrates' and Plato's attempted rebuttal of this relativist view; but it is easy to see how the old moral restraints slipped away, especially in politics.

These factors—unscrupulous political strife and the growth of moral relativism—reinforced each other. Thucydides, in a philosophically penetrating passage, points out that it affected even the language in which thinking had to be done. In his discussion of the effects of political violence he says 'In justifying their actions, they reversed the customary descriptive meanings of words.' He gives examples: what would have been called 'an irresponsible gamble' got to be called 'a brave and comradely venture'. This process, referred to in similar terms in the *Republic* (560d), is the same as that which in recent times has been called 'persuasive definition'. Its immediate result was to turn morality upside down; but indirectly it had the effect of stimulating Socrates and Plato to look instead for a way of finding *secure* definitions of moral words or of the things they connote. That is why we find them asking 'What then *is* courage?'; 'What *is* uprightness?', and in general 'What *is* goodness?'

It is easy to imagine the young Plato, under the influence of Socrates, being inspired by the hope of answering such questions; but in other respects he grew up in an atmosphere of disillusion culminating in disaster. Its effect on him will have been heightened by his upper-class upbringing. As we have seen, the Athenian aristocrats were by no means wholehearted supporters of the Empire; most of them admired Sparta for its orderly and stable system of government, on which Plato's political ideas are in part modelled; and there was at least a suspicion that treachery by members of this class had contributed to the final naval disaster for Athens at Aegospotami.

At any rate when Sparta came to settle the affairs of defeated Athens, although she did not, as some had expected, massacre the democrats, she secured her own interest by installing an oligarchic government, called by its enemies 'The Thirty Tyrants', among whom were two relatives of Plato's: Critias, his mother's first cousin, and Charmides, his maternal uncle. Both receive friendly treatment in his dialogues. The Thirty were indeed tyrannical and arbitrary: Plato records, in the *Apology* (32c), Socrates' courageous refusal to arrest a fellow-citizen, the democrat Leon, whom they had selected for judicial murder. Their government did not last long; it was ousted by a democratic regime, whose record was more moderate. Athens had lost her former glory; she did not, however, sink into complete ignominy, but took her share in the ups and downs of Greek mini-power politics.

We may conceive what effect these events—the collapse of a no longer inspiring imperialist democracy followed by the wretched performance of the opposing party—had on the young Plato. An able man of his class would naturally have sought a place in public life, and there is evidence that he started with this ambition; but since the chief qualification for success in politics was a total lack of scruple, it is not surprising that he was frightened off. He is said to have written poetry when young, and from the evidence of his writings (including a few poems) he would have made a good poet; but he came to see that there was another more lasting way of affecting men's minds, and thus, he hoped, the course of events. Socrates is expressing Plato's own attitude to politics when he says in the *Republic*, 'It would be like a man among wild animals, not willing to join in their crimes, nor able by himself to resist the savagery of all the rest; before he could help the city or his friends he would come to a sticky end without doing any good for himself or anybody else' (496d).

In 399 BC, after the restoration of the democracy, Socrates, Plato's idol, was tried on a charge of disbelief in the gods and corrupting the young, and condemned to death. The effect on Plato was profound and several of his dialogues are related to this event: Socrates' *Apology* or defence at his trial; the *Crito* in which he gives reasons for not making his escape after his condemnation, which would have been easy; and the *Phaedo*, in which he spends his last hours arguing for the immortality of the soul; and there are a number of smaller allusions. Plato seems to have resolved to devote his life to the exposition and development of Socrates' ideas.

Plato's distaste for political action can only have been strengthened by the outcome of his only active intervention in politics. This occurred not in his own city of Athens but at Syracuse in Sicily, at the court of Dionysius I, and of his son and namesake. We do not know why Plato first went to Sicily, when he was about forty; but it may have been as an offshoot of a purely philosophical visit to the neighbouring Italian cities, which boasted some distinguished philosophers, especially the followers of Pythagoras. When he was in Syracuse he formed a deep personal affection for the young Dion, whose sister was married to Dionysius I, and who himself married his own niece, her daughter. Plato later wrote a poem on Dion in which he called the relation 'love', and said that it had driven him out of his mind. According to Greek ideas there was nothing unusual about this, and the second remark seems no great exaggeration if we think of the things that Dion later persuaded Plato to do, against his own better judgement.

Dion became Plato's pupil and absorbed his doctrine. We do not know how long Plato's first visit to Sicily lasted. There is an improbable story that Dionysius caused him to be sold into slavery, whence he was ransomed by friends. He returned to Athens, and there founded a philosophical school called, from its location in the grove dedicated to the hero Academus, the Academy. In it Plato and his fellow-philosophers shared a common table and engaged in mathematics, dialectic (that is, philosophy) and other studies, all seen as relevant to the training of statesmen. It was not the first such institution, but was probably modelled on similar communities of the Pythagoreans in Italy. Aristotle was only one of its distinguished members, and it lasted for centuries.

When Plato was about sixty, Dionysius I died and was succeeded by his son Dionysius II, whose uncle Dion conceived the idea that the young ruler might be moulded by Plato into the philosopher-king of the *Republic*. This was an unpromising scheme from the beginning, and it is likely that Plato accepted the invitation to Syracus with reluctance and few hopes. But it was hard for him to resist the challenge, in view of what he had said in the *Republic* about such a philosopher-ruler being the only chance of rescuing the human race from its ills (473d). The young Dionysius was clever, but impatient of systematic instruction, and he no doubt had much else to engage his attention. Dion lost favour and was exiled, and Plato soon asked and received permission to return to Athens, where Dion joined him at the Academy. But Dionysius was still friendly to Plato, and there was an understanding that he and Dion should come back when the climate was more propitious.

Four years later Dionysius asked Plato to return, saying that Dion could come back after a year. He professed a continuing zeal for philosophy, and supported this claim with testimonials from eminent philosophers. Plato was pressed from all sides, and in the end consented. But Dionysius was no more tractable; while giving himself airs as a philosopher, he kept Dion in exile and confiscated and sold his property. Plato escaped with some difficulty from Sicily, and wisely refused to lend any support to Dion's attempt to recover his position by force. This attempt was at first successful, but Dion was later assassinated by a supposed friend, a fellow-member of Plato's circle, Callippus (who was not the only student of Plato's to become guilty of the political murder of a fellow-alumnus). Plato, his views about politics amply confirmed, kept out of them and devoted himself to his Academy.

2 *Plato's forebears*

To understand Plato we have also to look at the most significant of the earlier thinkers who may have influenced his ideas. Whether we call them philosophers or not is unimportant; the word has wider and narrower senses. At most a few fragments of their works survive, and nearly all our information comes from much later sources; so the Presocratic philosophers, as they are generically called, have been a happy battleground for scholars. From these disputes little has emerged which can be confidently relied on as true; all we can do here is to pick up a few ideas, attributed to one or other of these great men, which, *if* they were current in Greece by Plato's time, *may* have contributed to his intellectual background. It is on the face of it unlikely that all the ideas we find in his dialogues were newly-minted; and in fact there is quite a lot of evidence that they were not. Originality in philosophy often consists not in having new thoughts, but in making clear what was not clear before.

The earliest natural philosophers, starting with the shadowy figure of Thales in sixth-century Miletus on the eastern shore of the Aegean Sea, made cosmology their main interest. But the fact that the Greek word '*kosmos*', from which 'cosmology' is derived, had also a moral significance ('good order') may make us suspect that their motive was not, any more than that of their successors including Plato, mere scientific curiosity. Plato in the *Phaedo* attributes to Anaxagoras, one of these, the view that 'it is Mind which imposes *order* on all things and disposes each of them as it is *best* for it to be' (97c).

We find in these early thinkers the beginning of the urge to reconcile the 'One' and the 'Many', which is a recurring theme throughout Greek philosophy, above all in Plato. There confronts us a multitude of phenomena in the world as it presents itself to our senses; cannot some unifying principle be found to bring order into this chaos? The early cosmologists sought to find it by claiming that everything in the world was formed out of (or perhaps even *really* consisted of) some single material (Thales suggested water). This kind of solution was later abandoned; but the problem remained of finding some coherent reality which underlay the baffling diversity of the world (the 'manifold' as Immanuel Kant was later to call it). Plato had his own solution to this problem, as we shall see—a solution which depended not on physics but on logic, metaphysics and ethics.

An important step in the direction which Plato afterwards took may have been made by Pythagoras, of Croton in southern Italy (he was born on the island of Samos, not far from Miletus, probably in 570 BC). Since nothing of his work remains, and the stories about him are all suspect, it is even more difficult than usual to sieve out his ideas from those of his later disciples, with whom Plato was acquainted. For our purposes this does not matter; for if an idea which we find developed in Plato could have come from a Pythagorean source, it is less important whether that source was the Master himself. The chief danger to be guarded against is that of supposing that some idea came from the Pythagorean school to Plato, when in fact it went from Plato to the later Pythagoreans.

We may notice at least three suggestions which Plato may have picked up from the Pythagoreans. The first was that of a tightly-organized community of like-minded thinkers who should not only rule their own life together in accordance with strict principles, but provide guidance (even governance) for the polity in which they lived. Plato's political proposals could be said to be a result of the combination of this Pythagorean idea with the Spartan model of orderly government and discipline.

If the stories about Pythagoras are to be believed, he actually for a time came near to making real the dream which Plato was later to dream in his *Republic*—the ideal of the philsopher-ruler. Even if true, it did not last; for Pythagoras had to rely on persuasion, neither having nor seeking the absolute and secure power which Plato demanded for his philosopher-kings. We are told that in about 500 BC, after Pythagoras had been in Croton for some thirty years and in a position of power for some twenty, there was a revolution; many of his followers were killed and he himself had to flee. But twenty years is a long period of stability by Greek standards, if not by Plato's.

The Pythagoreans may also have been the source of the idea, central to Plato's thought, that mathematics, and abstract thinking generally, including logic, can provide a secure basis, not only for philosophy in the modern sense, but also for substantial theses in science and in morals. It is not certain whether either Pythagoras or Plato distinguished clearly enough between the important truth that mathematics and other abstract reasonings are a crucial ingredient in science, and the equally important error of thinking that they can by themselves establish conclusions of substance about the physical world. Aristotle accuses both, in very similar terms, of a related mistake (involving, to put it in his way, the failure to distinguish form from matter): the Pythagoreans, he says, attempt to construct bodies having physical properties like weight out of abstract geometrical or arithmetical entities like points, lines and numbers. It is arguable that in the *Timaeus*, where Plato seeks to found cosmology purely on mathematics (especially geometry), he lays himself open to this criticism.

A simpler illustration of the mistake is to be found in the *Phaedo*, where Plato slides from the logically-established truth that life and death are incompatible to the invalid substantial conclusion that the soul, being the principle of life, cannot perish (105–6). This Pythagorean mistake may have infected Plato's arguments about morality too, which sometimes seem to be conjuring substantial rabbits out of logical hats.

Thirdly, Plato became very Pythagorean in his mystical (or in a broad sense religious) approach to the soul and its place in the material world—although that was not the only source of these views, and both Plato and Pythagoras may have been influenced by ideas from the East and by the 'mystery religions' such as Orphism which spread through Greece in this period. The early Pythagoreans seem (though this has been disputed) to have been mind-body dualists; that is to say, they thought, as Plato was to think, that the soul or mind (*psȳchē*) was an entity distinct and separable from the body. This was consonant with primitive Greek thinking about the soul, as found, for example, in the earliest Greek poet Homer.

Empedocles of Acragas in Sicily, in the early fifth century, believed in the transmigration of souls, and it is possible that he got the doctrine from Pythagoras; Plato certainly makes use of it. The Platonic teaching about the soul, that before our birth it had acquaintance with objects in an eternal realm, and thus can, through mathematics leading to dialectic (philosophy), regain knowledge of them in this life, has what in ancient times passed for a Pythagorean stamp; and so does his denigration of the body and its base desires (the 'flesh' in St Paul's sense), and his consequent asceticism.

Two great philosophers, very different both from Pythagoras and from each other, but who lived at roughly the same time, also seem to have affected Plato profoundly. They took up opposite points of view on the problem of 'The One and the Many'. The first was Heraclitus, of Ephesus quite near Miletus, with whose more extreme disciple Cratylus Plato associated during his stay in Athens. Perhaps because of Cratylus, Plato treats Heraclitus as emphasising the diversity and changeability of the Many at the expense of the One; for Plato, Heraclitus is the archetypal believer in universal flux, who thinks that the utterly unstable manifold of phenomena that our senses purvey is all there is. Whether this was actually true of Heraclitus himself we shall never know; his few surviving fragments are extremely cryptic and are used by scholars to support widely varying interpretations.

Parmenides, by contrast, who was born somewhat later at Elea in southern Italy, went to the opposite extreme, denying the reality of appearances altogether. Though things in the world *seem* to be constantly changing and in motion, they logically cannot be. Parmenides' arguments (in verse) are much less clear than the more fragmentary survivals from those of his disciples Melissus and Zeno (not to be confused with Zeno the Stoic). This much is clear, however, that the fundamental premiss of the Eleatics (the name given to this group of philosophers, derived from that of Parmenides' city) was that 'Things which are not are not.' This they regarded as a logically necessary truth, which indeed it must be if there is no equivocation upon 'are not'. Unfortunately the Eleatics seem (committing the same kind of mistake as we have just noticed when discussing Pythagoras) to have meant different things by 'are not' in the subject and predicate of their premiss, taking this logical truth to establish a substantial conclusion, namely that void or empty space cannot exist; and therefore, since any movement requires an empty space for a thing to move into, that movement (and by a related argument change of other kinds) cannot take place. Zeno invented his famous paradoxes with the aim of proving the same point, that the belief in motion and change leads to logical absurdities. So the Eleatics concluded that, in spite of appearances, the universe is really solid throughout and immobile.

The work of Parmenides and his disciples represents the first thoroughgoing attempt to establish a cosmological system on the basis of rigorous logical arguments. Some may hail it as the beginning of metaphysics, others damn it as the first outbreak of metaphysical pseudo-science divorced from the observation of nature; but there is no doubt that it had immense influence. Zeno's paradoxes are still not all solved to everybody's satisfaction; and we find Plato puzzling about the difficulties raised by the Eleatics. He does this in the *Parmenides*, *Theaetetus* and *Sophist*, although by the third of these the problems have changed into ones about the alleged impossibility of making true negative statements. He shows thereby that he understands (as perhaps the Eleatics themselves did) that their origins lie in logical rather than cosmological difficulties.

In the whole of Plato's philosophy we may think of him as trying, by a more careful examination of the arguments, to find a synthesis between the Heraclitan or Cratylan view, which he accepted, that the world of appearances is a multifarious flux, and the Parmenidean doctrine that reality is one and unchanging. He found it, as we shall see, by postulating two worlds, a world of sense, always in flux, and a unified world of Ideas, not available to our senses but only to thought, which alone are fully knowable. But the two-world view itself can plausibly be attributed to Parmenides, together with the associated distinction, so important to Plato, between knowledge (which is of reality) and mere opinion (which is concerned with appearances).

One other fifth-century cosmologist must be briefly mentioned. Anaxagoras, a natural philosopher of the old school, was born in about 500 BC at Clazomenae not far from Miletus, and lived in Athens as a member of Pericles' circle. He, like Protagoras, another friend of Pericles, and like Socrates later, got into trouble for his philosophy; Anaxagoras and Protagoras escaped with exile, as Socrates could probably have done if his principles had not been so uncompromising, and as Aristotle did later when in similar trouble. We are told in Plato's *Phaedo*, in a passage I have already quoted (97c; see p.15), that Anaxagoras attracted Socrates' attention with his doctrine that Mind (*nous*) is the cause of all physical processes, but lost it when Socrates discovered that Anaxagoras made no *use* of Mind in explaining what happens, invoking grosser physical causes instead. But all the same he may have put into Socrates' or Plato's head (it is never certain whether the Socrates of the dialogues is the real Socrates) the idea that Mind had a place in explaining how the world works. This idea is prominent in dialogues like the *Timaeus* and the *Laws*, the second at least of which was written late in Plato's life.

It will be best to leave until Chapter 7 a discussion of the thinkers, called collectively the Sophists, against whom Plato was consciously reacting in much of his moral philosophy, and who appear, often but not always in savage caricature, in his dialogues. One of them, Protagoras, has been briefly mentioned already. They belong to the generation before Plato's; that is, they were roughly Socrates' contemporaries. Of Socrates himself (obviously by far the greatest influence on Plato's thinking) I shall say little, for the reason that his philosophy is so continuous with that of Plato that scholars have found it hard to decide which views belonged to which. We have some, but not much, independent evidence about what Socrates thought, for example from Aristophanes, Xenophon, and Aristotle. However, Aristophanes' portrayal is satirical and popular, and may have had a wider target than Socrates in particular; Xenophon was no philosopher, and therefore not in a position to understand at all deeply what was troubling Socrates; and it is not always clear, when Aristotle attributes a view to Socrates, whether he means the character in the dialogues or the historical person.

My own view, which is fairly orthodox, is that we can with some confidence attribute to Socrates a concern with the difference between opinion which merely happens to be correct and knowledge; with the search for secure definitions to turn the former into the latter; with a certain method of testing such definitions called *elenchos* or scrutiny; with the application of this method to practical decisions about how to live; with the question of whether goodness or excellence of character can be taught, and if so by what educative process; and with the possibility that excellence of character and knowledge of the truth about what was good were somehow inseparable, so that, if one could impart the knowledge, nobody who had it would willingly live badly. To all these doctrines we shall be returning.

On the other hand, I think that it is safer to attribute to Plato himself than to Socrates the cautious approach to moral education we find in the *Republic*, which insists on a thorough indoctrination in right opinions before a select few are introduced to philosophy and put on the path to knowledge; and his later doctrine about the soul, with its three parts and its communion with a world of Ideas separate from things in this world—a communion enjoyed in a former life, and, for those able to undertake philosophic study, in this. This last group of doctrines may well be based on Pythagorean ideas.

The extremely deep and difficult investigations of metaphysical and logical questions which occupy many of the later dialogues are fairly obviously the result of Plato's own perplexities; Socrates and the others who influenced him got him into these, and to some degree he got himself out of them. But their solution did not become clear before the work of Aristotle, if then; though there can be no doubt that the discussions in the Academy, in which he took part, and some of which are reflected in Plato's later dialogues, helped Aristotle on his way. But between the Socratic/early-Platonic caterpillar and the Aristotelian butterfly there intervenes a pupal stage; just what is going on behind the opaque surface of the chrysalis represented by these dialogues, and how much of the development was due to Plato, how much to Aristotle, scholars have not yet succeeded in determining, and probably never will.

3 *How Plato became a philosopher*

When we find somebody (whether it was Plato or Socrates) troubled by certain important questions for the first time in history, it is worth asking, 'Why *then*?' We have sketched Plato's situation in history and in the history of ideas; but we have so far only hinted at reasons why he, or anybody else, should have asked just the questions he did ask. But this is not hard to understand, especially to us, whose circumstances make the same questions tormenting. Although it may seem to us that the scale and pace of change today are greater than for Plato's contemporaries, they were, subjectively speaking, just as unsettled by it.

Suppose then that we ask what led Plato to put into the mouth of Meno, at the beginning of the dialogue named after him, the question 'Can you tell me, Socrates, whether goodness (virtue, excellence) is a thing that is taught; or is it neither taught nor learnt by practice, but comes to men by nature, or in some other way?' This is the question (also raised earlier in the *Protagoras*) which the whole of Plato's moral philosophy, and thus, indirectly, his other philosophy, is attempting to answer. Although Plato certainly had the philosophical temperament, and could get interested in philosophical questions purely for their own sake, moral phlosophy was what set him going, and it started as the philosophy of education.

It is clear from the rest of the *Meno* (perhaps the best dialogue for someone to read first if he wants to understand what made Plato into a philosopher) why Plato asked this question. A lot is made, as in several other dialogues, of the hit-or-miss quality of Athenian moral education: here were admirable citizens like Pericles, who wanted to do the best for their children, and taught them riding and wrestling and music, all very successfully; but to make them into good men was another matter. Somehow there did not seem to be any way of doing it that offered more than a fifty-fifty chance of success. Could there be a way? How familiar this all sounds!

As we have seen, life in the Greek cities, and especially the political life which engaged so much of their energies, was a pretty dirty game, and becoming more so. It was natural to find one of the causes of these evils in a failure of moral education: in particular, in the emergence of people into public life who were seeking their own good rather than that of the city. The mainspring of Socrates', and through him of Plato's, philosophical endeavours was the desire to diagnose the trouble and find a remedy.

The remedy that they were to propose comes out very clearly in the *Meno*. Right at the beginning, Socrates says that he cannot answer Meno's question, whether goodness (or excellence) can be taught, before he knows what it *is*. His point, brought out later, and already made in an earlier dialogue, the *Laches* (190b), is that one is bound to fumble in teaching anything unless one knows what one is trying to teach. But does anybody know this? If somebody had this knowledge, and so was able to teach men to be good men in the kind of way that riding-instructors teach them to be good horsemen or flute-teachers teach them to be good flautists, then by putting him in charge of the education of the young we should ensure a supply of good men in public life, instead of the present inferior crop.

But here Plato makes a very important distinction. It is possible to be a good man, in a manner of speaking, without *knowing* what it is to be a good man. For practical purposes, a man may lead an exemplary life on the basis of what Plato calls 'right opinion' or 'true belief'. This will lead him to do all the right things and give excellent advice to others. But this condition of unreasoned right living is an unstable one. Someone may start with all the best opinions and habits, and then something may happen to upset these (for example, his encountering new ideas propagated by some charismatic intellectual figure).

This, indeed, is exactly why the Athenians sent Socrates to his death: for 'corrupting the young'. They took him as a paradigm of the kind of 'sophist' (as these new intellectual gurus were called) who was leading the young astray. In this witch-hunt they were egged on by Aristophanes, who in his comedy *The Clouds* portrays Socrates as a sophist, turning the young away from their old good habits and putting all kinds of strange new ideas into their heads which undermined their morality; and the play ends with a powerful incitement of his audience to violence. But perhaps Socrates' attackers had got hold of the wrong man. If Plato was right, it was Socrates who was pointing the way to a solution of the problem.

In Plato's reconstruction of Socrates' defence at his trial, he makes him, after he has dismissed Aristophanes' caricature as mixing him up with teachers of a quite different stamp, go on later to narrate a story about himself. The Delphic oracle (a highly respected and authoritative source of religious doctrine and political advice) had said of him that he was the wisest man in Greece. In his efforts to discover what could be meant by this, he had engaged in many conversations with people who were reputed to know about all kinds of things, but who revealed, through their failure to give a satisfactory account of what they claimed to know, that they did not have *knowledge* at all. We may take some of the early dialogues as Plato's versions of encounters of this kind. Socrates concluded that the reason why the oracle called him the wisest man was that he alone knew that he did not know; the others thought they knew but did not.

Near the end of the *Meno* Socrates makes a related point, that although there are few things that he knows, one of these is that there is a difference between knowledge and right opinion (98b). The difference, he says, is that knowledge of anything is 'tied down' by the ability to give a reason for what we know, and this makes it, unlike right opinion, something abiding which will not run away. This demand for a 'reckoning of the reason' or 'account of the explanation' or 'definition of the cause' or 'explicit answer to the question "Why?"' (no one translation is adequate) is Socrates' and Plato's most central and seminal idea.

If we combine this with the point made already, that it is knowledge of what goodness is that enables us to teach it, we can already see the outlines of the proposal which Plato thought he got from Socrates. What we have to do is to find a way of knowing, as opposed to merely having opinions about, what things are, and above all what goodness is. We shall then be able, if we are allowed to, to pass on a stable kind of goodness to future generations. This is the programme of the *Republic*, and there are clear anticipations of it at the very end of the *Meno*.

Let us look more closely at the elements in this programme, in order to understand the task which Plato had set himself, and some of its problems. First of all, there is the idea that the teaching of goodness is somehow like the teaching of riding or flute-playing, which means that goodness itself is some kind of attainment like these. But is it? We use the same word 'good' for a good flautist as for a good man. Does it mean the same in both cases? To answer either 'Yes' or 'No' to this question can be highly misleading, because 'mean the same' is ambiguous. But at any rate Socrates and Plato were irresistibly attracted by the analogy between virtue or good living, and the arts and skills.

Plato, at any rate, saw quite soon that there were difficulties in this assimilation. In the early dialogue called the *Lesser Hippias*, a paradoxical analogy is presented between bad living and, for example, bad wrestling (374a). The wrestler who falls intentionally is a better wrestler than the one who falls because he cannot remain upright; by analogy one should argue that the man who says an untruth intentionally is a better man than one who does it unintentionally. The general point is that, if good living is a skill, then one shows one has it by one's ability to live rightly *if one wants to*. But most of us think that goodness consists in living rightly whether one wants to or not. In the Socratic manner, the paradox is just thrown at us, not resolved; but it clearly needs unravelling.

A related difficulty is presented in the first book of the *Republic* (332–3). If good living is a skill or art, what is it the skill to do? There seems no way of specifying the skill as 'the skill to do x' without making it also the skill to do the opposite of x. Another difficulty is this: if one has skill in or knowledge of wrestling, then one is a good wrestler. But is knowledge of goodness (that which, as Plato thought, would enable one to teach it) *sufficient* to make one a good man? As it has been put, is knowledge sufficient for virtue? Socrates seems to have thought so; but few people have believed him.

Another problem Plato had to face was that of what it is to know something, a problem closely bound up with the question of what the something is that we know. His Theory of Ideas (which claims that what we know has to be an eternally existing object) is Plato's answer to this question. And along with investigations into the status of the things known, Plato had to face problems about the person who is doing the knowing and about his relation to these things. His account of the soul or mind was to become the framework which held together his entire philosophy. The division of the mind into 'faculties' or 'powers' or even 'parts' enabled him to assign different kinds of mental activity to these different parts and thus, he thought, distinguish them more clearly. The mind was important to him for another reason too: as we have seen, he followed the Pythagoreans in regarding it as a separate entity from the body— an entity which could exist apart and independently. This enabled him, he thought, to solve the problem of how we can obtain knowledge about questions (in mathematics, for example) whose answers cannot be obtained by sense-perception (what later came to be called *a priori* knowledge). His solution was that the mind obtained knowledge of the eternal Ideas before it entered into the body at birth, and only had to recollect it in this life. It also enabled him to claim that after death we are exposed to the rewards and punishments so graphically described in the 'eschatological myths' at the end of several of his dialogues.

If these problems about knowing, the things known, and the knower could be solved, Plato thought that practical philosophy, which was his predominant concern and his incentive for undertaking all the rest of his inquiries, could be put on a secure basis. If it can be established that there are things which we can know for sure, and that the chief among these is the Good, then the gaining and imparting of this knowledge will be the means whereby we can not only lead good lives ourselves, but by education enable others to do the same. There remains the problem of setting up a political framework in which this education can take place; and to this problem Plato devoted his two longest dialogues, the *Republic*, written in middle life and before his disillusion in Sicily, and the *Laws*, written as an old man, as well as great parts of others. His view was that it could be done only by giving absolute power, not only over the educative process but also over the entire machinery of government, to those who had the knowledge.

It may be helpful at this point to give the reader an overview of the scope of Plato's dialogues. Though in the case of various dialogues there is dispute about their relative dating, or even in some cases about whether Plato himself or some disciple wrote them, there is fairly general agreement that they can be divided chronologically into groups having distinctive features. First comes a group of characteristically 'Socratic' dialogues. There are the *Apology* and the *Crito*, already mentioned, and then a group of short dialogues in which Socrates sets up puzzles, especially about particular virtues or good qualities and the relation of these to each other and to knowledge. The puzzles are not resolved in these dialogues; often they are taken up later by Plato, and many are discussed in greater depth by Aristotle.

Puzzle (*aporiā*) or paradox was a recognized method of philosophic inquiry from Zeno onwards, and still is; it can be used either, as by Zeno, to refute a theory by showing that it has unacceptable consequences, or, as most commonly by Socrates, and in modern times by Lewis Carroll, simply to set us thinking about a problem by showing to what apparently absurd results the apparently logical implications of commonly accepted notions or ways of speaking can lead. We may suppose that this method continued in use in Plato's Academy, and that many even of the later dialogues reflect it (though in them Plato is not so chary of positive conclusions); no doubt the puzzles were discussed *ad nauseam* among his students. Aristotle, a participant, produces elegant solutions of some of them. Concentrated examples of such a technique occur in the *Euthydemus*, whose combination of sophistication and *naïveté* has made it hard to date with confidence.

In this first group we may include, besides the dialogues just mentioned, the *Euthyphro*, *Laches*, *Lysis*, *Charmides*, *Theages*, *Greater* and *Lesser Hippias*, *Ion* and *Greater Alcibiades*.

Second in chronological order comes a group of longer dialogues, probably spanning the period of Plato's life immediately before and after his first visit to Sicily. This contains the *Protagoras*, *Meno*, *Gorgias*, *Phaedo*, *Symposium*, and *Phaedrus*, as well as that oddity the *Menexenus* (see p. 8). This was perhaps the most crucial phase in Plato's development; the Socratic puzzles about the virtues are discussed more deeply and connectedly; important positive and substantive doctrines are introduced concerning morality, education and politics; there are two marvellous disquisitions on love; and the 'Theory of Ideas', to be discussed in Chapter 5, makes a gradual appearance, with its insistence that to the moral and other qualities there correspond eternally existing entities, available to inspection by an instructed mind, which either are the models of such qualities, or give them to things by being present in them, or both.

Along with this development comes a strong dose of Pythagoreanism (plausibly connected by scholars with the visit to Italy and Sicily). Plato propounds the view that our souls are immortal and had access to these Ideas in a previous existence.

The *Republic* was probably also written during this time. Since its composition may have taken many years, it is unprofitable to speculate on its dating in relation to this second group (especially the *Phaedrus*). Many scholars think that its first book, which has the characteristics of the earliest group, started life as a separate piece, and that the rest was written much later. The topic of the whole dialogue is 'uprightness' or 'right living', and whether it is to be recommended as good policy for those seeking happiness; this leads Plato into large-scale proposals on how society should be organised (see Chapter 9). It also contains the first full-dress exposition of his views about the nature of knowledge and about philosophical method.

There is no agreement about the date of the *Cratylus*, devoted to the philosophy of language; but it is plausible to put it somewhere in this middle period. The rest of the dialogues, up to Plato's last work the *Laws*, show a trend away from the use of Socrates even as a mouthpiece for Plato's views; often he gets altogether displaced from the discussions, though in the *Philebus*, contrary to this trend, he again plays the chief role. In the *Parmenides* Socrates when young encounters the distinguished Eleatic philosopher of the preceding generation and his disciple Zeno, and, defending in a rather naïve way the Platonic Theory of Ideas, receives something of a trouncing; but he comes back with some telling criticisms of Parmenides' own system. It is natural to take this dialogue as an introduction to the series which includes the *Theaetetus*, *Sophist* and *Politicus* (or *Statesman*). In these, difficulties in the earlier Socratic or Platonic doctrines are penetratingly discussed, and an attempt is made to come to terms with the views of Protagoras, Heraclitus and above all the Eleatics. This leads Plato into very deep waters, into which we shall not be able in this little book to follow him. Plato's chosen philosophical method, called 'dialectic', is further developed, and new moves in it called 'collection' and 'division' (see p. 49) are explained and illustrated at length. The *Politicus'* main object is to expand on Plato's political theory, and it forms a kind of bridge between the *Republic* and the *Laws*.

Scholars disagree on the extent to which Plato modified, or even abandoned, his Theory of Ideas as a result of the criticisms voiced in the *Parmenides* (see p. 39). It is perhaps safest to say that he did not abandon it, but sought to preserve it by more careful exposition and restatement in other words, as he did in the case of the Socratic doctrine about the relation of knowledge to virtue. One of the bones of contention is whether the *Timaeus*, in which the Theory features in something like its earlier form, was written near the end of Plato's life, as used to be generally thought, or whether it belongs to the middle period. There are also passages in the *Politicus* (285d, e) and the *Philebus* (61d, e) which are at any rate couched in the language of the Theory.

The *Timaeus* is a work on cosmology, which has appended to it the *Critias*, an unfinished fragment about the lost island of Atlantis, the conquest of which by an earlier Athenian state governed in Plato's ideal manner was to have been the main subject of the dialogue. The town planning and administrative arrangements of Atlantis are described in engaging detail. The *Philebus*, almost certainly a late dialogue, returns to the subject of the rival merits of pleasure and thought as ingredients in the good life, and in the course of the discussion further pursues the exposition of the dialectical method and the problem of the One and the Many. Lastly the *Laws*, Plato's longest work and probably unrevised, expounds in detail his legislative proposals for his ideal state, somewhat modified from the *Republic*, in the direction (anticipated in the *Politicus*) of greater practicability.

4 *Understanding Plato*

After this necessarily brief survey of Plato's development, we are in a position to look at some of his ideas more closely. But first a warning is necessary. Anybody who takes up one of the early dialogues will have the impression that Plato is a very clear writer; and he certainly writes in a delightfully readable style. That, indeed, is one of the reasons why so many still read him. So the difficulty of really understanding him may not at first be apparent. The trouble is not so much that he writes entirely in dialogue form, so that he might not himself be meaning to endorse the views put into the mouth of one of his characters. Dialogues can be very clear; there is no difficulty, for example, in knowing what is going on in Berkeley's or Hume's. Nor is it that Socrates, the chief character in all the early dialogues, is usually unwilling to state his own views (which, we might assume, Plato would wish us to accept), and likes more to reduce those of others to absurdity. The main difficulty is one about Plato's situation in time: he comes in at the beginning of philosophy as we understand the term (what his predecessors except Socrates had been doing was not quite the same); and therefore he had to invent the method and the terminology as he went along. Not surprisingly, he did not become clear all at once, or sometimes even at all, about the issues he raised.

There is a style of interpretation, practised on Plato by many modern commentators, which goes like this. They first point to some passage in the dialogues whose meaning is not entirely clear. They then suggest various statements in modern English of what he might have meant, and draw consequences from each of them to which they think he would be committed if that were what he meant. If these consequences are absurd or inconsistent, they then, according to their temperaments, either write him off as a bad philosopher, or conclude that, since he was not a bad philosopher, he cannot have meant that.

Although the method has some resemblance to Socrates' treatment of his opponents, it is unfair in that Plato is not here to answer back, and is in any case unsound as a method of getting at what he meant. It is far safer not to attribute to Plato any proposition which cannot be translated into Greek, the language in which he did his thinking. If it cannot be, he cannot have thought that. One is handicapped when writing a short book about Plato in English, and I shall probably find myself committing the fault I have just been condemning, but to be on secure ground, if his own words are unclear or ambiguous, the most we can do is to imagine that we have him with us, put to him questions in Greek, and then speculate as to how he might answer them in Greek. If this method is followed, it will be found that many of the distinctions on which, as modern philosophers, we rightly want to insist, pass him by.

If we want to ask what Plato *would* have said, if he had lived now and had read Hume, Kant, Carnap, Wittgenstein etc., about questions for the posing of which these distinctions are necessary, we can, if we like, imagine additionally that we can teach him modern philosophical English and speculate as to what answers he would then give; but it *will* be speculation (good philosophical training though it is for ourselves), and cannot in any case pose as an interpretation of his views as expressed in the dialogues. What we can do is to look at those views, and then at the subsequent history of philosophy, and see what, in the hands of others, they *turned into*. There are many striking affinities between what Plato said and what later thinkers have said, even some who are not called Platonists; nearly all philosophers are heavily in debt to him. We can therefore, when reading Plato, often find the seed of some later idea. But it is seldom more than a seed.

Later thinkers who acknowledge debts to Plato, or, by contrast, who have reacted against him, often attribute to him views which have been suggested to them by reading him; but this is a dangerous game. Aristotle played it (perhaps with greater right than most, because he knew Plato personally and was taught by him). So did the Neoplatonists in late antiquity, our own Cambridge Platonists in the seventeenth century, and Hegel and other romantic philsophers in the nineteenth. And so do some modern philosophers of mathematics. It is by no means clear that Plato was a 'Platonist' in any of these senses. The problem is compounded by the fact that, although his thought has a remarkable unity, there are different aspects to it which different disciples have seized on.

Let us dramatise the two most prominent of these aspects by imagining that we are speaking not of one person but of two (which is indeed what one *would* imagine, if one compared some commentators with some other commentators). I shall call these two characters Pato and Lato. Pato is an advocate of what Aldous Huxley called 'the perennial philosophy'. He believes in a total difference in kind between the spiritual and the material, the immortal soul and the perishable body, the world of eternal Ideas and 'the world of matter and of sense' as Newman called it; and he endows this difference with a moral significance. The eternal verities are also eternal values, and the soul's task in its thousand-year cyclical journeys is to strive towards these and escape from the contamination of the flesh. These thoughts make Pato into the stern and ascetic moralist portrayed in Raphael's Vatican fresco; he would have been at home in a Zen Buddhist monastery, or even in Egypt with the desert fathers.

Lato seems at first entirely different. He is interested in science, esepcially in mathematics, and thus in logic and the philosophy of language. He taught Aristotle, and set him on the way to becoming the world's greatest logician and a notable biologist. He has learnt from Socrates to ask searching questions like 'What is justice (or The Just)?'—questions to which the answer would be a definition—and to submit proposed answers to destructive scrutiny, using logical and conceptual and linguistic techniques which he or Socrates invented. He follows Socrates in being an exposer of intellectual pretensions which are not founded on real understanding of what one is saying; but at the same time he encourages us to believe that if we *could* understand, reason would supply us with answers to the questions that trouble us. This intellectual midwifery, the sorting out of genuine from bogus offspring of the mind, makes the name 'Lato' appropriate, because Lato was the Greek goddess of childbirth, and Socrates claims in the *Theaetetus* to have learned the art from his midwife mother (149a).

The two characters are very different; so it is not surprising that the Patonists and the Latonists have given contrasting pictures of Plato. Readers of him will always be tempted to pick out those of his ideas which they find congenial, and forget about the others. In this book I am trying not to do that; but it is very hard. One expedient which I would recommend to anyone who wants to understand Plato is this: sometimes allow him to be unclear. There are many philosophical questions which had not arisen in Plato's time. No doubt, if he were going to be absolutely clear on some issues, he would have had to give a definite answer to such questions. But he did not; and it is historically sounder not to force upon him one answer or another, but rather to leave the questions unanswered, which means leaving his doctrine indeterminate at those points. It goes without saying that Plato was capable of making very clear and precise distinctions, and often does so, for the first time in philosophy, to good effect. But he had not made all that there are to be made; that would be too much to expect of somebody who was creating a whole new branch of inquiry.

We may illustrate this point, at the cost of anticipating questions which will occupy us later, from his treatment of the Socratic search for definitions. When Socrates asked questions like 'What is justice?' or 'What is The Just?', there are at least three things which we might take him as wanting. Does he want a definition of a word or of a thing; and if of a thing, of what *kind* of thing—of something we might come across in this world, or of something which is only available to thought? Let us try constructing a little dialogue to shed light on this question, without making Plato say anything which will not go into Greek.

ENGLISH STRANGER When Socrates says in the *Theaetetus* (147c) that mud (or clay) is earth mixed with water, is he saying what the *word* 'mud' means?

PLATO   Yes, of course. And *what* the word means, the thing mud, is what one has to be able to define if one is to show that one knows what mud is. As Socrates says, 'Do you think anybody understands the word for anything, if he doesn't know the thing, what it is?' (147b).

E.S.   But what is this mud he has to know? Is it what one gets on one's boots?

P.   How can you expect me to think that? One only gets *particular bits* of mud on one's boots, and one can touch and see them, but not know them in the sense I'm after. I am after what Mud is in itself, not after particular bits of mud. In the *Parmenides* I made Socrates reluctantly aware that, even with so down-to-earth a thing as mud, there is this Mud-in-itself that one has to know if one is to have knowledge what mud is (130c).

E.S.   So when Socrates says mud is earth mixed with water, is he defining a word or a thing?

P.   I don't see the difference. To define the word is to say what the thing is that it means. But this thing isn't what one gets on one's boots; it is what the mind has before it when one thinks of mud.

E.S.   Perhaps we could make the matter clearer if I asked you whether Socrates' definition is the sort of thing that would go into a dictionary. A dictionary is a collection of definitions rather like that first one you or your students compiled and which got into your works under the name *Definitions*. We have very big dictionaries now; the biggest is produced in Oxford and *it* defines 'mud' as 'a mixture of finely comminuted particles of rock with water' (you see, we like to be more exact nowadays). Other definitions in it which are very like those to be found in your *Definitions* are 'even: the latter part or close of the day' (cf. 411b); 'wind: air in motion . . . usually parallel to the surface of the ground' (cf. 411c). And you might find the following familiar: 'circle: a plane figure . . . bounded by a . . . circumference, which is everywhere equally distant from a point within, called the centre'; at least there is something very like this in that famous *Seventh Letter* attributed to you (342b).

P.   Your dictionary does sound as if it were after the same sort of things as I am after, namely statements in words of what other words mean; and of course what they mean are Ideas.

Without prolonging the dialogue, I think we can claim that it is simply not profitable to ask Plato the question 'Are you defining words or things?', because he would not understand what we were asking. In general it is very unclear, and contentious even among philosophers today, whether metaphysics, logic and linguistics are separate disciplines (we would not get a straight answer from either a logical positivist like Rudolf Carnap or an idealist like F. H. Bradley); and therefore it is not surprising that Plato cannot tell us which he is doing. But in what follows we may be able to shed a bit more light on another question, namely why he found the distinction between definitions of words and definitions of things difficult.

5 *Knowing things*

One of Plato's chief incentives to metaphysics was a nest of problems he thought he had encountered about knowledge. To understand his trouble, the first thing to get clear is, What did Plato think was the object of knowledge (that is, *what* somebody knows)? If the first of these expressions does not translate easily into Greek, the second does; and it is all right in Greek, and still quite natural in English, to say things like 'I know something.' 'Does the man who knows know something or nothing?' asks Socrates in the *Republic*; and, having got the obvious answer that he knows something, elicits the further answer that this something is an entity, an existing thing (476e).

As we shall see, Plato did not clearly distinguish between *what exists* and *what is true* (at least not in his earlier work; the distinction is at least hinted at in the *Timaeus* (29c)), and this may have been an extra source of confusion. It is easy to slip from the correct idea that what is known must be true to the mistaken idea that what is known must exist. If we speak in this way of an object of knowledge, we are implying that knowledge is some sort of relation between two things: the knower, that is the person who knows, or his mind or knowing faculty, and an object, that is the thing known, or what he knows. The relation can be thought of as like that between us (or our eyes) and a bird when we see a bird. This way of thinking about knowledge, natural though it is, can lead to a lot of trouble.

If the question 'What is this thing that we know?' is once raised, a modern philosopher is likely to answer 'The truth of a proposition' or, more simply, 'That (for example) five is a prime number', or 'That pigs can't fly.' For those of us who speak in these terms the status of the 'things known' called truths or propositions will be highly obscure, and has troubled many moderns; but it did not trouble Plato, because he did not look at the matter in this way. If he had, he would have been less tempted to (as the professionals say) 'hypostatize', or 'reify', the objects of knowledge (that is, suppose that they are existing things); for, although some philosophers have postulated entities out in the world called propositions, they take a bit of swallowing.

We may note that, even on a propositional view of knowledge, problems arise of a somewhat Platonic sort. Whenever we make a statement, it has to be *about* something (its subject). In the *Sophist* the Eleatic Stranger says 'If it weren't about anything, it wouldn't be a statement at all; for we showed that to be a statement, but one about nothing, is impossible' (263c). This true point is familiar from modern discussions. But it raises difficulties in the case of statements with abstract subjects, such as 'The circle is a plane figure, etc.' This is not a statement about any particular circle or even about any specific kind of circle; but unless we can identify what the person who makes it is talking about, how can we be sure he is talking about anything?

But Plato was not attracted by a propositional view of knowledge. This was partly because of some features of Greek idiom, which, in combination with other traps, led him to posit, as the objects of knowledge, Ideas existing in an eternal realm which are not propositions but *things*. I shall use the word 'Idea', with a capital 'I', to translate Plato's '*ideā*' and '*eidos*' (sometimes also translated 'Form'); but it must be understood that he meant by these a kind of object independent of the mind, with which the mind could become acquainted, and not anything merely mental (i.e. existing only in the mind).

The first feature of Greek idiom which may have misled Plato is this. Greek tends to put what looks like a direct object after verbs of knowing. It says, commonly though not always, 'I know *thee* who thou art'. The dialogues are full of examples of this construction. Given its possibility, it was easy for Plato to think of knowledge as a relation between a knower and a *thing*, the thing being not a proposition but rather the thing denoted by the subject of the 'that'-clause or the indirect question, as in 'I know Meno, who he is', or 'I know Meno, that he is rich' or '. . . whether he is rich'.

There are cases in which it is perfectly natural and indeed correct to use 'know' with a direct object. We can know stories, and know geometry, for example. With some other related verbs it is even easier. 'Understand', but not 'know', is used even in English in a way that could capture the meaning of Plato's Greek in some contexts, as in 'He understands justice (i.e. what it is)'; and the commonest word for 'understand' in Greek is also one of Plato's favourite words for 'know'. Since we can also speak of understanding the *word* 'just', this does something to explain Plato's difficulty, already noticed, in separating definitions of words from definitions of things.

But Plato more commonly uses a different model from these, also natural in English as in Greek: the model of what is now often called 'knowledge by acquaintance'. It is common nowadays to distinguish the kind of knowing expressed by '*savoir*', '*wissen*' and '*scire*' from that expressed by '*connaître*', '*kennen*' and '*cognoscere*' ('I know that pigs can't fly' from 'I know Meno' and 'I know Athens'). Significantly, though Greek has a word cognate with (that is, related etymologically to) the second set of verbs for knowing, it does not use it, any more than English uses 'know', to make this distinction, but allows it indiscriminately to govern direct objects, or 'that'-clauses, or both combined ('I know Meno, that he is rich'), or the equivalent participial construction ('I know Meno, being rich', as Greek puts it); and similarly the verb which is cognate with '*wissen*' is used in all these ways. It is also cognate, like '*ideā*' and '*eidos*', with the Greek and Latin words for 'see', thereby making it even easier for Plato to think of knowing as being, like some kind of mental seeing, a direct acquaintance with an object or thing. So Plato, when he wants to say something about other kinds of knowledge, often recurs to the model of knowledge by acquaintance. I have already given an example from the beginning of the *Meno*; near the end of the dialogue he does the same, illustrating the difference betwen knowledge and true opinion by the example of knowing the road to Larissa, as opposed to having opinions about it (71b, 97a). Plato is here setting out a theory about knowledge which is supposed to hold for all sorts of knowledge; but he illustrates it by a case of knowledge by acquaintance—acquaintance with a physical thing, namely a road.

It may have been in part this tendency of the Greek language which led Plato to posit a *thing* or *entity* such that knowledge is a relation between us and it, and to think of this entity as being somehow *like* Meno or Athens or the road to Larissa, which we

know in the perfectly ordinary sense of being acquainted with
them, and yet mysteriously somehow *unlike* them. It had to be
unlike them, because knowledge must be of what is true, and
moreover (Plato thought) reliably and abidingly true. Because
the Greek word for 'true' (like the English) sometimes means
'real' (see p. 41), and because we cannot know what is false, he
thought that what we know has to be real. And thinking, as he
did, that we could not really know anything unless we had the
right to be sure of it, the only candidates he could admit as
objects of knowledge in the full sense had to be things which
were not merely real, but *necessarily* real, and therefore eternal
and indestructible. If we have knowledge of other things (for
example, the things we see and touch) it is not of the full-
blooded kind.

Plato hankered, in his search for real knowledge, after the
kind of certainty which the truths of mathematics have; but
because he was after things and not truths, the things had to be
necessarily existing things. Looked at in this light, even the road
to Larissa does not really qualify (it might be washed away, as
roads in Greece sometimes are).

There are other linguistic traps too for Plato. Greek had no
separate words for 'word' and 'name'. Thus it was easy for Plato
to suppose that the way in which a word like 'man' got its
meaning was the same as that in which a proper name like
'Meno' got its meaning—by there being an object of which it is
the name (the Idea of Man). This has been called the 'Fido'—
Fido theory of meaning: the view that for any word to have
meaning is for there to be some entity to which it stands in the
same relation as the name 'Fido' does to the dog Fido.

Another trap was the facility with which Greek formed
abstract nouns by adding the definite article to the neuter
adjective. We still do this (influenced by Plato) when we speak
of 'The Right and the Good' (the name of a book on ethics by Sir
David Ross); but it is not natural in English. It became extremely
common in the political and other rhetoric of Plato's time, as can
be seen by reading almost any of the speeches in Thucydides.
Where we should speak of knowing what rightness is, or
alternatively of what 'right' means, it is easy in Greek, because
of the factors already mentioned, to speak of knowing the Right,
and thus fail to distinguish between these possibly different

things. And from this it is a small step to saying, as Plato was tempted into saying, that the Right which we know is a really and necessarily existing thing, which has to perfection the quality of rightness (for if the Right is not right, what is?).

This view that the Ideas themselves have the properties of which they are the Ideas is known by scholars as the doctrine of *self-predication*, or, alternatively, of *paradigmatic Ideas*. The notion of the Idea as a paradigm or ideal example of the quality in question occurs in Plato as early as the *Euthyphro* (6e), and we can see how seductive it is. And no doubt the temptation offered by this Greek way of expressing abstract nouns was reinforced by a still older way, personification. Aeschylus' avenging Furies mockingly predict that if they gave up their task, people would say 'O Right! O thrones of the Furies!' And of course the goddess Right must always be right, as the lady on top of the Courts of Justice is always just.

Plato, to his credit, came to see that self-predication leads to paradox. In the *Parmenides* (132) he presents the famous 'Third Man' argument. To simplify this a bit: if for something to be a man is for it to resemble the Idea of Man, and if for things to resemble one another is for them to share a common characteristic of which the Idea is the perfect example, then will not there have to be a third man, the Idea by resemblance to which both the first man and the second (the original Idea) are called men; and shall we not need a fourth man to account for the resemblance between these three; and so *ad infinitum*?

It is by no means clear whether this criticism, either in my simplified form or in the various different forms in which it occurs in Plato and Aristotle, is valid and unavoidable. So Plato is perhaps not to be blamed if he did not abandon his Theory of Ideas in the light of it; but all the same it *is* a mistake to suppose that for words to have meanings is (always at any rate) for there to be entities for which they stand. If we know how to use a word in speaking and thus communicating with one another, it has a meaning; and knowing how to use it is not knowing some solid chunk of eternal verity of which it is the name, but knowing the conventions for its use, and in particular what, according to these conventions, is implied by somebody who uses it in a statement. To know what 'circle' means or what a circle is is to know that if we call anything a circle we are implying that it is a plane figure of a certain sort; and in order to know this we do not have to know any celestial entities.

It is hard (for me at any rate) not to think that another factor contributed to Plato's taking this false trail. Some people have a more vivid mental imagery than others; they think more in pictures. Those who lack this gift often find it hard to understand the thought of those who have it. That Plato had it nobody could doubt who read the similes and myths which enliven his dialogues. When he speaks of 'seeing' one of these entities called Ideas, he is thinking of something very like literal seeing, only done with what he calls in the *Republic* 'the mind's eye' (533d). Elsewhere he speaks of 'grasping' Ideas. We have grown accustomed through the long use of such terms in philosophy and common parlance (along with such technical terms as 'intuition', which means, literally, 'looking') to thinking of them as very weak, threadbare metaphors; and translators often, when Plato says 'look', translate 'investigate' or 'reflect' or the like. But for Plato they were hardly metaphorical at all. Here is a passage from the *Phaedo*, keeping Plato's visual and tactual language:

> The soul, when it uses the body to look at something, by sight or hearing or some other sense . . . is dragged by the body among things which never stay the same, and it itself gets lost and disturbed and tipsy, just like a drunk, from contact with such things . . . But when it looks by itself, on its own, it goes in the other direction, to the pure, the eternal, the immortal, the unchanging, and, because of its affinity with them, joins their company, whenever it is by itself and can do so; it ceases its wanderings and is with them and ever unchanging like them, from contact with such things. And this condition of the soul is called wisdom. (76c, d)

It is clear from such passages, which are very common in the dialogues, that Plato thought of the difference between ordinary sight and touch on the one hand, and the mind's sight and grasp of the eternal Ideas on the other, as lying in a difference in the objects and in the organs of perception, and not in a difference in the kind of relation between knower and known. Knowledge or wisdom is a kind of mental looking—a vision of the Eternal.

But Plato did not think that *everything* which we see or grasp with our mind gives us knowledge; for believing too (in the sense of having opinions) is a mental activity of the same general kind, and opinions or beliefs can be false. The obvious account, within this framework, of false belief is to say that it is the seeing or grasping with the mind of false objects—things which 'are not'. And here the framework got Plato into great trouble, from which he may never have extracted himself completely.

The trouble arises through thinking of truth and falsity in beliefs as properties of the thing believed. Plato frequently uses the words which we translate 'true' and 'false' as if there were no difference between the sense in which we speak of a true statement and that in which we speak of a true (as opposed to forged or in general spurious) Vermeer. The spurious object of belief 'is not' what it purports to be; and Plato, because he did not initially distinguish between the 'is' which means the same as 'exists' (as in 'The British Empire is no more') and the 'is' which expresses predication (the copula, as in 'He is tall'), gets into difficulties about whether, when we have false beliefs, we are seeing or grasping or saying what 'is not', and therefore whether when we do this we have anything at all before the mind. But if we have nothing before the mind, how can we be believing anything at all. The upshot seems to be the paradoxical one that we cannot have false belief.

Plato inherited these difficulties from the Eleatics. He grapples manfully with them in the *Theaetetus* and the *Sophist*; but the beginnings of them can be seen in the *Republic*, where he says that knowledge is of what is, belief is of what is and is not, and ignorance is of what is not (477a). His conception of knowledge and belief as kinds of mental seeing of genuine or spurious objects led him inevitably into these troubles; and scholars do not agree on the extent to which he eventually got himself out of them.

It is not even clear that he always thought of belief as a kind of *mental* seeing; the 'things believed' in the *Republic* are, typically though not always, objects perceived by the senses; so perhaps he did not distinguish clearly between seeing one of these objects with the eyes and believing it (to exist). By the time of the *Republic* he is distinguishing between knowledge and belief by distinguishing between their objects (478a); but earlier, in the *Meno*, he speaks as if the same thing, the road to Larissa, could be an object either of knowledge or of belief, and finds the difference between them in the greater abidingness of knowledge, secured by a 'reckoning of the reason' for what we know (the reason being, he implies, the Idea, and the reckoning, the defining of it—97a, see p. 46). This suggests a definition of knowledge very similar to one which has been popular, but also controversial, recently: 'true belief which has a rational ground'. Plato later in the *Theaetetus* raises difficulties against such a definition; but it is not clear whether they led him finally to abandon it (201cff.).

By positing the existence of Ideas as real abiding entities visible to the mind, and therefore qualified to be objects of knowledge in the fullest sense, Plato thought he had resolved the problem of 'The One and the Many' which had been an incentive to philosophy ever since the early cosmologists. Even if the Heracliteans were right about the sensible world—even if, that is to say, it is, considered in itself, a multifarious, unintelligible flux—still we can reason about it if we use not our senses but our minds. As he says in the *Theaetetus*, 'Knowledge lies not in the effects [of the senses] upon us, but in our reasoning about them. For it is, it seems, possible in the case of the latter to lay hold on reality and truth, but not in the case of the former' (186d). This reasoning puts us in touch with the eternal Ideas, which have each of them a unity (the one Man as contrasted with the many particular men or the many different kinds of men—it is not clear always which he means). And they also have jointly a unity among themselves, by all partaking of the Idea of the Good (see p. 49). The Ideas, therefore, have the perfect, eternal, unchanging oneness for lack of which Parmenides denied reality to the objects of sense.

Having got thus far, Plato may have been tempted to find the hallmark of knowledge in the clarity and distinctness of its objects. 'If this very thing becomes clear', he says at one point in the *Phaedo*, 'you won't look any further' (106b). If, he might have said, we can with our mind's eye discern some Idea very clearly, is not that a certificate that it exists and that we have knowledge of it? To his great credit, unlike Descartes, he resisted this temptation. He did not rely on the self-evidence of intuition. Following Socrates, he insisted that we have to establish the credentials of claims to knowledge by submitting them to a rigorous testing procedure; and to this we must now turn.

6 Definition, dialectic and the good

As we have seen, it was Socrates' practice to ask people who were thought to have knowledge, 'What is . . . ?', where the gap is to be filled by a word for something which they claimed to know about (courage, for example, in the case of the gallant soldier Laches). In Plato's early dialogues this happens constantly. What often happens after that is that the victim offers some answer, and this is then submitted to scrutiny (*elenchos*); the Greek word also means 'audit'. This frequently starts with Socrates complaining that he has been given the wrong sort of answer. Usually this is because the respondent has given one or more examples of the thing in question, instead of saying what the feature is which they all have, which makes them examples of it.

Thus in the *Meno*, where goodness is what is being inquired into, Socrates asks for 'a single form, the same in them all, in virtue of which they are goodnesses, to which someone who is answering the question, what goodness may be, can well look and point it out' (72c). The word translated 'form' is '*eidos*', which is the standard word later for Plato's Ideas; but we do not need to ask whether by this stage he is insisting, as Socrates himself probably did not, on the substantial and separate existence of the Ideas. Nor do we need to ask whether Plato has distinguished between the fault of offering *kinds* of goodness in lieu of a definition of goodness, and that of offering *particular instances* of goodness; the former interpretation suits mos⟨ passages. At least we can say that Socrates is asking for some kind of definition (whether a definition of a word or of a thing, it is, as we have seen, not profitable to ask); and Aristotle gives him, rather than Plato, the credit for introducing this move.

I say 'credit'; but recently Socrates has been attacked for seeking definitions, and has even been accused of committing therein a 'Socratic Fallacy'. There are two lines of attack which must be distinguished. The first of them points out that words have a multiplicity of subtly varying uses, and that it is a mistake to suppose that there will always be some *one* common element, *the* meaning of a word ('game' for example), wherever it occurs. There may be only a 'family resemblance' between different things we call games: think, for example, of roulette, tournament chess and the game of pretending to be an aeroplane, and ask what one feature they have in common with all games which things other than games do not have.

Without going into this criticism in detail, it can be shown that it is not very damaging to Socrates' main enterprise. Granted that it may be the case that no one common element will be found, nevertheless it remains important to seek to understand what we are saying, especially when we are arguing; for if we do not understand what we are saying, we shall not know which steps in an argument are valid and which are invalid. It may be that our understanding cannot be captured in cut-and-dried definitions, a single one for each word, but that was not Socrates' or Plato's main point. They were acquainted with the phenomenon of ambiguity, and if it is more complex than they thought, it still does not diminish the importance of understanding.

The other line of attack would be more damaging if it could be sustained. '*Before* we start trying to define a word', it may be said, 'we have in some sense to know how to use it. We have *either* to be able to point to examples of its correct use, *or* to be able to explain its meaning in words. If we can do neither of these things, we cannot even start. But pointing to examples is a perfectly legitimate way of starting, and Socrates does wrong to ban it. When the word that is being asked about is a moral word, Socrates' move can be very harmful. For instance, we all know how to pick out examples of courage, but many of us find it hard to define the word. If Socrates asks us what courage is, and we cannot provide an answer which satisfies his rigorous standards, we may come to think that we don't know what it is, or wonder whether the acts we thought had it in fact had it, or even whether there is such a thing; and this may be bad for our moral characters. Socrates therefore really is corrupting the young.'

Behind this criticism lies a theory about meaning which must now be brought out into the open. The most famous modern statement of this claims that 'if language is to be a means of communication there must be agreement not only in definitions but, queer as this may sound, agreement in judgements also'. You and I cannot be using a word in the same way unless there are some uses of it which we agree to be correct, and this implies that we agree on at least some substantial and not merely verbal questions. Unless, for example, there are some things we agree to be pigs, we cannot be using the word 'pig' in the same way. This may be true of certain classes of words; but that it is true of all words has not been established. In particular, it is highly disputable in regard to value words. Is it not possible for you and me to be in radical disagreement on how one ought to behave, so that we cannot find *any* 'ought'-statement on which we could agree, and yet be using the word 'ought' in the same way? If we did not mean the same by the word, our attempts to voice our disagreements would founder; for when I said 'He ought' and you said 'He ought not', we should merely be at cross purposes.

However, it is not necessary for us to insist on this point in order to defend Socrates. For he could easily grant initially that we do have a 'right opinion', or at least a consensus, right or wrong, that such and such acts are courageous, and that this enables us to get along all right with the word; but go on, first to deny that this right opinion amounts to knowledge (it does not have the necessary certitude or abidingness), and secondly to say that what would give it this more reliable quality would be some sort of deeper understanding of what we say. What is being challenged, in this criticism, is the Socratic-Platonic distinction between knowledge and right opinion. The basis of the attack is that right opinion (in Greek *orthē doxa*, the etymological ancestor of 'orthodoxy') ought to be enough for the upright man.

If the attack were justified, then perhaps philosophy itself ought never to have started. For what above all got philosophy started was Socrates' and Plato's insistence that right opinion is not enough; it is utterly unstable and unreliable unless it is turned into secure knowledge by 'a reckoning of the reason'. 'A reason' is what Socrates is asking for in his 'What is . . . ?' questions. If we could understand the words used in setting out the problems that trouble us, we might then go on to find secure solutions to them. That really is what philosophy is about, and so those who press this attack are revealing themselves as antiphilosophers, like the Athenians who put Socrates to death on substantially the same grounds. As a great modern philosopher of mathematics, Gottlob Frege, put it, echoing Socrates and speaking of people who held that definitions were unnecessary in mathematics: 'The first prerequisite for learning anything is thus utterly lacking—I mean, the knowledge that we do not know.'

In default of this deeper understanding, popular agreement is not enough, and is often (especially at times of moral uncertainty like Plato's and our own) not forthcoming. It is to be noted that Euthyphro, in a dialogue which has been singled out for attack, is in *disagreement* with the rest of his family on whether he would be doing his religious duty if he prosecuted his father for the manslaughter of a servant who had murdered another servant. If it was a real case, there was no doubt dissension about it in the city at large. In such a case there is no orthodoxy to appeal to, and we have, however much we should like the comforts of moral assurance, to think the thing out for ourselves. This is what Socrates and Plato are trying to find a way of doing, and the importance of their endeavour for the theory and practice of moral education is, as we shall see, immense.

We must now ask how Plato thought the Socratic question could be answered—what philosophical method he was proposing. As we have seen, he had rejected the mere clarity of a thought as a certificate of its correctness, and was not going to rely on general assent either. Instead, he demanded what he called 'a reckoning of the reason' for thinking it. And this was to take the form 'The . . . is—', that is, some kind of definition. This is what Plato called 'an account (*logos*) of the being' of something. The phrase was adopted by Aristotle, and is the lineal ancestor of the modern expression 'essential definition'. But it is important when reading Plato to keep in mind that it means no more than an answer to the Socratic question 'What is . . . ?'. Plato thought that the thing about which the question was asked was an eternally existing entity, an Idea, and that the definition was a description of this entity. It is doubtful whether Socrates thought this, and Aristotle did not. Those who follow

William of Occam in thinking that such entities ought not to be multiplied more than we have to will seek to discard Plato's separately existing and eternal Ideas, while salvaging all that they can of his philosophical enterprise. This aim probably motivated Aristotle, and it is indeed remarkable how much can be salvaged.

Socrates' method of 'scrutiny' consists in eliciting from his victims answers to his questions, and then demolishing them by showing them to be inconsistent with other opinions which the victims are not willing to give up. Often these are generally accepted views. An example is the first definition of 'rightness' or 'uprightness' considered in the *Republic*: 'Truthfulness, and the giving back of anything that one receives from anybody' (331c). This is rejected because it would have the consequence that, if one had been lent some weapons by a friend, and he had gone mad, it would be right, or upright, to give them back to him.

Unfortunately there are two ways of taking this argument, which have not been generally distinguished, and were not by Plato. Is he saying that any definition which runs counter to the opinions of its proposer, or to received opinion, is to be rejected? This would invite the objection that the opinions might be wrong, and not the definition. However, Plato is generally thought to be proposing such a method of refutation.

He would be on safer ground if he were saying that any definition which can be shown to run counter to the linguistic usage of native speakers is to be rejected. The argument would then go: 'All of us would call the act of giving back the weapons to the madman "not right"; this universally held opinion, whether or not it is *correct*, is certainly not *self-contradictory*; so the definition, which makes it self-contradictory, must be wrong.' On this way of taking the argument, the method is sound by the usual canons of scientific method: a linguistic hypothesis about the meaning of a word has been advanced, and is refuted by showing that the linguistic facts do not square with it. We have already noticed the difficulty of attributing to Plato a clear distinction (if such exists) between linguistic or logical enquiries into the meanings of words and metaphysical enquiries into the things the words mean. He certainly often speaks in the latter way, and it was therefore difficult for him to distinguish, for example, between people's opinions about the nature of the *thing* called 'rightness' and their native ability to use the *word* 'right' correctly.

What is fairly clear, moreover, is that he failed, as many moderns still fail, to make a further distinction. This is the distinction between on the one hand substantial opinions about questions of morality or even of fact, and on the other questions about what rightness, etc. are (whether these latter are thought of as questions about language or about the nature of things). It is perhaps the greatest fault in Plato's way of putting the questions he was asking, as demands for accounts of the *being* of things, that it can make us confuse substantial questions with verbal ones. To revert to a previous example, there is a substantial question about mud, namely how it is, as a matter of fact, composed (a question that is answered by putting it into a centrifuge; earth and water will be the result). There is also a question, 'What is mud?', which, as we have seen, could be taken *either* for a question about the Idea of Mud *or* for one about the word 'mud'. On neither interpretation is it about the thing mud in the down-to-earth sense of what gets on one's boots or what goes into the centrifuge. But it is easy to take the question about the Idea for a more substantial question than it really is, and Plato probably did so.

In moral questions especially, it is very easy (people still constantly do it) to confuse questions about correct use of words with substantial moral questions. If we ask 'What is uprightness?' we might be asking for a definition of a word, concept or Platonic Idea, and, if so, we ought perhaps to be satisfied with the answer which Plato gives in *Republic* IV, 'Doing one's own duty' (433a). On the other hand, we might be asking for a specification of what our duty is; and in that case we should need to be given the precepts for living which Plato provides in the rest of the *Republic*. Plato was probably not as clear as he should have been about the difference between these two sorts of question. But at least he seems to have seen the need for asking both.

The Socratic method of scrutiny is further developed by Plato, who uses the name 'dialectic' for the developed form of it. It is sometimes said that Plato's method changed but that he used the name 'dialectic' for whatever method he at any one time preferred. This is an exaggeration; his method did develop, but retained a recognisable resemblance to that of Socrates. In the *Republic* he says:

> Then do you call 'a dialectician' the man who demands an account of the being of each thing. And the man who does not have that, in so far as he cannot give an account to himself and to another, to that extent will you deny that he has understanding (*nous*) of it? . . . And then the same applies to the Good. A man who cannot give a determinate account of the Idea of the Good, separating it from everything else, and battling through all the scrutinies of it, being eager to scrutinise it by reference not to opinion but to its real being, and who cannot in all these scrutinies come through with his account unscathed, will you say that a man like that knows neither the Good nor any other good thing (if he gets hold somehow of some simulacrum, he gets hold of it with his opinion, not with knowledge)? (534b, c)

The relation of this to Socrates' method of scrutiny is obvious. And so is the importance of separating what you are defining from everything else, the method later to be known as 'division', which is insisted on as early as the *Euthyphro* (12d), and is indeed ascribed by Xenophon to Socrates.

In later dialogues the method is developed still further, but not in such a way as to cut it off from its Socratic ancestry, which Aristotle, who took over a lot of this from Plato, also shares. The development is chiefly in the method proposed for setting out in a systematic form the definitions which were the answers to Socrates' questions. This form came later to be called '*definitio per genus et differentiam*'; in order to say what something is, one has first to give its genus, assigning it to the class of things into which one has *collected* everything that resembles it generically, and then *divide* up the genus into species, saying what differentiates each, including the thing in question. This method has been immensely influential in biology, from Aristotle to Linnaeus and beyond. Fully worked-out examples of it are given by Plato in the *Sophist* and the *Politicus*.

Before leaving the subject of definition we must explain why the Good plays such an important part in Plato's scheme. He calls it in the *Republic* 'the greatest thing we have to learn' (505a).

The reason is in essence simple, but because it was not explicitly stated in Plato's surviving works, commentators have not always understood it. The Idea of any class of things (for example men) was thought of by Plato as a perfect (that is, supremely good) specimen or paradigm of the class. This is involved in the doctrine of self-predication which has already been mentioned. To know what Man is, is not to know what it is to be any old kind of man, but rather what it is to be a good or perfect man. Similarly, to know what the Circle is, is to know what it is to be a good or perfect circle, not just any circle that a slovenly schoolmaster might draw on the blackboard.

This means that in order fully to know what it is to be a man or a circle, we have to know what it is to be a good man or a perfect circle; and thus that knowledge of the being of anything involves knowledge of the goodness or perfection of a good thing of that kind, and (Plato would have added) vice versa. Thus knowledge of the Good will comprehend knowledge of the goodnesses or perfections of every kind of thing, and thus of their specific natures. This line of thought involves two confusions. The first is between 'good man' in the sense of 'typical specimen of the class *man*', and 'good man' in the sense of 'man having the good qualities demanded in men'. A typical man is not necessarily a morally good man. The second is that of thinking that what it is to be a good man or a good circle is determined by the meaning of 'good' (by the Idea of the Good, as Plato would have put it); it is in fact determined by the standard for goodness in those two classes of thing, which, as Aristotle saw, is different in the two cases.

Aristotle, however, follows Plato in finding a very close link between the essential nature of a species of thing and the perfection of that thing, the end to which its whole development is striving (in Aristotle's terms, between the formal and the final cause). And Aristotle's notion that we can explain everything by giving its purpose goes back, through Plato, to Anaxagoras, who according to a passage in the *Phaedo* from which I have already quoted (97c) suggested that Mind orders all things as it is for the best that they should be—an idea which, according to Plato, Anaxagoras made no use of, but which Socrates took to heart. Since in the *Phaedo* explanation in terms of purpose (of what is for the best) is put alongside explanation in terms of the Ideas which make things what they are, it is natural for Plato to speak, as he dces in the *Republic*, of the Good as the source of all being, and of our knowledge of it (509b).

Plato, because he thought of the objects of knowledge as things, and of our knowledge of them as a kind of mental seeing, goes on to represent the hierarchy of Ideas as a kind of quasi-physical chain with the lower items 'attached' to the Good at the top. By looking at (or grasping) this chain we can see (feel) the connections. The chain contains only Ideas; that is to say, nothing from the world of sense is admitted into it (511b, c). This was Plato's way of putting the correct point, further elaborated by Aristotle, that true, certain knowledge (by which he meant knowledge of necessary truths) cannot be had by observation of nature; it can only be of what we can show to be true by giving the required definitions.

Plato here gets near to the notion, much used by some recent philosophers but also disputed by others, of analytic truth. His most important claim in this area could be put into modern dress as the claim that the truths of logic and mathematics, and philosophical truths generally, do not rest on observation of particular things and events, but on definitions available to thought. But, as we saw, it is usually dangerous to try to put Plato into modern dress; that was not how it looked to him, because he was, he thought, talking not about *propositions* and how they are derived or known, but about things inspected with the mind's eye. Whereas for us a definition is one kind of analytically or necessarily true proposition, for him it was a description of a mentally visible and eternally true object.

7 Education and the good life

We saw that Plato's search for an adequate account of knowing was motivated, at least in part, by the belief that only this could discriminate right opinion about how to behave from error, and make it secure from deviance. We have now reached a point at which it can be explained more fully how he hoped to achieve this. But we must first look briefly at the educational scene in Athens. In the *Meno* he purports to record a conversation between Socrates and some others shortly before his trial, which took place when Plato was about 28; and this gives a good picture of the situation as it would have impressed itself on Plato. It is suggested that if goodness were teachable there would be teachers of it, and it is asked who these might be. Socrates, in an ironical spirit, suggests that if we are looking for *professional* teachers of goodness or excellence, we can find them in the people known as *sophists* (91b).

This word is connected with '*sophos*', commonly translated 'wise', but often better rendered as 'clever'. '*Sophos*' covers any kind of skill or dexterity, physical or intellectual, artistic or political, and is often a term of commendation—more so than its near equivalent '*deinos*', which can mean 'clever' in a neutral or even hostile sense, but literally means 'terrible' (as in the French '*enfant terrible*'). As the intellectual life of Greece blossomed there came into being a class of people who can be compared, at any rate in their effect on society, with the intellectual gurus of our own day. To these people the name 'sophists' came to be especially applied; it means that they themselves were clever, and that they could impart this cleverness, especially rhetorical skill, to young men who were prepared to pay them handsomely enough. In the *Protagoras* 'sophist' is defined as 'a master of the art of making people into clever speakers' (312d).

In popular estimation Socrates counted as a sophist, and he suffered for the supposed sins of the whole class; but he differed from them in not claiming to be able to make people clever or impart any other kind of excellence, but only to talk with them and perhaps help to birth any good notions that they might themselves bring forth; and also in not taking any money. The sophists held a variety of doctrines, and no doubt made significant contributions to the thought of that intellectually exciting period. But in one way it is not important what their doctrines were; by making young people think at all about problems to which, in the opinion of their elders, there were right answers such as ought not to be questioned, they were thought to have unsettled an entire generation. In this sense, at least, Socrates was the most sophisticated of the sophists, and by their own lights the Athenians did right to put him to death.

In the *Meno* the suggestion that the sophists can count as teachers of goodness is summarily rejected by the traditionally-minded democrat Anytus (the man principally responsible for the prosecution of Socrates). Even one of the sophists themselves, Gorgias, is quoted as saying that he cannot make men good, only clever. Instead, Anytus suggests that the right person to teach young men goodness would be any decent Athenian gentleman (like himself, we are to understand). Socrates then gives him the usual treatment, pointing out that these decent people do not seem to make much of a go of educating their own sons. The same point is made in the *Protagoras* (324d).

The traditional Greek education which a boy would get from any decent gentleman in any Greek city was probably not unlike that prescribed, in a bowdlerised form, in the earlier part of Plato's *Republic*. Plato has made important alterations: he has censored certain passages in Homer and the other poets; and the emphasis is more on the conscious formation of character and less on the learning of accomplishments like wrestling and music-making for their own sakes. But there cannot have been any radical difference in what the boys would actually have done. There would be variations from city to city: in one the mix would include more 'music' (including the performing arts as well as literature); in another more 'gymnastic' (athletics with an eye to military training). In Sparta the whole thing was highly organised as in the *Republic*; in other cities less so. But it is obvious that in the *Republic*, in his primary education, Plato is consciously taking over, with modifications, the traditional

Greek education in 'music and gymnastic' such as any well-born
Greek boy could expect to receive, and such as Socrates says in
the *Crito* that he himself received when young (50e).

This old education did not mix very well with the new
education offered by the sophists. The old education aimed
primarily at training the character, the new the intellect. A
person who was successfully educated in the old way at its best
would have the virtues which had made Athens what she was:
the virtues extolled by the 'Right Argument' in Aristophanes'
Clouds. We must not put it too high; we have only to look again
at the *Meno* and find Themistocles, who was actually a wily devil
with a far from spotless reputation, being cited as a supremely
good man (93b). But Themistocles was very *successful*, and
commanded the Greek fleet in its most decisive victory over the
Persians, and so his sins (like Nelson's) were forgiven.

The well-born, well-educated Greek was not a paragon of
virtue by Christian standards. He often wanted to make a hit in
politics, and do something notable for the city; at worst he was
ambitious to a degree which we should condemn; he wanted to
be able to entertain lavishly (Aristotle rates 'magnificence' as one
of the virtues, meaning by it having the wherewithal and the
aptitude for living in style); he wanted to put his opponents in
their places, and even worse; and generally to have that thing
which sounds so weak when translated into English, 'honour';
but not only, it must be added, for achievements which we
should call honourable.

The education provided by the sophists still aimed at what
was called goodness or excellence, but in a very different way.
By training not the character but the intellect it aspired to enable
its products to pursue just those ambitions which the traditional
upbringing cultivated, but pursue them with far greater hope of
success. A principal means to this was a training in rhetoric,
giving an ability to persuade courts and assemblies, and thus get
one's political way. The new education played on the weaknesses of the old: the old produced ambitious but fundamentally
upright people; the new fostered the ambitions, and held out
greater hopes of realising them, but paid less attention to
uprightness. Readers who doubt this should look at the *Theages*,
and see what that young man, who takes Socrates for a sophist,
hopes to get from him (125–6).

There is another side to the question. Intellectual education is not a bad thing. Aristotle puts the matter very well in the course of his mature reflections on this subject. Intellectual ability, cleverness, is morally neutral; it all depends on a man's character. If his character leads him to pursue good ends, intellectual ability will enable him to achieve them more readily; if his ends are wicked, he will also more readily achieve *them*. The situation which Plato faced was one in which a new education and an old education confronted each other, not quite as opponents one of which was good and the other bad, as Aristophanes made out, but rather as two factors which actually worked together for ill but could, if reformed on lines which he was to suggest, work together for good. In the *Gorgias* a contrast is drawn between the right and the wrong kind of rhetorician, and in the *Sophist* between the right and the wrong kind of sophist. The right kind in both cases is the philosopher who, because he *knows* the Good and everything which depends on it, can really educate people instead of just pandering to their desires and ensnaring them.

The basis, therefore, of Plato's educational reforms is Socrates' distinction between knowledge and opinion. This theme runs through the whole, not only of Plato's, but of Aristotle's moral philosophy. In Plato's ideal city the scheme is that character-training should precede intellectual training. This diverges from Socrates' practice even as portrayed by Plato in such dialogues as the *Theages* and the *Charmides*; he shows Socrates having intellectually very educative conversations with young men and offering to do it on a regular basis. In the *Gorias* Plato puts into the mouth of a critic, and does not deny (how could he?), the accusation that it was Socrates' practice to 'whisper with three or four young men in a corner' (485d); and although Aristophanes is wrong in portraying Socrates as the founder of a 'school' in any institutional sense, he is no doubt right in implying that young people were his disciples.

Plato's developed view was different; we should first implant, by entirely non-intellectual training, right opinion leading to right habits and dispositions, and only then will it be safe, at a much later age, to introduce people to philosophy, in order that they may acquire knowledge of the Good which determines which opinions are right. The only kind of intellectual training that the young get in his Republic is mathematics, a morally safe discipline. And philosophy is not for everybody, but only for those gifted people who are capable of it, and who can safely be entrusted with the running of the educational process, and indeed of the entire state. This they are to do in the light of the knowledge which they attain, in order that the society may be one in which the good life can be lived (see p. 64).

Aristotle took over this distinction between goodness of character and goodness of intellect; and he quotes Plato as saying that people should be brought up from their early years to like and dislike what they ought to like and dislike. Aristotle's view, a development of Plato's, was that if they have acquired the habit of right desire they will be able to recognise *that* such and such actions and characters are good, but they may still not know *why* they are; they will not have 'goodness in the full sense', for which the intellectual quality of wisdom (*phronēsis*) is a necessary condition.

On one point Aristotle corrects Socrates' view in the *Meno* (88c): the intellectual quality is only a necessary condition of goodness in the full sense, and not identical with it; the qualities of character are needed as well. But by the *Republic* Plato himself was implying this. Those who have the 'that' but not the 'why' are in the same position as the good men without knowledge in the *Meno*, and as those in the *Republic* who have had the primary education but have learnt no philosophy. They lack the 'reckoning of the reason' which alone can make knowledge of the Good, and therefore goodness, secure. In the Platonic state this security has to be provided by others, those who do have the knowledge.

We see then that Plato has incorporated reformed versions of both the traditional and the sophistic education into his proposed educational system. A purged system of character-formation will be succeeded, at a safe age and for sound pupils, by a development of the intellect; and each will be supervised by people who, because they know what goodness is, know what they are about, unlike both the good Athenian gentlemen and the clever sophists.

8 *The divided mind*

There is a group of doctrines, usually attributed to Socrates, in taking over which Plato encountered difficulties which caused him to modify his views, in particular his views about the mind. The most basic of these doctrines is one about the relation of the Good to desire. Not all its versions are identical. Aristotle, almost certainly endorsing Platonic views, puts it thus: 'the Good is what everything is after'. In the *Gorgias* Socrates says 'We desire the good things', and adds that whatever else we desire, we desire for the sake of these (468c). In the *Philebus* he says (in this late dialogue certainly expressing Plato's own views) 'Everything that knows [the Good] chases and pursues it, desiring to acquire and possess it' (20d). A version passed into medieval philosophy in the maxim 'Whatever is sought, is sought under the appearance of good.'

The doctrine can be given either a logical interpretation: if you are not disposed to choose something, you cannot really be thinking it the best (to think better *is* to prefer, and to prefer *is* to be disposed to choose, other things being equal); or else a psychological one, in terms of what always, by natural necessity, happens: everything as a matter of inevitable fact does choose what it thinks to be best. Plato had probably not distinguished between those interpretations, and I must confess to a doubt whether the latter, if its obscurities were removed, would turn out to be different from the former.

A related doctrine, which Plato also clung to until the end (it occurs in the *Laws*, 731c and 860d), is that, as it is commonly translated, 'Nobody willingly errs.' A translation which makes the doctrine sound self-evidently true is 'Nobody makes mistakes on purpose'; but unfortunately the *Laws* version cannot be translated in this way, since the words used mean 'Nobody willingly is not upright.' Most probably Socrates was misled by the self-evidence of the doctrine in one version into taking the more substantial version to be self-evident too.

Also related is the doctrine, already mentioned, that goodness is somehow like a craft or skill. We saw the Aristotle rightly rejected the view expressed by Socrates early in the *Meno* that goodness is the same thing as wisdom. Wisdom (which Plato equated with knowledge and with skill, two concepts which even as late as the *Politicus* he did not distinguish) is, says Aristotle, only a *necessary condition* of *goodness in the full sense*. This may also represent Plato's mature view, as we shall see.

Allied to these views is the doctrine known to scholars as 'the unity of the virtues', the view that, properly speaking, if we have any kind of goodness, we have all kinds. This might seem to follow from the premiss that wisdom and goodness or virtue are identical; for if all the virtues are identical with wisdom, they must be identical with each other. But this is too quick; courage and uprightness, for example, might each be identical with a different *kind* of wisdom, namely wisdom concerning the areas in which those virtues are exercised; and then they would not be identical with each other. Plato gives his mature views on the question in the *Laws*; virtue is one, in that it is a genus to which all virtues belong; but the species of it differ. But he still stresses the fundamental importance, for good life, education and government, of understanding the common genus (964ff.) And it is probable that he went on thinking, as Aristotle did, that one cannot have virtue *in the full sense* (cannot be, in the words of the end of the *Meno*, 'the real thing in respect of virtue') without this understanding.

But can one have the understanding without the virtue? Only, Plato came to think, if the understanding somehow failed to be in full control of us. In the *Republic* (435ff.) he gives his considered solution to the difficulty raised by the Socratic doctrine that nobody willingly errs, a doctrine which he had defended in the *Protagoras* as part of the group of doctrines we have been considering. The solution lies in thinking of the mind or soul as divided into parts which do not necessarily see eye to eye (a doctrine also found in the *Phaedrus*). For example, when people are thirsty they still may not drink, because 'there is in their soul that which bids them drink, and also something else which forbids them, and prevails over the other'. He calls the former part desire, and the latter, reason; and he adds a third part called spirit, the seat of anger, which is the natural ally of reason against desire. The good ordering of our lives which is called virtue depends on the right schooling of the two lower parts so that they obey the reason, in the same way as good government depends on the lower orders obeying wise rulers.

The way in which this partition of the mind is supposed to solve the problems raised by the Socratic doctrines is this: We can say that one part of the mind has knowledge of the Good, but may not be fully in control of the other parts. Plato had denied in the *Protagoras* that this was possible (352b). 'Self-mastery' and its opposite are, according to the *Republic*, misnomers: in the strict sense it is absurd to speak of someone being the master of himself, because then he would also be the slave of himself, and he surely cannot be both (430e), even though common parlance, and Plato himself earlier in the *Gorgias*, talks that way (491d). But it does make sense to speak of one part of him being master, or not being master, of other parts. So we can say that self-controlled people are those whose reason is in control of their desires. But not all people are in this sense self-controlled, and of those who are not it will make sense to say that they know (with their reason) the Good, but that their baser desires, which are seeking something else under the misapprehension that it is good, defeat the reason, so that bad action rather than good, vice rather than virtue, results.

Plato did not at first divide up the mind or soul in this way. In the *Phaedo*, the soul is represented as 'most like to that which is homogeneous and indissoluble' (80b); it is natural to take this as an insistence on the unity of the soul, and this unity is indeed used in the proof of immortality. The baser desires which lead us to wrong-doing are in this dialogue assigned in St Paul's fashion to the body or 'flesh'.

But even in the *Phaedo* Plato shows that he is not wholly satisfied with this way of putting the matter, and rightly. For desires are conscious states, and the soul or mind is supposed to be the seat of consciousness. A lump of flesh does not have desires: my throat does not have desires when I am thirsty; *I* have them, as part of my conscious experience. By the time he wrote the *Philebus* Plato was expressing this point very clearly (35c); he proves it from the fact that desire is of something not physically present, which therefore cannot be apprehended by the bodily senses, but only envisaged by the mind. The premiss at least of this argument is stated already in the *Symposium* (200); this is probably near in date to the *Phaedo*.

Plato had therefore, if he was to adopt the 'internal conflict' solution, to divide up the soul. But he did so with reluctance, and at the end of the *Republic* he again, when insisting on the immortality at least of the rational part of the soul, seems to be saying that it is indivisible, only we can hardly see whether it is or not because of the impurities, the mutilations and the accretions which cling to it like barnacles owing to its association with the body (611). Since both these ways of drawing up the lines of battle between the good and the evil in us are metaphors, it is perhaps not fair to Plato to insist that he decide between them.

But the solution of dividing up the self (which has continued to attract psychologists all the way to Freud) runs into more serious difficulties than this. First of all, does it leave the self enough of a unity to match our commonsense conviction that it is a single 'I' that has both the conflicting motives? If 'it is no more I, but sin that dwelleth in me', am I sinning at all? Even more seriously, what is supposed to be the role of reason (or of conscience if that is different)? Is it its function to know the Good, or to desire it? Plato is very insistent that each part of the soul, like each part of the city, has it own function; but there seem to be two different functions here.

Aristotle was aware of this difficulty, of which David Hume in the eighteenth century was to make much. Aristotle divided up the mind or soul in a somewhat Platonic but more complicated way; but he put all the motivative faculties into one part and all the cognitive and in general intellectual faculties into another; and he said of the intellect or reason that 'by itself it moves nothing; it is only when it is in pursuit of an end, and is concerned in action, that it moves anything'. Aristotle wrestled with this problem, inherited from Plato, of how the cognitive and motivative functions can somehow *combine* to produce action; he was driven a long way towards Hume's position that 'Reason is perfectly inert', while struggling, like Plato, to avoid Hume's conclusion that it 'both is and ought only to be the slave of the passions, and can never pretend to any other office than to serve and obey them'.

If Plato had been consistent in separating off the cognitive part of the mind, he would have given it no motivative function. But then, as Hume saw, it would have been totally powerless to make us do anything, except in the service of some desire which had its origin in one of the other parts of the mind. The result would be that in his effort to explain how we could be weak-willed and follow desire in despite of reason, Plato would have made it impossible for us to follow reason in despite of desire. In the *Phaedrus* he uses the simile of reason, the charioteer, controlling two horses, spirit and appetite (246, 253ff.) Even in that simile it is the horses that do the pulling; and Plato has left it unclear what, in reality, correspond to the bridle and the spur. Perhaps all that reason can do is show the horses how to get where *they* want to go.

Actually he is not fully consistent, and so escapes this conclusion. Sometimes he escapes it by making the spirit, if well conducted, the ally of reason, providing the motive force which reason, strictly understood, could not provide. More typically he gives to reason itself a motivative power, claiming, as in a passage already quoted, that merely to know the Good is automatically to be attracted by it, so that the same faculty of reason fulfils both the cognitive and the motivative roles. In the same way, in the *Politicus*, the body of the king has small strength; he manages to govern because of the understanding *and power* of his soul or mind (259c).

Whether this is a possible solution depends on whether there could be such a thing as Plato thought the Good to be. To fulfil its dual role of object of knowledge and object of desire it would have to be such that, once discovered, it automatically excited desire. If anybody did not desire it once discovered, it would not be the same thing which he had discovered. Two people logically could not both discover this same thing, and one desire it, one not. 'We needs must love the highest when we see it' would then become a logically or metaphysically necessary truth—and that not because 'highest' is a value word, so that to call something 'the highest' is already to express love for it. For if that were so, before we thought of something as the Good, we should have to be already being attracted by it; desire as well as cognition would have to be involved in the 'discovery' of it; and that is ruled out by a consistent separation of reason from motivation. Rather, the Good has to be something determined independently of our wills: propositions describing it have to be factually descriptive. And yet our wills have somehow to be automatically engaged in its pursuit once discovered; propositions about it have therefore to be prescriptive as well.

Whether we can follow Plato in believing in the existence of such a thing will depend on how seriously we take the objections of some modern thinkers to the existence, or even the coherence, of the notion of 'objective prescriptions'—that is to say, of propositions which can somehow at one and the same time both be objectively established as true, independently of how anybody is motivated or disposed, *and* carry a prescriptive force. Whatever side we may take in modern disputes on this issue, it is clear that Plato, in his doctrine of the Good as an eternally existing entity, beyond being but at the same time the source of being, as he says in the *Republic* (509b), did believe in something very like what is now called objective prescriptivity; but, perhaps fortunately for him, he did not have such unwieldy words with which to express it.

9 *The authoritarian State*

Given Plato's views about knowledge of the Good, and about the role of education in making possible a good life, it is easy to see how he came by his highly authoritarian political doctrines. We can become good men and lead a good life by one of two means. Either we acquire right opinions about the best way to live, or we acquire knowledge. Both, as he says in the *Meno* (98), will serve the limited purpose of living a good life; but right opinion can never be reliably imparted, and will never be secure against corrupting influences, unless somebody—either a man himself or those who teach and subsequently rule him—has not merely right opinion but knowledge: knowledge of the Ideas, which are the explanations of why things are as they are, and are also, because of the dependence of the other Ideas on the Good, explanations of how it is best that they should be. The possessors of this knowledge are the only people who can determine what kind of life is good, and thus the only people who can provide the education (even the primary education which imparts only right opinion) and the governance which are the necessary conditions of the good life.

Given these premises it seems obvious that, if the good life is to be lived in a particular society or state, its institutions will have to be framed in such a way as to further this education, and that this will come about only if those who have the knowledge are put firmly in charge of the machinery of government. Anybody who objects to Plato's authoritarian views will have to find some flaw in this argument; and the best way to understand the strengths and weaknesses of the argument is to look for the flaws. We shall see that the argument is more secure than it looks at first sight, and that to reject it involves rejecting some views which are still widely held.

Let us first look at the political institutions which Plato actually recommends, and then see what justifications he can find for their adoption. The *Republic* contains his first full-scale design for an ideal state, though it is concerned with much else besides, and is, on this as on other questions, a bit sketchy and programmatic. The citizens are to be divided into two classes, and the higher of these subdivided again into two, making three in all. They correspond to the three 'parts' into which man's mind is divided, reason, spirit and appetite; to each class those people are assigned in whom these mental characteristics respectively predominate. It is presumed that heredity will do most of the work of assignment between classes; but Plato makes a point of saying that, if there are any misfits, promotion or demotion is to take place.

The small class of rational people is to rule the state with the support of the 'spirited' or soldier class, from whom the rulers themselves, called 'guardians', are selected during the common process of education which both classes initially share. The masses in the lowest of the three classes are excluded from any part in government; their role is to obey, and to supply the community's needs by engaging in useful trades. Scholars dispute whether Plato intends them to share in the education provided for the guardians and soldiers, but his silence on the question seems to imply that he does not.

The first stage in this education, as we have seen, comprises training in the arts and in athletics with a view to the formation of good character and right opinions, firmly implanted. Intellectual education, the cultivation of the reason as a qualification for ruling, will not otherwise be safe. Mathematics, an essential preliminary to philosophy, is offered to the children but not forced on them. They are also taken as spectators to see battles, mounted on horses for their safety, so that when they come to fight they may do so bravely. By the age of thirty a select few, who have proved themselves in all the branches of the earlier education, are judged fit for the study of philosophy for five years, after which they serve in the lower offices of state, civil and military, for fifteen years. At fifty, 'the survivors, the best of them,' are 'compelled to turn their mind's eye' to the Idea of the Good, and then take their turns for what remains of their lives ordering the city, and the individual citizens, and themselves, using the Good as their model. When not thus occupied, they can indulge in the pleasures of philosophy (540).

The innovation which Plato thinks will seem most startling is that women are to share all this, both the education (including athletics) and the responsibility of government, on equal terms with men. It must be remembered that the Greeks in Plato's time engaged in athletics naked. The picture of Californian beaches which this may suggest is quickly dispelled; we learn that the sex life of all is to be strictly regulated, mating being forbidden except at special festivals and between selected partners at the discretion of the rulers, with a eugenic purpose. Children are to be held in common, as in a strict kibbutz, treating all grown-ups as equally their parents.

The life of the two higher classes is as austere as in Sparta; Plato is insistent here and elsewhere that ruling as such is a disagreeable activity, to be undertaken not for personal advantage but for the good of society as a whole. This was perhaps Plato's greatest contribution to political theory; a much commoner view was that political power is desirable not only for its own sake but also for the material advantages that the powerful can obtain. Plato, by contrast, envisages the rulers ruling unwillingly, and only for fear of being ruled by somebody worse than themselves (347c). Being neither pleasure-seeking nor ambitious, the true philosopher, alone qualified to rule through his knowledge of the Good, can leave the pursuit of material pleasures to the lower orders.

Hardly any detail is given in the *Republic* of how the government of the ideal state is actually to be carried on. In particular, the relation of the rulers to the laws remains somewhat obscure. In the *Crito*, an early work, Socrates is made to enjoin and himself exemplify a highly reverential attitude to law; although he has been unjustly condemned to death, it would be wrong for him to break the laws by fleeing into exile, because the laws could then accuse him of going back on a compact with them from which he had benefited in the past (50). Did Plato in the *Republic* intend that his rulers should have this same attitude of implicit obedience to the laws? The question is discussed and clarified in a later dialogue, the *Politicus*, to which Aristotle's discussion owes much (293ff.) In an ideal state with ideal rulers, Plato thinks, the rulers ought not themselves to be bound by the laws, but should be able to alter them *ad hoc* to fit individual cases, just as a doctor fits his treatment to the condition of each patient. Any attempt to lay down laws by which the rulers themselves were to be bound would lead to an inability to suit measures to particular cases and to a ban on all innovation however beneficial. *Provided that the ruler possesses the art of ruling*, he should be free to adapt the laws to his knowledge of the Good.

Only in inferior imitations of the ideal state, which lack rulers with this knowledge (and such are indeed hard to find), is universal obedience to the laws, even by the rulers, insisted on. Those who do not have knowledge of the Good have to be controlled by laws. This includes the lower classes even in the best of states; for them the absolute obedience commended in the *Crito* is still appropriate. The judges are to be subordinate to the government: Belloc's 'Lord Chief Justice of Liberia / And Minister of the Interior' held a combined office which would have had a counterpart in Plato's city, in which the judiciary is 'the guardian of the laws and the servant of the kingly power' (305c).

By the time Plato wrote the *Laws* his pessimism had gone further, no doubt increased by his experiences in Sicily and the lack of progress, by Platonic standards, in the politics of the Greek cities. The main speaker plays the role of a lawgiver, of a type which was in demand when new Greek colonies were founded, and to which the Academy provided some recruits, as we have seen. By his mouth Plato sets out a lengthy, elaborate and detailed set of laws, which must have appeared extremely severe and rigid even to a Greek reactionary. They are not to be departed from, although at the end there seems to be provision for amendment by the supreme Nocturnal Council in the light of the Idea of Virtue.

In this second-best city, as Plato recognises it to be (875), the rulers are 'servants of the law' (715d). But in an ideal city it would not be so. The ideals of the *Republic* remain in another respect too; although in both works great inequality of power is prescribed, the distribution of wealth, though not actually inverted as in the *Republic* so that the rulers are poorer, remains moderately egalitarian; and it does not depend on one's income-group whether one becomes a ruler, but only on one's merit as judged by the existing rulers. The philosopher-king ideal survives (711).

A modern liberal will certainly find these suggested institutions extremely repellent. Let us then ask how he might seek to undermine Plato's argument. He might, first of all, attack the more picturesque features of the Platonic metaphysics. He might dismiss as mythological the view that there is a celestial world of eternally existing Ideas, visible to the eye of the mind provided that it has been suitably schooled. The claim that only those with this superior mental vision are competent to guide others by education and firm government might thus be defeated. Unfortunately matters are not so easy for the liberal. We can show this by restating the Platonic authoritarian argument without the mythology. In order to establish it, it is not necessary for Plato to adopt a mental-vision-of-eternal-objects theory of knowledge. Of the two alternative caricatures of Plato invented in Chapter 4, Pato clearly believed in such a theory, and he was a political authoritarian. What will be more interesting to the liberal is to see whether the more modern-seeming Lato would have to have the same political views. Lato is a linguistic philosopher. Are there views about language, especially evaluative language, which can have such extreme political implications?

It would not be unfair to attribute to Lato a view about evaluative and in particular about moral language which is still widely accepted: the view that moral and other evaluative statements state objective facts about the world, which are capable of being known. This extremely respectable position is variously known as ethical objectivism, cognitivism or descriptivism—terms which do not mean the same as each other, but whose differences in meaning need not concern us here. Lato certainly believed in the 'objectivity of values'; but he could allow us, if we wanted, to dismiss as mythological the metaphysical scaffolding wherewith Pato sought to support it. It is enough for Lato to claim that, when I say that a certain way of life is good, I am claiming to state an objective fact.

If this were granted, the question then arises of how such claims are to be assessed for truth or falsity. How do we settle whether the way of life *is* good? Various sorts of objectivist give different answers to this question; but whatever method of settling these evaluative questions is proposed, the next question will be whether everybody is equally able to operate it, or whether some are better than others at determining questions about value. For if some are better than others, will not the Platonic authoritarian conclusion follow that these superior people should be given the say in all important political decisions? If what we are after is the good life, must we not leave the ordering of our lives to those who *know* what it is?

The crucial fact here, when we ask whether all are equally good at answering questions about values, is that people *differ* about such questions. This point was discussed in Plato's school, and indeed, if the *Greater Alcibiades* is a genuine work of Plato's, as it probably is, discussed by Plato himself. The same views as are there expressed are in any case implicit in the *Theaetetus* (170d), the *Phaedrus* (263a) and elsewhere. The argument is closely bound up with the analogy between the good life and arts and skills. In the *Alcibiades* Socrates is made to point out that, whereas 'the many' are all in agreement about how to speak Greek (for example, they do not disagree about how to apply the words 'stone', 'stick', 'man' and 'horse', and therefore all qualify as competent teachers of the use of these words), when it comes to assessing the merits of men or horses, or in general making value judgements, they do differ, and therefore we cannot say that they are all competent teachers about such evaluative matters. There is, rather, a select class of people who know (that is, who have the appropriate skill) and are therefore competent teachers. This conclusion is applied to questions about what is right or wrong, on which Alcibiades has pretended to instruct the Athenians in their Assembly (111).

If it is once agreed that only some, not all, people are qualified to pronounce on questions of value, then the Platonic authoritarian argument is well under way. And it seems that this argument requires only two premisses: that values are objective, and that people differ about them. It looks as if the second premiss is obviously true, and as if, therefore, anybody who wishes to avoid the authoritarian conclusion will have to reject the first. Unless, that is, we take the pessimistic view that *nobody* knows the objective answers, though these do exist. Short of divine guidance, there would then be no hope of getting our politics right; but although in the *Meno* Plato rather playfully attributed to divine guidance such successes as had been achieved hitherto, he hoped for something more reliable (99c).

It is possible to think of various ways in which a liberal might seek to escape the authoritarian conclusion while remaining an objectivist. These moves rely on two distinctions, that between means and ends and that between questions of substance and questions about the meanings of words. We shall see that the first distinction does not help the liberal against Plato if he remains an objectivist, but that the second enables us to liberalise Lato, if not Pato, in a way that could conceivably have commended itself to Plato himself if, as was not the case, he had been clear about both distinctions. But it leaves him no longer an unmixed objectivist.

It might be suggested that if we distinguish between the end (the good life) and the political and other means to it, we can say that the knowledgeable élite is indeed more competent than the rest of the population to judge of means, but not of ends. Everybody is, in the last reckoning, the best judge of whether his own life has been a good one for himself; but people can be wildly mistaken about what political, social and economic arrangements are most likely to bring it about that the maximum number of people attain this satisfaction with their own lives. But if this is so, we shall maximise satisfaction by finding out (perhaps by democratic vote, or less crudely by sociological researches) what manner of lives will most satisfy various sorts of people, and then leaving it to the experts to see to it that lives of those kinds are achieved.

To this suggestion there are at least two objections. The first is that it is not likely in practice to lead to a very liberal form of government. At any rate a great many of the vexed questions in politics are questions of means, even if we differ about ends too. And secondly, in any case, questions of means and ends in politics are thoroughly tangled up with one another. To take a simple example: imagine that we are all agreed that it is a desirable end to raise the general standard of living (in the crudest material and measurable terms). It will hardly be a liberal society if, having agreed upon this end, we leave the means to it in the hands of experts. For one thing, if the experts pursue this end single-mindedly, they will find themselves doing things inimical to *other* ends which their subjects hold dear, such as personal liberty; but if they try to meet this objection by securing prior agreement to a comprehensive basket of ends, with a

weighting or priority attached to each, the sheer political imprac-
ticability of such a procedure will at once become apparent. They
are more likely to succeed by submitting themselves to the
judgement of their subjects at the end of a given term of office,
and asking for re-election if their measures have in the outcome
advanced what the subjects think to have been in their interest.

Such an arrangement, however, ought not to commend itself
to an objectivist liberal any more than it would to Plato. For the
question about ends remains pressing. If values are objective, as
both Pato and Lato think, then judgements about the ends
which ought to be pursued (that is, about the character of the
good life) will be objective too, and will have, on the preceding
argument, to be left to experts. So the first liberal escape-route is
closed.

A more promising line starts from a distinction which Pato
would find difficult, but into which Lato might be coaxed if we
had him with us. The question 'What is the Good?' can be taken
in at least two ways. It can be taken as an inquiry into the
meaning of the *word* 'good', or as an inquiry into the qualifying
properties which entitle us to call a thing of a certain kind (or, as
perhaps Plato would have thought, of any kind) good. Plato had
not had the advantage of reading the sixth chapter of Aristotle's
Nicomachean Ethics I, and therefore made the mistake of thinking
that the qualifying properties which make things of all kinds
good are the same; but it is easy to see that the properties that
make a good strawberry good are not the same as those which
make a good motorcycle good.

However, leaving this difficulty on one side, let us take
separately, as Plato does not, the question of the meaning of the
word 'good' and that of the qualifying properties which entitle
us to call things good. The failure to make this distinction is the
source of the view, commonly called descriptivism, which has
been almost universal in moral philosophy until recently: the
view that the two questions which I say have to be distinguished
are really the same question. This is no place to argue that they
are not the same question (that two people may mean the same
by 'good' but use different qualifying properties for assessing
goodness in, for example, cheeses). I shall merely assume for
the sake of argument that there is a distinction, and then see
how it helps with our present problem.

If the question 'What does the phrase "the good life" *mean*?' is a different question from 'What properties make a life good?', then interesting possibilities open up. We have to ask: If Socrates puts the question 'What is the good life?', which of these questions does he mean us to answer? The first question, about the meaning, looks a good candidate for handling by means of the Socratic method of scrutiny. Various definitions or explanations of the meaning will be proposed, and tested against the understanding we all have of how words are rightly used. If we can find an account of the meaning which satisfies this test, then we can proceed to use the phrase, in full awareness of its meaning and therefore its logical implications, in argument about the other question, the question about the properties which make a life good. Our achievement so far would be a philosophical one, reached by the analysis of concepts, without any assumptions of substance about what *does* constitute a good life. If Plato were simply suggesting that this is a necessary and useful contribution on the part of the philosopher, we could perhaps all agree.

But then we have to ask: What bearing will the philosophical, conceptual inquiry so far outlined have upon the answer to the second question, 'What properties make a life good?' That will depend, obviously, on what account of the meaning of 'good' has stood up to the scrutiny-test. Without launching into a survey of rival theories in moral philosophy, let us at least envisage the possibility that the successful account of the meaning of 'good' and of other such words might put into our possession certain logical weapons—certain canons of argument about the question of what kinds of life are good—which could help us settle that question. In that case, Plato's programme would have been in part vindicated. The philosopher would have made an important contribution, not merely to the question of meaning, but also to moral and political ones.

Unfortunately Plato did not bequeath to us an account of the meaning of 'good'; and his account of other moral concepts or Ideas is not sufficient for us to extract canons of moral argument. We can only speculate about what he would have said if he had given a full explanation of the concepts used in moral argument. It is fairly safe to say that the account would have included certain elements. In the first place he would have insisted on the objectivity of statements about the good life, at least in the sense that fully informed and rational people would not disagree about what it consisted in. But he would also have insisted that statements about the good life were prescriptive, in the sense that to accept that a certain way of life would be good would be already to be motivated towards pursuing it.

It is not obvious that, when 'objectivity' is taken in this minimal sense, the notion of an objective prescription (see p. 62) is incoherent, though it probably is incoherent if it is taken in the more usual sense, in which a statement is said to make an objective claim if it is factual or descriptive. Probably Plato would have claimed it in this stronger sense; but even in the weaker sense it could serve to support his political views. For if there are prescriptions on which all rational and informed people would agree, and if only a certain section of the population are rational and informed, ought we not to crown them as philosopher-kings and let them coerce and indoctrinate the others, for their own good, into obeying these prescriptions?

The conclusion could be avoided if we abandoned objectivity, if not entirely, at any rate as regards judgements made by people about *their own* good. Let us suppose that everybody is the best judge of what is good for *him*, in the sense of what most satisfies *him*. We could then avoid the most illiberal aspects of Plato's paternalism by confining the role of his rational rulers to the tasks, first of determining what outcomes would maximally reconcile the divergent interests of all their subjects, thus ensuring for them the greatest possible satisfaction, and secondly of finding the means most conducive to bringing about these outcomes. And we could allow the subjects to dismiss the rulers by popular vote if they proved unsuccessful in this role, and elect others. Given his background, it is unlikely that Plato would have agreed with this democratic solution, but it is consistent with his main philosophical views as interpreted by Lato, except that the claim that value judgements are objective has to be interpreted in a rather weak sense. Philosophy is left with a crucial role, but it is not allowed to dictate to people what they are to find good in life.

Two further points may be made, the first in Plato's favour, the second not. First, as has often been pointed out by recent writers, we are unlikely to be able to escape being ruled by a ruling class of some kind; 'the iron law of oligarchy' is fairly well established by a study of history. If there are going in any case to be relatively few people who have the power of government and exercise its functions, even in a democracy, then Plato is surely entirely right in holding that it will be best if they receive, before they attain this position of power, an education which will enable them to exercise it wisely. Though Pato may be wrong in requiring a deep study of the eternal verities and values, Lato is on safer ground when he asks that they acquire an understanding of the language they use when they debate the crucial moral and other evaluative questions that confront the statesman. For if they do not understand the questions they are asking, they will hardly be able to answer them rationally. If Lato were to claim that this is all the education that is necessary for rulers, he would be going too far, for they need other qualifications besides philosophy. But in fact even in the *Republic* this claim is not made—only that such understanding is a supremely important part of the equipment of a ruler.

Secondly, we must make more allowance than perhaps Plato does for human fallibility. Even if we grant him that there is a skill of ruling which could in theory equip its possessor to make all the right decisions, it may be a skill which no human being will ever attain, and perhaps a skill by the exercise of which he will be corrupted. Plato is in fact fairly pessimistic about this, as can be seen by reading between the lines of the *Republic*, and by looking at the much less ambitious demands made of his rulers in the *Laws*. But Plato does not recognise, as he should, that if rulers are fallible their claim to absolute power is less strong. As Sir Karl Popper rightly insisted, it may be more important to have institutional means of limiting the harm that unwise rulers can do, and removing them without violence if they fail to secure the good of their subjects.

10 *Plato's achievement*

If the first of Europe's philosophers whose works survive does not have the same towering dominance as its first poet, Homer, that is not any reflection on Plato's genius. His actual achievement in his own field was as great. It is merely that we know a little more about what went before. Despite this, he, like Homer, presents to us the appearance (albeit a misleading one) of arising out of nothing, and also of a certain primitiveness which his marvellously polished style does not altogether conceal. He has a greater claim than anybody else to be called the founder of philosophy as we know it. But what, exactly, did he found? The answer will depend on who 'we' are; it will be different for Patonists and Latonists, and even that crude division does not do justice to the complexity of Plato's make-up, and of his influence on the subsequent history of philosophy.

Of the two Platos that we distinguished, it is difficult to think that the achievement of Pato was as great as that of Lato. The 'perennial philosophy' is perennial just because it is a very natural expression of human thinking about the mind and about values; it has appeared in many places at many times in different forms, and Plato's mind-body dualism, with its associated belief in the immortality of the soul, and his particular treatment of the objectivity of values, are not markedly different from anybody else's. What is unique in him is the progress from these quasi-religious speculations, which could have remained, as they have in others, vapid and evanescent, towards a much tougher, more precise logical and metaphysical theory, a moral philosophy and a philosophy of language; these were not entirely new, but, through discussion and criticism of them, they engendered the lasting achievements of Aristotle in those fields, and thus shaped the entire future of philosophy.

Let us start with Plato's development of the topic of 'The One and the Many'. We have seen how the early cosmologists sought an explanation of the bewildering variety of things in the world by seeking for them some common ground or reason. The search started with the question, 'What were their origins?'; went on to the question 'What are they all made of?'; but then divided. Natural scientists went on asking this second question in ever subtler forms and have been answering it ever since. But by this time problems had arisen which could not be answered by this method, and which demanded an entirely different sort of inquiry, whether we style it metaphysics or logic. For the puzzles generated by Parmenides could not be solved without asking 'What are they all?' in a quite different sense. This new inquiry, whether we call it conceptual or logical or even linguistic, consists in asking about the meanings of the words we use, or, to put it in a way more congenial to Plato, about the natures (in a quite different sense from the physical) of the things we are talking about. The Many are to be understood, not by seeking their physical constituents, nor even the efficient causes of their motions and changes, but by isolating and understanding the Idea to which we are referring when we use a certain word. This is to know in the deepest sense what it *is* to be a thing of a certain kind.

Plato had grasped the truth that conceptual understanding is different from natural science, and just as important. He had succeeded in distinguishing from each other the four different types of explanation (the four different kinds of 'Why?'-questions and their answers) which were duly classified by Aristotle in his doctrine of the 'four causes'. Of these we have just mentioned three:

1 The *material* cause, or explanation of the material constitution of a thing;

2 The *efficient* cause, or cause in the narrower modern sense, which made a thing do what it did;

3 The *formal* cause, or explanation of its form—of what it is to be that kind of thing;

and he also, as we shall see in a moment, distinguished

4 The *final* cause, or explanation of the purpose for which something comes to be as it is.

Plato was more interested in formal and final causes than in the other two kinds, and thought that they would both be understood by getting to know the Idea of the kind of thing in question. This association of the formal and final causes (having its origin in Plato's doctrine about the Good, already discussed) may have been a mistake; but, if so, it was a very momentous one which was taken over by Aristotle and by many philosophers to this day. The notion that what it *is to be* a thing of a certain kind (its essence) is logically tied to what a thing of that kind *ought to be* (its purpose) still has its adherents.

To have distinguished the four kinds of explanation would have been achievement enough, but Plato went further. He saw that there was a question about how we could claim to *know* the answers to the formal and final 'Why?'-questions. We may concede that in his theory of knowledge knowing is treated too much like mental seeing, and the objects of knowledge too much like objects of ordinary vision, being different from them only in being seen by the mind and not the eyes, and in having a perfection and abidingness which the objects of ordinary vision do not have. But nevertheless the Theory of Ideas does represent Plato's way of stating some very important discoveries.

The first of these is that the sort of knowledge we are after both in science and in mathematics and logic is something universal. A causal law or a mathematical or logical theorem, if it holds at all, holds for all similar cases. That moral principles too have to be universal is a feature of them whose importance has to be acknowledged even by those who do not follow Plato in his cognitivism—do not, that is, allow themselves to speak of moral *knowledge*.

The second is that all these disciplines including morality are capable of being structured into systems in which more general concepts or statements form the grounds of more specific ones. For both Plato and Aristotle this truth was expressed in their doctrine that in order to say what a thing is, we have to say to what genus it belongs, and then to say how it is differentiated from the other kinds of things in that genus. This is summed up in the Platonic method of dialectic, employing 'collection' and 'division' (see p. 49). We must never forget that the word Plato used for his Ideas, '*eidos*', is the same word, and with very much the same meaning, as we translate 'species' when we meet it in

Aristotle's logic. Plato's description in the *Republic* (511) of the way in which the Ideas are subordinated to one another in a hierarchy may sound too crudely physical to us (it is almost as if he were looking with his mind's eye at a lot of quasi-visible onions strung together in a rope); but this was his way of putting the thought that a discipline has to be logically ordered if its propositions are to be *connected* (the metaphor survives) with each other.

In this and other ways Plato's investigations of the Socratic 'What is . . . ?' questions led him a very long way into the disciplines of logic and metaphysics. Aristotle's systematisation of logic—above all his theory of the syllogism which dominated logic for many centuries—could never have been achieved without Plato's insights.

Plato also, as we have seen, avoided a trap into which he might easily have fallen, given his assimilation of knowing to mental seeing: that of thinking, as Descartes seems to have thought, that the clarity and distinctness of the vision was a certificate of its correctness. Instead, by recognising the difference betwen knowledge and right opinion, he was led to demand, as a qualification for knowledge, the ability to give and defend a reason or explanation for the thing known. This explanation normally took the form of a definition (ideally of the type just described). However, the importance of this distinction transcends Plato's particular theory of definition. Whenever anybody, whether in science or mathematics or moral philosophy, makes some statement on the basis of mere intuition, hoping that we will share the intuition and therefore agree with it, he should be disciplined by means of the Socratic-Platonic demand that he 'give an account' of what he has said. Even now too many philosophical frauds are unwilling to face the auditors in this way.

So far we have not, in this chapter, made much of any distinction between on the one hand science and mathematics, and on the other morals and politics. This is in accordance with Plato's practice; he thinks that all are subject to the same disciplines and methods, although in the application of them to this imperfect world rigour may be lost. But those who now wish to make a sharp distinction between evaluative and factual propositions, and thus between the methods appropriate to morality and science, do not have to part company with Plato completely even here. For one of the most remarkable things about him is how, even though he never wavered in his objectivism, and constantly assimilated moral to other kinds of knowledge, he also recognised quite early, following Socrates, the special feature of value judgements which distinguishes them from factual ones, their prescriptivity. This comes out above all in his equation of thinking something good with desiring and therefore being disposed to choose it, and thus in his acceptance, albeit in a modified form, of the links between knowledge and goodness which had led Socrates into paradox.

Nor did the prescriptivity of value judgements die with Plato. It is implicit in Aristotle's statement that the Good is what everything is after; and also in his doctrine known as the 'practical syllogism'. The conclusion of a piece of practical reasoning, he saw, can be an action just because its premisses contain a value judgement which is prescriptive. He insists that practical wisdom, our guide in matters of evaluation and action, is 'epitactic' (meaning 'prescriptive')—a word he takes over, with the distinction it implies between active prescription and mere passive judgement, from Plato's *Politicus* (260b). The same intimate connection between value judgements and action became important again in the eighteenth century with the work of Hume, who found in it an obstacle to the founding of morality on reason, and of Kant, who thought he had surmounted the obstacle; and it is still important today.

Plato was also the first person in history to attempt a systematic account of the structure of the mind. His account is no doubt crude compared with Aristotle's, let alone with what a satisfactory explanation of 'mental' phenomena would require. And he did not see the necessity for saying precisely what, in more literal terms, the metaphor of 'parts of the mind' really means. All the same, he started a very important and fruitful line of inquiry, and had much more excuse for his crude partition of the mind than some recent thinkers like Freud. Although it is hard to take seriously, as constituents of 'the mind', entities like 'the intellect' and 'the will' (to use modern descendants of Plato's terms), the distinctions which have been made in this kind of way do nevertheless need making.

They need making, above all, in order to emphasise the

importance of disciplined thought, if we are to have a satisfactory way of answering any of the more difficult questions that face us. Although we have to allow credit to Plato's predecessors, and especially to the Sophists, for bringing into emphasis the intellectual side of man's nature, we owe to Plato and Socrates more than to anybody else the idea, which has been current ever since, that man will have more success in almost everything he undertakes if he learns to *think* better.

This brings us to what, I am sure, Plato himself thought of as his most important practical contribution: his educational theory. He believed firmly that there could be a body of knowledge or understanding whose attainment and handing down would make possible the orderly solution of political problems such as had brought Athens and all Greece into chaos. In this he taught the world a valuable lesson. If we could fully understand the problems, which involves understanding first of all the words in terms of which they are posed, and then (even harder) understanding the situations and the people that generate them, we should be on a way to their solution. This, at any rate, is a more hopeful line than attributing them to human wickedness which can never be eradicated. Even the wicked can be coped with if we understand what makes them do what they do. Socrates did not think he had attained this understanding, and even Plato was not all that optimistic; but he saw it as the only way out of the troubles of Greece, and founded an institution, the Academy, which he thought would help towards attaining it.

His bolder plans for political reform are more questionable, and more tentative. If the education of the intellect, preceded by a thorough schooling of the will, is necessary in order to put human society to rights, how can this come about? Plato here took a short cut. If absolute power could come into the hands of good and wise men, would not that do the trick? We have seen how much of good sense can be extracted from this bold suggestion. It is not wholly devoid of merit, but simply ignores the difficulty (indeed the practical impossibility) of finding suitable incumbents, and the further difficulty of reconciling absolute power, however wise its possessor, with the attainment of ends which nearly everybody (and who shall say they are wrong?) will include in their requirements for the good life, above all liberty. When Plato, impressed with the practical difficulties, goes on in the *Laws* to subject human and fallible rulers to a rigid code, he only makes matters worse. In its final form the Platonic proposal shares many features with the Holy Inquisition.

Nevertheless, Plato's political theory presents the liberal with a challenge which he has to face, and in facing which he will find himself having to answer questions which too many liberals ignore. If some ways of organising society are better than others, in the sense that they do better for the people who live in the society, even on their own reckoning; and if some politicans and others are doing their very best to prevent it being organised, or kept organised, in these better ways, what am I to do about them, if not seek the power to frustrate their malign endeavours? If I think I know how a wise dictator would arrange things, ought I not to try to become a wise dictator? Plato has his answer to this question; what is the answer of the liberals?

Plato did not see his political proposals realised, nor perhaps did he expect to. His only excursion into politics, in Sicily, was a disaster. But a change did come over men's minds as a result of his thought. Greek political morality did not improve, it is true; nor was the Roman much better. But though the practice of politics remained as dirty as before, it is fair to claim that, gradually, through the work of Plato and his successors, the Stoics, Christians and others, ideals of a new and better sort came in the end to be current.

The rhetoric of present-day politics is still mostly nothing but rhetoric; but rhetoric does influence people (even its authors), and cause things to happen which otherwise would not. Our political rhetoric is permeated now by ideals which were simply non-existent in the rhetoric of Plato's day. This can be seen by comparing almost any political speech nowadays with almost any speech reported from the fifth and fourth centuries BC. Politicians do not always do what they commend in their speeches; but sometimes they do, and that has made a difference to the world. Part of this difference we owe to Plato. In the end he made many people see that personal or even national ambition and success are not the most important things in life, and that the good of other people is a worthier aim. For this we can forgive him for being also the father of political paternalism and absolutism.

Further reading

Readers who want to study what others have said about Plato will find nearly all the bibliographical information and guidance that they need in the fourth and fifth volumes of W. K. C. Guthrie's *A History of Greek Philosophy* (1962–78), which is also itself both helpful and readable, though enormously long. My own debt to it will be obvious. The earlier volumes, especially that on Socrates, are useful for Plato's predecessors. Those whose taste is for philosophically more sophisticated books might well try I. M. Crombie's *An Examination of Plato's Doctrines* (1962) or J. C. B. Gosling's *Plato* (1973) in the 'Arguments of the Philosophers' series. J. Barnes's *The Presocratics* (1969) in the same series is also good. Sir Karl Popper's *The Open Society and its Enemies* vol. 1 (1945) and Gilbert Ryle's *Plato's Progress* (1966) are two highly readable but also highly controversial books, the first on Plato's politics, the second on his philosophical development. There are a number of good multi-author volumes of essays, among them *New Essays on Plato and Aristotle* (ed. R. Bambrough, 1965), *Studies in Plato's Metaphysics* (ed. R. E. Allen, 1965) and *Plato* (ed. G. Vlastos, 1971). The latter's own *Platonic Studies* (1973) are also to be commended.

All these books are written mainly for specialists. The general reader is better advised to stick to Plato; and for this purpose there is a number of series of translations of single dialogues, some with excellent introductions, and a convenient omnibus volume of all the dialogues (*Plato*, ed. E. Hamilton and H. Cairns, 1961). More advanced, but very useful, are the volumes of translations with commentary in the Clarendon Plato series. However, accurate translation of Plato's Greek is often difficult, and nobody who bases his interpretations on translations, rather than the Greek text, can claim authority.

References

All references in this book to Plato are to the pages of Stephanus' edition as printed in the margin of the standard Oxford Classical Text of Plato (ed. J. Burnet, 1900–7) and of nearly all translations. In the references below the figures on the left refer to pages of this book. References to Aristotle are to the pages, columns and lines of Bekker's edition, also followed by most modern editions and translations.

Page

7. Thucydides II 35.

9. *The Polity of the Athenians* is wrongly attributed to Xenophon and printed with his works.

10. Herodotus III 38.

11. Thucydides III 82. For persuasive definition see C. L. Stevenson, *Ethics and Language* (1944), ch. 9.

17. Aristotle, *On the Heavens*, 299–300.

18. Heraclitus and Cratylus are discussed by Plato in *Theaetetus* (esp. 179ff.) and *Cratylus* (esp. 439ff.).

20. Aristophanes, *The Clouds*. Xenophon, esp. *Memoirs of Socrates*. Aristotle, esp. *Metaphysics* 987b1, 1078b17, *Eudemian Ethics* 1216b2, *Nicomachean Ethics* 1144b18ff. 1145b23ff. For Socrates' moral influence see Lysias' speech against Aeschines his disciple, fragment xxxviii in Budé edition (ed. Gernet and Bizos, 1955).

26. On Recollection see my 'Philosophical Discoveries', *Mind* 69 (1960), §viii, repr. in *Plato's Meno*, ed. Sesonske and Fleming (1965), *The Linguistic Turn*, ed. R. Rorty (1967), and my *Essays on Philosophical Method* (1971).

27. Lewis Carroll's philosophical use of paradox is delightfully illustrated in P. L. Heath, *The Philosopher's Alice* (1974).

32. J. H. Newman, *The Dream of Gerontius* (1868).

36. On this chapter, see M. Furth, 'Elements of Eleatic Ontology', *Journal of History of Philosophy* 6 (1968), and my own 'A Question about Plato's Theory of Ideas', in my *Essays on Philosophical Method* (1971) (also in *The Critical Approach*, ed. M. Bunge, 1964).

39. For 'Fido' see G. Ryle in *British Philosophy in the Mid-Century*, ed. C. A. Mace (1957).

44. Both sorts of attackers appeal to L. Wittgenstein, *Philosophical Investigations* (1953), esp. §66ff., 242. For the first attack, see J. R. Bambrough, 'Universals and Family Resemblances', *Aristotelian Society Proceedings* 51 (1960/1).

45. For the second attack, see M. Nussbaum, 'Aristophanes and Socrates on Learning Practical Wisdom', *Yale Classical Studies* 26 (1980), and P. T. Geach, 'Plato's *Euthyphro*', *Monist* 50 (1966), repr. in his *Logic Matters* (1972).

45. Wittgenstein, *Philosophical Investigations*, §242.

46. G. Frege, *Foundations of Arithmetic*, trans. J. L. Austin (1959), p. iii.

48. Aristotle, e.g. Categories 1a2.

48. On the two ways of taking the argument, see my 'The Argument from Received Opinion' in my *Essays on Philosophical Method*, pp. 117ff.

50. On the Good, see my 'Plato and the Mathematicians', op.cit. pp. 94–6, repr. from *New Essays on Plato and Aristotle*, ed. R. Bambrough (1965).

53. On this chapter, see my 'Platonism in Moral Education: Two Varieties', *Monist* 58 (1974).

57. Plato in Aristotle, *Nicomachean Ethics* 1104b11.

58. Aristotle, *Nicomachean Ethics* 1094a3, 1172b14.

59. Aristotle, ibid. 1144b17–32.

61. The biblical quotation is from St Paul, *Epistle to the Romans*, ch. vii.

61. D. Hume, *A Treatise of Human Nature* (1739), III I i; II 3 iii.

63. On 'objective prescriptivity' see J. L. Mackie, *Ethics: Inventing Right and Wrong* (1977), ch. 1, commented on in my *Moral Thinking* (1981), pp. 78–86.

67. H. Belloc, *The Modern Traveller* (1898).

71. I have tried to sort out the distinction between the meaning of moral words and the criteria for their application in my *The Language of Morals* (1952), esp. chs 6ff.; see also my *Freedom and Reason* (1963), ch. 2.

74. K. R. Popper, *The Open Society and its Enemies*, vol. 1, esp. ch. 7.

ARISTOTLE

JONATHAN BARNES

Contents

For Richard Robinson

1 *The man and his work*

Aristotle died in the autumn of 322 BC. He was sixty-two and at the height of his powers: a tireless scholar, whose scientific explorations were as wide-ranging as his philosophical specu-lations were profound; a teacher who inspired—and who con-tinues to inspire—generations of pupils; a controversial public figure who lived a turbulent life in a turbulent world. He bestrode antiquity like an intellectual colossus. No man before him had contributed so much to learning. No man after him could hope to rival his achievements.

Of Aristotle's character and personality little is known. He came from a rich family. He was a bit of a dandy, wearing rings on his fingers and cutting his hair fashionably short. He suffered from poor digestion, and is said to have been spindle-shanked. He was a good speaker, lucid in his lectures, persuasive in conversation; and he had a mordant wit. His enemies, who were numerous, made him out to be arrogant and overbearing. His will, which has survived, is a generous and thoughtful docu-ment. His philosophical writings are largely impersonal; but they suggest that he prized both friendship and self-sufficiency, and that, while conscious of his place in an honourable tradition, he was properly proud of his own attainments. As a man, he was, I suspect, admirable rather than amiable.

But that is unprofitable speculation; for we cannot hope to know Aristotle as we may know Albert Einstein or Bertrand Russell—he lived too long ago. One thing, however, can be said with certainty: Aristotle was driven throughout his life by a single overmastering desire—the desire for knowledge. His whole career and his every activity testify to the fact that he was concerned before all else to promote the discovery of truth and to increase the sum of human knowledge.

He did not think himself singular in possessing such a desire, even if he pursued his object with a singular devotion: he believed that 'all men by nature desire to know'; for each of us is, most properly speaking, to be identified with his mind, and 'the activity of the mind is life'. In an early work, the *Protrepticus* or *Exhortation to Philosophy*, Aristotle announced that 'the acquisition of wisdom is pleasant; all men feel at home in philosophy and wish to spend time on it, leaving all other things aside'. (Philosophy for Aristotle is not an abstract discipline engaged in by cloistered academics. It is, quite generally, the search for knowledge.) And in the *Nicomachean Ethics* he argues that 'happiness'—the state in which men realise themselves and flourish best—consists in a life of intellectual activity and contemplation. Is not such a life too godlike for a mere man to sustain? No; for 'we must not listen to those who urge us to think human thoughts since we are human, and mortal thoughts since we are mortal; rather, we should as far as possible immortalise ourselves and do all we can to live by the finest element in us—for if it is small in bulk, it is far greater than anything else in power and worth'.

A man's noblest aim is to immortalise himself or imitate the gods; for in doing so he becomes most fully a man and most fully himself. And such self-realisation requires him to act on that desire for knowledge which as a man he naturally possesses. Aristotle's recipe for 'happiness' may be thought a little severe or restricted, and he was perhaps optimistic in ascribing to the generality of mankind his own passionate desire for learning. But his recipe came from the heart: Aristotle counsels us to live our lives as he himself tried to live his own.

One of Aristotle's ancient biographers remarks that 'he wrote a large number of books which I have thought it appropriate to list because of the man's excellence in every field': there follows a list of some 150 items, which, taken together and published in the modern style, would amount to perhaps fifty substantial volumes of print. And that list does not include all of Aristotle's writings—indeed, it fails to mention two of the works, the *Metaphysics* and the *Nicomachean Ethics*, for which he is today most renowned.

That is a vast output; yet it is more remarkable for its scope and variety than for its mere quantity. Aristotle's genius ranged widely. The catalogue of his titles includes *On Justice*, *On the Poets*, *On Wealth*, *On the Soul*, *On Pleasure*, *On the Sciences*, *On*

*Species and Genus, Deductions, Definitions, Lectures on Political
Theory* (in eight books), *The Art of Rhetoric, On the Pythagoreans,
On Animals* (in nine books), *Dissections* (in seven books), *On
Plants, On Motion, On Astronomy, Homeric Problems* (in six books),
On Magnets, Olympic Victors, Proverbs, On the River Nile. There
are works on logic and on language; on the arts; on ethics and
politics and law; on constitutional history and on intellectual
history; on psychology and physiology; on natural history—
zoology, biology, botany; on chemistry, astronomy, mechanics,
mathematics; on the philosophy of science and the nature of
motion, space and time; on metaphysics and the theory of
knowledge. Choose a field of research, and Aristotle laboured in
it; pick an area of human endeavour, and Aristotle discoursed
upon it. His range is astonishing.

Of his writings only a fifth has survived. But the surviving
fraction contains a representative sample of his studies, and
although the major part of his life's work is lost to us, we can
still form a rounded idea of his activities. Most of what has
survived was never intended to be read; for it is likely that the
treatises we possess were in origin Aristotle's own lecture-
notes—they were texts which he tinkered with over a period of
years and kept for his own use, not for that of a reading public.
Moreover, many of the works we now read as continuous
treatises were probably not given by Aristotle as continuous
lecture-courses. Our *Metaphysics*, for example, consists of a
number of separate tracts which were first collected under one
cover by Andronicus of Rhodes, who produced an edition of
Aristotle's works in the first century BC.

It should not be surprising, then, that the style of Aristotle's
treatises is often rugged. Plato's dialogues are polished literary
works, the brilliance of their thoughts matched by the elegance
of their language. Aristotle's surviving writings for the most part
are terse. His arguments are concise. There are abrupt transitions, inelegant repetitions, careless allusions. Paragraphs of
continuous exposition are set among staccato jottings. The
language is spare and sinewy. The style is accounted for only in
part by the private nature of the treatises; for Aristotle had
reflected on the appropriate style for scientific writing and he
favoured simplicity. 'In every form of instruction there is some
small need to pay attention to language; for it makes a difference

with regard to making things clear whether we speak in this or that way. But it does not make *much* of a difference: all these things are show and directed at the hearer—which is why no one teaches geometry in this way.' Aristotle *could* write finely—his style was praised by ancient critics who read works of his that we cannot—and some parts of the treatises are done with polish and even panache. But fine words butter no parsnips, and fine language yields no scientific profit.

The reader who opens his Aristotle and expects to find a systematic disquisition on some philosophical subject or an orderly textbook of scientific instruction, will be brought up short: Aristotle's treatises are not like that. But reading the treatises is not a dull slog. Aristotle's style has a vigour which on intimate acquaintance proves no less attractive than Plato's lovely prose. And the treatises reveal their author's thoughts in a direct and stark fashion: we can, as it were, overhear Aristotle talking to himself.

Above all, Aristotle is tough. It is best to take up a treatise and imagine that you had to lecture from it yourself. You must expand and illustrate the argument, make the transitions clear, set aside some material for another time and another lecture, add a few jokes, subtract a few *longueurs*. Aristotle can be vexing. What on earth does he mean here? How does this follow from that? Why can't he be a little more explicit? One ancient critic claimed that 'he surrounds the difficulty of his subject with the obscurity of his language, and thus avoids refutation—producing darkness, like a squid, in order to make himself hard to capture'. Every reader will, from time to time, think of Aristotle as a squid. But the moments of vexation are far outnumbered by the moments of excitement and elation. Aristotle's treatises offer a unique challenge to their readers; and once a reader has taken up the challenge, he would not have the treatises in any other form.

2 *A public figure*

Aristotle was no intellectual recluse: the life of contemplation which he commends is not to be spent in an armchair or an ivory tower. Although never a politician, he was a public figure and lived often enough in the public gaze. But he died far from the main centres of Greek life. In the spring of 322 he moved to Chalcis, on the island of Euboea, where his mother's family had property; and in the last months of his life he lamented the fact that he had become isolated and cut off.

The preceding thirteen years he had spent in Athens, the cultural capital of the Greek world where he had taught regularly in the Lyceum. Aristotle believed that knowledge and teaching were inseparable. His own researches were carried out in company, and he communicated his thoughts to his friends and pupils, never thinking to retain them as a private treasure-store. He thought, indeed, that a man could not claim to know a subject unless he was capable of transmitting his knowledge to others, and he regarded teaching as the proper manifestation of knowledge.

The Lyceum is often referred to as Aristotle's 'school'. It is tempting to think of it as a sort of university: we imagine timetables and lecture-courses, the enrolment of students and the granting of degrees, and we surround Aristotle with all the formalities of our own educational system. But the Lyceum was not a private college: it was a sanctuary and a gymnasium—a sort of public leisure centre. An old story tells that Aristotle lectured to his chosen pupils in the mornings and to the general public in the evenings. However that may be, arrangements in the Lyceum were surely less formal than those of a modern university. There were no examinations, no degrees, no set syllabus; probably there were no official enrolments—and no fees.

Aristotle combined teaching and research—his lectures must

often have been 'research papers', or talks based on his current research interests. He did not work alone. Various friends and colleagues joined him in his scientific and philosophical enterprises. We know little about Aristotle's research arrangements, but I incline to think that we should picture a group of friends working in concert, rather than a Teutonic professor masterminding the projects of his abler students.

Why did Aristotle suddenly abandon the pleasures of the Lyceum and retire to remote Chalcis? He said that 'he did not want the Athenians to commit a second crime against philosophy'. The first crime had been Socrates' trial and execution. Aristotle feared that he might suffer Socrates' fate, and his fears had a political basis.

During Aristotle's lifetime, Macedonia, under the rule first of Philip II and then of his son, Alexander the Great, expanded its power and came to dominate the Greek world, depriving the small city-states of their liberty and independence. Aristotle had lifelong connections with Macedonia. His father, Nicomachus, had been a physician at the Macedonian court and a friend of Philip's father, Amyntas; and in his will Aristotle named Antipater, Alexander's viceroy in Greece, as his executor. The most celebrated episode in the Macedonian connection began in 343 when Philip invited Aristotle to Mieza as tutor to the young Alexander. A rich romance later surrounded that happy coupling of prince and philosopher; but we can hardly hope to penetrate the veil of legend and discover how far Aristotle influenced his ambitious and unlovely charge. (We do know that he wrote a book entitled *Alexander, or On Colonies*.)

Alexander died in June of 323. The Athenians, ever jealous of their autonomy, rejoiced, and anti-Macedonian feeling became strong and violent. Aristotle was not a Macedonian agent, and the political theory he taught in the Lyceum was, if anything, hostile to the Macedonian interest. None the less, he was associated with Macedonia. (There is no reason to doubt the story that the Athenians had once set up an inscription in his honour, recording that he 'had served the city well . . . by all his services to the people of Athens, especially by intervening with King Philip for the purpose of promoting their interests'.) Aristotle had Macedonian friends: that was enough to set democratic Athens against him. He found it prudent to leave the city.

Willy-nilly, Aristotle was a public figure. To us, looking back from the vantage point of history, Aristotle is the Prince of Philosophers. Whether his contemporaries regarded him in that light we do not know; but that he enjoyed a certain renown in Greece can be stated with some assurance. An interesting sidelight on his public career is shed by a broken inscription found at Delphi: since 'they drew up a table of those who won victories in both Pythian Games and of those who from the beginning organised the contest, let Aristotle and Callisthenes be praised and crowned; and let the Stewards transcribe the table . . . and set it up in the temple'. The inscription was engraved in about 330 BC.

Aristotle allegedly wrote to his friend Antipater in the following vein: 'as for what was voted to me at Delphi, of which I am now deprived, this is my attitude: I am neither greatly concerned by the matter, nor quite unconcerned'. It seems that the honours granted to Aristotle in 330 were later withdrawn. The inscription itself was discovered by archaeologists in a well—it may have been thrown there in 322 BC in a fit of anti-Macedonian pique.

The fact that Aristotle was invited to draw up the victory-lists at Delphi is evidence that by the early 330s he had some reputation as a man of science. For the work demanded serious historical research. Victors in the Pythian Games, which were second in importance only to the Olympics, had their names and achievements preserved in the Delphic archives. Aristotle and Callisthenes (who was his nephew) sifted through a mass of ancient records; from that material they had to determine a correct chronology, and then produce an authoritative list. The list was of interest not only to the sporting man. In Aristotle's day historians could not anchor their narratives to a universally employed chronological system (as modern historians use BC and AD). Chronological accuracy depended on the use of catalogues, whether of state officers or of athletic victors.

The index of Aristotle's writings contains the title *Pythian Victors*. Alongside it are other titles testifying to similar projects of detailed historical scholarship: *Olympic Victors*, *Didaskaliae* (a *catalogue raisonné* of the plays produced at the Athenian festivals), *Dikaiomata* (a collection of legal submissions made by various Greek cities, prepared by Aristotle to enable Philip to settle boundary-disputes). Of Aristotle's historical researches, the most celebrated are the *Constitutions of States*, 158 of them in all. A few fragments of the *Constitutions* have survived, and at the end of the last century a papyrus was discovered which contained almost the complete text of the *Constitution of the Athenians*. The work consists of a brief constitutional history of Athens, together with an account of current Athenian political institutions. Aristotle, who was not himself a citizen of Athens, had burrowed in the Athenian archives and familiarised himself with Athenian politics. His researches produced a compact and well-documented history of one aspect of Athenian life. Judged by modern critical standards, the work is of uneven quality; but the *Constitution of the Athenians*, which represents only a small fraction of Aristotle's historical researches, illustrates well the scope and detail of his scientific studies.

3 *Zoological researches*

Aristotle began teaching in the Lyceum in 335 BC. The thirteen years from 335 to 322 constituted his second Athenian period. His first period in Athens had lasted for twenty years, from 367 to 347. In 347 he suddenly left the city. No reason for his removal is reliably reported; but in 348 the northern town of Olynthus had fallen to the Macedonian army, and on a wave of hostile reaction Demosthenes and his anti-Macedonian allies had come to power in Athens: it is most probable that political issues exiled Aristotle in 347 as they would again in 322.

However that may be, in 347 Aristotle and a few companions sailed eastwards across the Aegean and settled at Atarneus, a town with which Aristotle had family ties. The ruler of Atarneus was Hermias, a good friend both of philosophy and of Macedonia. Hermias gave Aristotle and his friends 'the city of Assos to live in; and they spent their time there in philosophy, meeting together in a courtyard, and Hermias provided them with all they needed'.

Aristotle stayed in Assos for two or three years. He then migrated to Mytilene in nearby Lesbos, where he met Theophrastus, who was to become his greatest associate and pupil. Shortly after that he returned to his native city of Stagira, where he remained until he answered Philip's royal summons.

Hermias received a bad press in antiquity: he was reviled as a tyrant, a barbarian and a eunuch. But he served Aristotle nobly, and Aristotle admired him in return. When, in 341, Hermias was betrayed and put to death in grisly fashion by the Persians, Callisthenes wrote an encomium on him, and in his memory Aristotle composed a hymn to virtue. Aristotle married Hermias' niece, Pythias, who was the mother of his two children, Pythias and Nicomachus. Whatever the character of Hermias may have been, science is in his debt. For it was during Aristotle's years of travel, between 347 and 335, and in particular during his stay in the eastern Aegean, that he undertook the major part of the work on which his scientific reputation rests.

For if Aristotle's historical researches are impressive, they are nothing compared to his work in the natural sciences. He made and collected observations in astronomy, meteorology, chemistry, physics, psychology; but his fame as a research scientist rests primarily on his work in zoology and biology: his studies on animals laid the foundations of the biological sciences; and they were not superseded until more than two thousand years after his death. The enquiries upon which those great works were based were probably carried out largely in Assos and Lesbos; at all events, the place-names which occur from time to time in the biological treatises serve to localise their observations and point to the eastern Aegean as a main area of research.

The facts which Aristotle so assiduously uncovered were displayed in two large volumes, the *History of Animals* and the *Dissections*. The *Dissections* has not survived. It was concerned, as its name implies, with the internal parts and structure of animals; and there is good reason to believe that it contained— and perhaps largely consisted of—diagrams and drawings. The *History of Animals* has survived. Its title (like the titles of several Aristotelian works) is misleading: the word 'history' transliterates the Greek word '*historia*' which means 'enquiry' or 'research', and a better translation of the title would be *Zoological Researches*.

The *Researches* discuss in detail the parts of animals, both external and internal; the different stuffs—blood, bone, hair and the rest—of which animal bodies are constructed; the various modes of reproduction found among animals; their diet, habitat and behaviour. Aristotle talks of sheep, goats, deer, pigs, lions, hyenas, elephants, camels, mice, mules. He describes swallows, pigeons, quails, woodpeckers, eagles, crows, blackbirds, cuckoos. His researches cover tortoises and lizards, crocodiles and vipers, porpoises and whales. He goes through the kinds of insect. He is particularly informative about marine creatures—fish, crustacea, cephalopods, testacea. The *Researches* range from man to the cheese-mite, from the European bison to the Mediterranean oyster. Every species of animal known to the Greeks is noticed; most species are given detailed descriptions; in some cases Aristotle's accounts are long, precise and astonishingly accurate.

Zoology was a new science: where should Aristotle, confronted with such a copious supply of data, make a start?

First, let us consider the parts of man; for just as people test currency by referring it to the standard most familiar to them, so it is in other cases too—and man is of necessity the animal most familiar to us. Now the parts of man are clear enough to perception; nevertheless, in order that we may not break the proper sequence, and in order that we may rely on reason as well as perception, we must describe his parts—first the organic parts, then the uniform parts. Now the chief parts into which the body as a whole divides are these: head, neck, torso, two arms, two legs.

Aristotle begins with man, because man is most familiar, and can be used as a reference point. Much of what he says will, he is aware, be perfectly well known—it may seem childish or pedantic to record that men have necks between their heads and torsos. But Aristotle wants to give a full and orderly account, even at the cost of apparent *naïveté*; and in any case, the discussion quickly becomes more professional. The following passage will give some flavour of the *Researches*.

The octopus uses its tentacles both as feet and as hands: it draws in food with the two that are placed over its mouth;

and the last of its tentacles, which is very pointed and the only one of them which is whitish and bifurcated at the tip (it uncoils towards the *rhachis*—the *rhachis* is the smooth surface on the other side from the suckers)—this it uses for copulation. In front of the sac and above the tentacles it has a hollow tube by which it discharges the sea-water which gets into the sac whenever it takes anything in with its mouth. In moves this tube to right and to left; and it discharges milt through it. It swims obliquely in the direction of the so-called head, stretching out its feet; and when it swims in this way it can see forwards (since its eyes are on top) and has its mouth at the rear. As long as the animal is alive, its head is hard and as it were inflated. It grasps and retains things with the underside of its tentacles, and the membrane between its feet is fully extended. If it gets on to the sand, it can no longer retain its hold.

Aristotle goes on to discuss the size of the tentacles. He compares the octopus to the other cephalopods—cuttlefish, crayfish and the like. He gives a detailed description of the internal organs of the creature, which he has evidently dissected and examined with minute care. In the passage I have quoted he refers to the phenomenon of 'hectocotylisation'—the bifurcation in one of the tentacles of the male octopus, by means of which it copulates with the female. Aristotle himself was not entirely certain of the phenomenon (at any rate, elsewhere he denies that the octopus uses its tentacle for copulation); but he was correct, and the facts which he reports were not rediscovered until the middle of the nineteenth century.

It is easy to become starry-eyed over the *Researches*, which are on any account a work of genius and a monument of indefatigable industry. Not surprisingly, sober scholars have felt it incumbent upon them to point out the defects in the work.

First of all, it is said that Aristotle often makes errors of a crude and unscientific kind. A notorious example concerns the copulation of insects. Aristotle asserts more than once that during copulation the female fly inserts a tube or filament upwards into the male—and he says that 'this is plain to anyone who tries to separate copulating flies'. It is not: the assertion is wholly false. Another example concerns the bison. After a true but somewhat vague description of the beast, Aristotle observes that it is regularly hunted for its meat, and that 'it defends itself by kicking, and by excreting and discharging its excrement over a distance of eight yards—it can do this easily and often, and the excrement burns so much that it scalds the hair off the hounds'. A splendid picture, but quite absurd: Aristotle was taken in by some tipsy huntsman's after-dinner stories.

Secondly, Aristotle is accused of failing to use 'the experimental method'. The observations he reports are, most of them, amateur; they were made in the open and not in the laboratory. There is no evidence that Aristotle ever attempted to establish correct experimental conditions or to make controlled observations; there is no evidence that he tried to repeat his observations, to check them or to verify them. His whole procedure seems appallingly slapdash.

Finally, Aristotle is criticised for ignoring the importance of measurement. Real science is essentially quantitative, but Aristotle's descriptions are mostly qualitative. He was no mathematician. He had no notion of applying mathematics to zoology. He did not weigh and measure his specimens. He records a layman's impression of how things look rather than a professional's accurate description of how they are.

Now there is certainly some truth in all those charges—Aristotle was not infallible. But the charges are grossly misplaced. The first charge is unexciting. There are numerous mistakes in the *Researches*, some to be explained by the fact that Aristotle possessed few technical instruments and some to be put down as plain errors of observation or judgement. (His most influential error gave rise to the theory of 'spontaneous generation'. Some insects, Aristotle asserts, 'are generated not from parent creatures but spontaneously: some from the dew that falls on leaves . . . some in mud and dung when they putrefy, some in wood (either on plants or in dead wood), some in the hair of animals, some in animals' flesh, some in their excrement'. Aristotle had observed lice on the head and worms in dung; but he had not—for want of care or for want of instruments—observed the phenomena with sufficient accuracy.) But the errors are greatly outnumbered by the insights—and what scientific work has ever been free of error?

The *Researches* contain one passage which is often said to

report an experiment. Aristotle is describing the early development of chicks in the egg. He records in considerable detail the stage of growth reached by the embryo on successive days. Evidently, he took a clutch of eggs all laid on the same day, removed one a day from the brooding hen, cracked it open, and chronicled the daily changes he observed. If we are to believe the implications of the text, he did this not only for the domestic hen—the case he describes in detail—but for other birds too.

The description of the chicken embryo is one of the many remarkable passages in the *Researches*; but it is not the report of an experiment (Aristotle, so far as we know, did not control the conditions in which the eggs were incubated). Nor is it typical of the *Researches* as a whole, where such dated and consecutive observations are rare. But that is hardly odd: the fact is that the 'experimental method' is of no particular importance to the sort of research that Aristotle was engaged upon. Aristotle was inaugurating a new science. There was a superabundance of information waiting to be collected, sifted, recorded and systematised. Experimental evidence was not required. Nor, in any case, is experiment appropriate in descriptive zoology. You do not need the 'experimental method' to determine that man has two legs or even to exhibit the hectocotylisation of the octopus. Aristotle himself was well aware that different sciences call for different methods. Those who accuse him of failing to experiment are victims of the vulgar error that all the sciences must be approached by the experimental path.

It is sometimes said in reply to the third charge that Aristotle's zoology is non-quantitative because he did not possess the technical devices upon which quantitative science relies: he had no thermometer, no finely calibrated scales, no accurate chronometer. That is all true; but the point should not be exaggerated. Greek shopkeepers regularly weighed and measured dead meat, and there was no technical reason why Aristotle should not have weighed and measured it live. Nor is it relevant to observe that Aristotle was no mathematician. Although he did not himself contribute to mathematical progress, he was well acquainted with the work of his contemporaries (mathematical examples and references are common enough in his writings); and in any case it requires no mathematical expertise to introduce measurement into science.

The *Researches* do, in fact, contain plenty of indeterminately quantitative statements (this animal is larger than this, this creature emits more semen than the other). There are also a few determinately quantitative observations. Of the two main types of squid, Aristotle remarks that 'the so-called *teuthoi* are much larger than the *teuthides*, growing to a length of up to 7½ feet; some cuttlefish have been found three feet long, and the tentacles of the octopus sometimes attain that size or even longer'. Aristotle seems to have measured the cephalopods. He could well have weighed them and given their other vital statistics, but he chose not to do so. And that was not an error but a wise choice. As Aristotle clearly saw, it is form and function rather than weight and size which matter in his kind of zoology. The length of an octopus's tentacles, which varies from specimen to specimen, is of little scientific interest; it is with the structure of the tentacles, and with their functional role in the animal's life, that the scientist is concerned.

The *Researches* are not flawless, but they are a masterpiece. Nowhere else does Aristotle show more vividly his 'desire to know'.

4 *Collecting facts*

Aristotle was a research scientist, and much of his time was devoted to original and first-hand study: he recorded his own observations, and he carried out dissections himself. But he could not have based all his multifarious descriptions on personal research, and like any other seeker after knowledge he borrowed other men's observations and culled other men's flowers. What, then, were Aristotle's research methods? How did he approach his work?

A pleasant story has it that Alexander the Great, 'inflamed by a desire to know the natures of animals', arranged for 'several thousand men throughout the whole of Greece and Asia Minor to be at Aristotle's disposal—everyone who lived by hunting or falconry or fishing, or who looked after parks, herds, apiaries, fishponds or aviaries—so that no living creature should escape his notice'. It is, alas, unlikely that Alexander ever did anything of the sort; but behind the story lies the fact that in the *Researches* Aristotle makes frequent reference to the reports of bee-keepers and fishermen, of hunters and herdsmen, of all those engaged in agriculture and animal husbandry. Bee-keepers are experienced in the ways of bees, and Aristotle relied on their expertise. Fishermen see things which landlubbers never observe, and Aristotle sought information from them. He was properly cautious in using their information. Some people, he says, deny that fish copulate; but they are wrong. 'Their error is made easier by the fact that such fish copulate quickly, so that even many fishermen fail to observe it—for none of them observes this sort of thing for the sake of knowledge.' Nevertheless, much of Aristotle's work is based partly on the testimony of such professionals.

In addition, Aristotle had written sources at his disposal. The Greek doctors had made some study of human anatomy, and Aristotle uses their writings in his treatment of the parts of man—his detailed account of the vascular system includes long quotations from three of his predecessors. In general, Aristotle's researches included a comprehensive programme of reading: 'he worked so hard . . . that his house was called the House of the Reader'. And he had a large library: 'He is the first man we know to have collected books, and his example taught the Kings of Egypt how to put together a library'.

Book-learning was of relatively little importance to Aristotle in his zoological researches, for there were few books from which he could learn anything. But in other disciplines there was much to peruse. Aristotle recommends that 'one should make excerpts from written accounts, making lists separately for each subject, e.g. for the good, or for animals', and the index of his books shows that he himself prepared various compilations of that sort. Many of his own discussions begin with a brief history of the question at issue, setting out in summary form the opinions which his predecessors had advanced. When discussing the nature and variety of causes in the *Metaphysics* he observes that we have given sufficient consideration to this subject in the *Physics*; nevertheless, let us also set down the views of those who have preceded us in the enquiry into existing things and in the philosophical investigation of reality; for it is plain that they too say that there are certain principles and causes. Thus, as we proceed, that will be useful to our present enquiry; for either we shall find some further kind of cause, or else we shall be more firmly convinced of those we have just mentioned.

Aristotle wrote several essays in intellectual history. His early work *On Philosophy* contained a full account of the origins and development of the subject; and there were monographs on Pythagoras, on Democritus, on Alcmaeon, and others. Only fragments of these works have survived; but the summary histories in the treatises no doubt drew upon them. Judged purely as history those summaries are not beyond criticism; but their specific purpose was not to set out a narrative or to chronicle the story of an idea. They were designed to provide starting-points for Aristotle's own investigations and checks upon his own speculations.

There were not always past enquiries to consult. At the end of one of his logical treatises, Aristotle writes that

> in the case of rhetoric there was much old material to hand, but in the case of logic we had absolutely nothing at all until we had spent a long time in laborious investigation. If, when you consider the matter and remember the state from which we began, you think that the subject is now sufficiently advanced compared to those other disciplines which have developed in the course of tradition, then it remains for all of you who have heard our lectures to forgive our omissions and to thank us warmly for our discoveries.

The note of self-satisfaction is not typical of Aristotle; and I cite the passage not to show that Aristotle could on occasion give himself a merited pat on the back, but rather to indicate, by contrast, that his customary procedure was to build upon the work of his predecessors. He could not do that in logic; and he could do it only to a limited extent in biology. In other subjects, 'which have developed in the course of tradition', he gratefully accepted all the tradition offered him.

Reliance on tradition, or the use of past discoveries, is a sensible procedure for any intellectual enquirer. But in Aristotle it goes a little deeper than that. He was highly conscious of his own position at the end of a long line of thinkers; he had a strong sense of intellectual history and of his own place therein.

The point bears upon two characteristic features of Aristotle's thought. First, he insists on the value of what he calls 'reputable opinions'. Something believed by all or most men—at any rate by all or most clever men—is reputable and must, he thinks, have something to be said for it. In the *Topics*, a work primarily concerned with reasoning from and about 'reputable opinions', he advises us to collect such opinions and to use them as starting-points for our enquiries. In the *Nicomachean Ethics* he implies that, in practical philosophy at least, reputable opinions are the end-points as well: 'for if the difficulties are solved and the reputable opinions remain, sufficient proof of the matter will have been given'. The best our investigations can hope to achieve is a winnowing of the reputable opinions, which will blow out the chaff of falsity and leave behind the grains of truth.

Aristotle's advice to attend to reputable opinions is more than the banal suggestion that before beginning research you should see what other men have done. Men desire by nature to discover the truth. Nature would not have given men such a desire and left it impossible of satisfaction. Hence if men generally believe something—if a thing is reputable—that is a sign that it is more likely to be true than false.

Secondly, Aristotle had a clear idea of the importance of tradition in the growth of knowledge.

In all cases of discovery, those things which are taken over from others who have earlier laboured upon them make gradual progress later at the hands of those who have taken them over, whereas what is discovered at the very beginning customarily makes but little advance at first—and yet it is far more useful than the later increase which depends upon it. For the beginning is doubtless the most important thing of all, as they say. And that is why it is hardest; for the greater it is in power, the smaller it is in magnitude and the harder to see.

But once it is discovered, it is relatively easy to add to and increase the rest.

Or again:

Investigation of reality is in a way difficult, in a way easy. An indication of this is that no one can attain it in a wholly satisfactory way, and that no one misses it completely: each of us says *something* about nature, and although as individuals we advance the subject little if at all, from all of us taken together something sizeable results—and, as the proverb has it, who can miss a barn-door? . . . And it is fair to thank not only those whose beliefs we share, but also those whose views were more superficial; for they too contributed something— for they prepared things for us. If Timotheus had not existed, we should lack a great deal of lyric poetry; but if Phrynis had not existed, Timotheus would not have done so. It is the same with those who have expressed views on reality. For from some we have taken over certain opinions, and others were the causes of the existence of those men.

The acquisition of knowledge is arduous, and science grows slowly. The first step is the hardest, for we have there nothing to guide our journey. Later, progress is easier; but even so, as individuals we can contribute little to the growing pile of knowledge: it is collectively that the ants amass their anthill.

---

5 *The philosophical background*

Aristotle was an indefatigable collector of facts—facts zoological, astronomical, meteorological, historical, sociological. Some of his political researches were carried out during the final period of his life when, from 335 to 322, he taught at the Lyceum in Athens; much of his biological research was done during the years of travel, between 347 and 335. There is reason to believe that his collecting activities were just as brisk during the first period of his adult life, the years between 367 and 347: that period is yet to be described.

So far, we have seen Aristotle as a public figure and as a private researcher; but that is at most half the man. Aristotle, after all, is reputed to have been a philosopher, and there is nothing very philosophical about the jackdaw operations I have so far described. Indeed, one of Aristotle's ancient enemies accused him of being a mere jackdaw:

> why did he turn away from the further exhortation of the young and incur the terrible wrath and enmity both of the followers of Isocrates and of some other sophists? He must surely have implanted a great admiration for his powers, from the moment when he abandoned his proper business and for those reasons was found, together with his pupil, collecting laws and innumerable constitutions and legal pleas about territory and appeals based on circumstances and everything of that sort, choosing . . . to know and teach philosophy and rhetoric and politics and agriculture and cosmetics and mining—and the trades performed by those who are ashamed of what they are doing and say they practise them from necessity.

The accusation is puffed up with rhetoric and contains some absurd falsifications: Aristotle never devoted much study to cosmetics. But it is still worth pondering. Aristotle's studies in 'politics and agriculture' are impressive, the *Constitutions* and the *Researches* are magnificent works; but how are they connected with *philosophy*? It will take a long story to answer that question.

Aristotle was born in 384, in the northern Greek town of Stagira. His father died when Aristotle was still young, and he was brought up by his uncle Proxenus, who had connections with Atarneus. Nothing is recorded about Aristotle's early education; but since he came from a rich and learned family, he no doubt received the sort of literary and gymnastic training which was normal for a well-born Greek. In 367, at the age of seventeen, he left Stagira for Athens, where he joined the brilliant group of men who worked and studied in the Academy under the leadership of Plato. In one of his lost works Aristotle told how a Corinthian farmer had happened to read Plato's

Gorgias and 'at once gave up his farm and his vines, mortgaged his soul to Plato, and sowed and planted it with Plato's philosophy'. Is that fictionalized autobiography? Perhaps the young Aristotle read Plato's dialogues in Stagira and was seduced by Dame Philosophy. However that may be, the move to Athens and the Academy was the crucial event in Aristotle's career.

The Academy, like the Lyceum, was a public place, and Plato's school was no more a modern university than was Aristotle's. Yet there were some differences between the two establishments. Plato owned a private estate near the Academy. His lectures and discussions were not, as a rule, public. Indeed, Plato's school appears to have been a fairly exclusive club. In 367 Aristotle took out membership.

Plato himself was no polymath. He did not pretend to the range which his most famous pupil was to attain. Rather, he limited his own researches to philosophy in the narrow sense— to metaphysics, epistemology, logic, ethics, political theory; and the Academy was primarily a school of philosophy. But Plato was not blinkered. He encouraged other men's researches in other subjects, and he gathered about him the most talented minds in Greece.

Mathematics was certainly studied in the Academy. Plato, himself no mathematician, was keenly interested in the methods of mathematics; he set his pupils mathematical problems and urged them to study the mathematical sciences. It is probable that natural science too was studied. Plato's *Timaeus* contains speculation of a scientific nature, and a comic dramatist guyed the young Academicians thus: 'In the gymnasium of the Academy I heard some absurd and extraordinary arguments; discussing nature, they were distinguishing sorts of animals, and kinds of tree, and species of vegetable—and then they tried to discover to what species the pumpkin belongs.' Plato was interested in problems of classification; and those problems had some bearing upon Aristotle's later attempts at biological taxonomy.

Again, the Academy found a place for rhetoric. It was in that subject that Aristotle first made a name for himself. In about 360 he wrote a dialogue, the *Gryllus*, on the subject of rhetoric, in which he attacked the views of Isocrates, a leading orator of the day, an educator and professional pundit. One of Isocrates' pupils, Cephisodorus, replied with a long counterblast—the first of many polemics to be directed against Aristotle. (Cephisodorus accused Aristotle of wasting his time in collecting proverbs—evidence that by 360 Aristotle had already begun his compilatory activities.) Some years later, in his *Protrepticus*, Aristotle defended the ideals of the Academy against the more pragmatic notions of Isocrates' school, and Isocrates himself replied in his *Antidosis*. Despite this deep division, Aristotle was able later to praise Isocrates' style of writing.

Rhetoric continued to interest Aristotle. The first drafts of his treatise on *Rhetoric*, which, unlike the *Gryllus* and the *Protrepticus*, still survives intact, may well go back to those early years in the Academy; and the final touches were not put to the work until the latest period of Aristotle's life. Rhetoric and the study of literature are closely connected: Aristotle wrote a historico-critical book *On the Poets* and a collection of *Homeric Problems*. Those studies too may have been undertaken in the Academy. They showed Aristotle to be a serious student of philology and literary criticism, and they formed part of the preparatory work for the *Poetics*, in which Aristotle sketched his celebrated account of the nature of tragedy, and for the third book of the *Rhetoric*, which is a treatise on language and style.

Rhetoric is also connected with logic—indeed, one of Aristotle's main claims in the *Gryllus* was that rhetoric should not excite the passions by fine language but should rather persuade the reason by fine argument. Plato himself was greatly interested in logic, or 'dialectic' as it was called; and the Academicians indulged in a sort of intellectual gymnastics in which set theses were to be defended and attacked by means of a variety of stylised arguments. Aristotle's *Topics* were first outlined in his Academic years. The work lists the various argument-forms (*topoi*—hence *Topics*) which the young gymnasts used. The *Sophistical Refutations*, an appendix to the *Topics*, catalogues numerous fallacies which they had to recognise and to solve.

Aristotle remained in Athens as a member of Plato's Academy for twenty years. In 347, the year in which Plato died, he left Athens for Atarneus: he was thirty-seven, a philosopher and a scientist in his own right. What, in those two formative decades, did he learn? What aspects of Academic philosophy influenced him and gave shape to his own later views?

He had a profound love for Plato. On Plato's death he wrote a moving elegy in which he praised him as a man 'whom it is not right for evil men even to praise; who alone or first of mortals proved clearly, by his own life and by the course of his arguments, that a man becomes good and happy at the same time'. But you may love a man while rejecting his beliefs. Aristotle was certainly no thorough-going Platonist. Plato's views are strongly criticised in Aristotle's surviving treatises, and criticisms were made while Plato was still alive. 'Plato used to call Aristotle the Foal. What did he mean by the name? Clearly it was known that foals kick their mothers when they have had enough milk.' Ancient critics accused the Foal of ingratitude, but the criticism is absurd—no teacher requires his pupils to sub-scribe from a sense of gratitude to his own doctrines. Whether or not Aristotle *believed* Plato's theories he was certainly influenced by them. I shall pick out five points which together determined much of Aristotle's philosophical thought, and turned him into a philosophical scientist rather than a mere collector of agricultural information.

First of all, Plato reflected deeply on the unity of the sciences. He saw human knowledge as a potentially unified system: science, for him, was not the random amassing of facts; it was the organisation of facts into a coherent account of the world. Aristotle, too, was a systematic thinker, and he shared whole-heartedly in Plato's vision of a unified theory of science, even if he disagreed with Plato about the way in which that unity was to be achieved and exhibited.

Secondly, Plato was a logician. I have already quoted Aristotle's claim that he was a pioneer in the science of logic, and it is true that Aristotle turned logic into a science and invented the discipline of formal logic. But Plato, both in his dialogues—most notably in the *Parmenides* and the *Sophist*—and in the 'dialectical' exercises he encouraged in the Academy, had prepared the ground for Aristotle. He had investigated the foundations of logic, and he required his pupils to train themselves in the practice of argumentation. Aristotle's study of rhetoric in the Academy, and his closely related interest in 'dialectic', started him on the subject he was to make his own.

Again, Plato was concerned with problems of ontology. ('Ontology' is a grandiose name for a part of general metaphysics: an ontologist attempts to determine what sort of things really exist, what are the fundamental entities of which the world consists.) Plato's ontology was contained in his theory of Ideas or Forms. According to that theory, the ultimate realities—the things on which the reality of everything else is somehow dependent—are abstract universals. It is not individual men and individual horses—Tom, Dick and Harry; Surrey, Barbary and Bucephalus—but the abstract forms of Man or manhood and of Horse or horseness which constitute the basic furniture of the real world. The theory is not easy to understand; what matters here is that Aristotle rejected it, and that he spent much of his philosophical activity in developing an alternative ontology.

Fourthly, Plato thought of scientific knowledge as a search for the causes or explanations of things. In his view, the notions of science and knowledge were intimately tied to that of explanation, and he discussed the types of explanation that might be given and the conditions under which phenomena could and should be explained. Aristotle inherited that concern. He too ties knowledge to explanation. His scientific endeavours were directed not merely to observing and recording, but above all to explaining.

Finally, there is the question of knowledge itself. How can we acquire knowledge in the first place? By what channels do we come to know and understand the world? Why suppose, indeed, that we know anything at all? The part of philosophy which deals with such questions is customarily called epistemology ('*epistēmē*' is the Greek for 'knowledge'). Epistemology matters to any philosopher who is concerned with science and our grasp of reality, and epistemological theories will be determined, in part at least, by issues in ontology. Many passages in Plato's dialogues are given to epistemological discussion. Here, too, Aristotle followed in his master's footsteps.

Knowledge must be systematic and unified. Its structure is given by logic, and its unity rests at bottom on ontology. It is essentially explanatory. It poses deep philosophical problems. All that, and much more, Aristotle learned in the Academy. However profoundly he disagreed with Plato's detailed elaboration of those five issues, he was at one with Plato in principle. In the next few chapters I shall sketch Aristotle's views on these subjects. By the end of the sketch it will be possible to see why

Aristotle is much more than a collector of facts—why he is a philosopher-scientist.

6 *The structure of the sciences*

The most developed of Greek sciences was geometry. Euclid's work was done after Aristotle's death, but Euclid himself built on the researches of his predecessors, and those predecessors had given at least some thought to what was to become the distinctive feature of Euclid's own geometrical science. In a word, Euclid's geometry is an axiomatised system: he selects a few simple principles, or axioms, which he posits as the primary truths of his subject; and from those axioms he derives, by a series of logically compelling deductions, all the other truths of geometry. Geometry thus consists of derived truths, or theorems, and primary truths, or axioms. Each theorem follows logically—though often by way of a long and complex chain of reasoning—from one or more of the axioms.

The notion of an axiomatic system is elegant and intellectually attractive. Plato was attracted to it, and he suggested that the whole of human knowledge might somehow be set out as a single axiomatised science. From a small set of primary truths, every other truth might be logically deduced. Knowledge is thus systematic and unitary—it is systematic because it can be presented axiomatically, unitary because all truths can be derived from a single set of axioms.

Aristotle was no less impressed than Plato by the power of axiomatisation, but he did not believe Plato's optimistic claim that all knowledge could be founded upon a single set of axioms. For he was equally impressed by the apparent independence of the sciences. Mathematicians and doctors, biologists and physicists, work in different domains, discuss different objects, and follow different methods. Their disciplines rarely overlap. Nevertheless, Aristotle felt the need for system: if human knowledge is not unitary, it is surely not a mere disconnected plurality either. 'The causes and principles of different things are different—in one way; but in another way, if you speak universally and by analogy, they are all the same.' The axioms of geometry and the principles of biology are mutually independent—but they are the same 'by analogy': the conceptual apparatus and the formal structure of all the sciences are the same.

Aristotle divided knowledge into three major classes: 'all thought is either practical or productive or theoretical'. The productive sciences are those concerned with the making of things—cosmetics and farming, art and engineering. Aristotle himself had relatively little to say about productive knowledge. The *Rhetoric* and the *Poetics* are his only surviving exercises in that area. (*Poetics* in Greek is *'poiētikē'*, and that is the word translated as 'productive' in the phrase 'the productive sciences'). The practical sciences are concerned with action, with how men are to act in various circumstances. The *Ethics* and the *Politics* are Aristotle's chief contributions to the practical sciences.

Knowledge is theoretical when its goal is neither production nor action but simply truth. Theoretical knowledge includes all that we now think of as science, and in Aristotle's view it contained by far the greatest part of the sum of human knowledge. It subdivides into three species: 'there are three theoretical philosophies—mathematics, natural science and theology'. Aristotle was intimately acquainted with contemporary mathematics, as any student of Plato's would be, and Books XIII and XIV of the *Metaphysics* are acute essays on the nature of numbers; but he was not a professional mathematician and did not pretend to have advanced the subject.

Natural science includes botany, zoology, psychology, meteorology, chemistry, physics. (The term I translate as 'natural science' is *'phusikē'*, often misleadingly transliterated as 'physics'. Aristotle's *Physics* is a treatise about natural science as such.) Aristotle thinks that the objects of natural science are marked off by two characteristics: they are capable of change or motion (unlike the objects of mathematics) and they exist 'separately' or in their own right. (The second point will be examined in a later chapter.) The greater part of Aristotle's life was devoted to the study of such objects.

Nevertheless, natural science is not the best of sciences. 'If there are no substances apart from natural substances, natural science will be the primary science; but if there are changeless substances, the science of them will be prior and will be the primary philosophy'. There are such substances, and they are divine. Theology is thus prior to natural science: 'the theoretical sciences are preferable to the rest, and this to the other theoretical sciences'. The term 'theology' should be used cautiously here. Primary philosophy 'must be the theoretical study of the primary principles and causes of things', and Aristotle follows a long Greek tradition in calling those primary substances 'divine'. I shall say a little about Aristotle's divinities in a later chapter; here it is enough to observe that he usually identifies them with parts of the heavens, so that 'theology' might well seem to be a branch of astronomy.

Two things for which Aristotle cared greatly appear to have escaped the net: metaphysics and logic. Where are they to be placed in the system of the sciences? Both seem to be theoretical, and both are treated by Aristotle as in some way identical with theology.

According to Aristotle, 'there is a science which studies being *qua* being and the things that belong to this in its own right'. (We call the science 'metaphysics', and Aristotle studies it in his *Metaphysics*. But Aristotle never uses the term 'metaphysics', and the title '*Metaphysics*' means literally 'What comes after natural science'.) The phrase 'being *qua* being' has a pleasantly esoteric ring to it, and some scholars have turned it into an abstruse and abstract item. In fact Aristotle means something neither abstract nor abstruse. 'Being *qua* being' is not a special kind of being; indeed, there is no such thing as being-*qua*-being at all. When Aristotle says that there is a science which studies being *qua* being, he means that there is a science which studies beings, and studies them *qua* being; that is, a science which studies things that exist (not some abstract thing called 'being'), and studies them *qua* existing.

The little word '*qua*' plays an important role in Aristotle's philosophy. There is nothing mysterious about it. Pooh-Bah, in *The Mikado*, is, among other things, Chancellor of the Exchequer and Private Secretary to Ko-Ko. He has different attitudes in his different capacities. As Chancellor, he urges a frugal wedding-ceremony for Ko-Ko and his bride; as Secretary, he recommends a splurge. He does one thing *qua* Chancellor or under his Chancellor's hat, another *qua* Secretary or under his Secretarial hat. In the former case the cares of State are relevant to his advice, in the latter his recommendation is determined by different considerations. Similarly, to study something *qua* existent is to study just those features of the thing which are relevant to its *existing*—and not any of the many other features of the thing; it is to study it under its existential hat. Everyone who does not study fictions studies 'beings', things that exist; the student of being *qua* being studies just those aspects of existent things which belong to them in virtue of the fact that they exist.

The study of being *qua* being is thus supremely general: everything that exists falls within its purview (contrast entomology or phonology, which are restricted to insects and to linguistic sounds), and the properties it investigates are those which absolutely everything must have. (Thus Book X of the *Metaphysics* discusses what it is to be *one* thing. *Everything* is *one* thing; by contrast, only some things are monopterous or consonantal.) Aristotle engages in this highly general study in various books of the *Metaphysics*. Several of his logical writings, both extant and lost, were also devoted to it.

Metaphysics, in Aristotle's view, is the primary philosophy, and hence it is identified with theology. But how, we may wonder, can a science which studies absolutely everything be the same as a science which studies only a special and highly privileged class of things? Aristotle anticipated the question. He suggested that theology 'is universal because it is primary'; and he appears to mean that if you study the primary substances on which all other entities are dependent, then you will implicitly be studying *all* existents *qua* existent. Not everyone has found that suggestion compelling, and Aristotle's primary philosophy is sometimes thought to consist of two quite distinct parts, a general metaphysics which studies beings *qua* being, and a special metaphysics which studies the principles and causes of things.

As to logic, Aristotle's successors were unsure of its status. Some later philosophers held that logic was a 'part' of philosophy—a discipline to be set alongside mathematics and natural science. Others, including Aristotle's own followers, stated that logic was a 'tool' of philosophy—something used by philosophers and scientists, not an object of their studies. (The Greek for 'tool' is *'organon'*: that is why later Aristotelians gave the collective title *Organon* to Aristotle's logical writings.) It seems clear that logic is *both* a part *and* a tool of philosophy. The old dispute rested on the false belief that logic could not be both things at once.

Aristotle himself did not discuss the position of logic in his scheme of things. He argues that the student of being *qua* being will study 'the things called axioms in mathematics' or 'the first principles of deduction'; 'for they belong to everything that exists, and not to some particular kind of thing separately from the others'. And he holds that the logician 'assumes the same shape as the philosopher' or discusses the same range of things as the student of primary philosophy. Logic, being an entirely *general* science, should thus be subsumed under metaphysics or theology. But there are passages in which Aristotle seems to imply that logic is not to be so categorised; and indeed, having said that the logician 'assumes the same shape as the philosopher', he immediately adds that his is for all that a distinct profession.

The structure of human knowledge, according to Aristotle, can be exhibited in a diagram, thus:

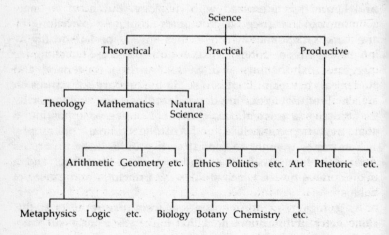

The scheme exhibits the structure and arrangement of the sciences, and shows its author to have been a self-conscious systematiser.

7 *Logic*

The sciences—at any rate the theoretical sciences—are to be axiomatised. What, then, are their axioms to be? What conditions must a proposition satisfy to count as an axiom? Again, what form will the derivations within each science take? By what rules will theorems be deduced from axioms? Those are among the questions which Aristotle poses in his logical writings, and in particular in the works known as the *Prior* and *Posterior Analytics*. Let us first look at the rules for deduction, and thus at the formal part of Aristotle's logic.

'All sentences are meaningful . . . but not all make statements only those in which truth and falsity are found do.' 'Of statements, some are simple, that is, those which affirm or deny something of something, and others are composed of these, and are thereby compound sentences.' As a logician, Aristotle is interested only in sentences that are true and false (commands, questions, exhortations and the like are the concern of the student of rhetoric or linguistics). He holds that such sentences are all either simple or compounded from simple sentences, and that simple sentences affirm or deny something of something— some *one* thing of some *one* thing, as he later insists.

That much Aristotle adopted from Plato's *Sophist*. In his *Prior Analytics* he goes beyond Plato in several ways. Simple sentences of the sort logic deals with are called 'propositions', and propositions are analysed into 'terms'. If a proposition says or denies P of S, then S and P are its terms—P the predicate term, S the subject term. Propositions are either universal or particular: they affirm or deny P either of every S or of some S. Thus 'Every viviparous animal is vertebrate' affirms *being vertebrate* of all viviparous animals; and 'Some oviparous animals are not san-guineous' denies *being sanguineous* of some oviparous animals. Thus we have four types of simple proposition: universal affirm-atives, affirming P of every S; universal negatives, denying P of every S; particular affirmatives, affirming P of some S; and particular negatives, denying P of some S.

Furthermore, propositions come in a variety of moods: 'every proposition expresses either that something applies or that it necessarily applies or that it possibly applies'. Thus 'Some calamaries grow to a length of three feet' expresses the thought that *being a yard long* actually holds true of some calamaries. 'Every man is necessarily constituted of flesh, bones etc.' says that *being corporeal* holds necessarily of every man—that a thing *could not be* a man without being made of flesh, bones etc. 'It is possible that no horses are asleep' states that *being asleep* possibly belongs to no horses—that every horse *may* be awake. These three moods or 'modalities' are called (though not by Aristotle) 'assertoric', 'apodeictic' and 'problematic'.

That, in brief, is Aristotle's doctrine of the proposition, as it is found in the *Analytics*. All propositions are simple or com-pounded of simples. Every simple proposition contains two terms, predicate and subject. Every simple proposition is either affirmative or negative. Every simple proposition is either uni-versal or particular. Every simple proposition is either assertoric or apodeictic or problematic.

The doctrine of the *Analytics* is not quite the same as that of the short essay *On Interpretation*, a work in which Aristotle reflects at greater length on the nature and structure of simple propositions. And as a doctrine it is open to various objections. Are *all* propositions either simple or compounded from simples? 'It is now recognised that the octopus's last tentacle is bifurcated' is surely a compound proposition—it contains as a part of itself the proposition 'the octopus's last tentacle is bifurcated'. But it is not compounded *from* simples. It consists of a simple proposi-tion prefixed by 'It is now recognised that', and 'It is now recognised that' is not a complete proposition at all. Again, do all simple propositions contain just *two* terms? 'It is raining' seems pretty simple. But does it contain *two* terms? Does it affirm *raining* of 'it'? Or what of the sentence 'Socrates is a man'? That surely contains a predicate and a subject. But it is neither universal nor particular—it does not predicate *man* of 'all' or of 'some' Socrates; for the term *Socrates* is not a general term, so that (as Aristotle himself observed) the phrases 'all' and 'some' do not apply to it.

Consider, finally, such sentences as 'Cows have four stomachs', 'Humans produce one offspring at a time', 'Stags shed their antlers annually'—sentences of the sort that Aristotle asserts in his biological writings. It is not true that *every* cow has four stomachs—there are deformed specimens with three or five apiece. Yet the biologist does not want to say merely that *some* cows happen to have four stomachs, or even that *most* cows do. Rather, he claims, correctly, that *every* cow *by nature* has four stomachs (even if in fact some do not). Aristotle stresses that in nature many things hold 'for the most part', and he believes that most of the truths of the natural sciences will be expressible by way of sentences of the form 'By nature, every S is P', sentences which are true if for the most part Ss are P. But what exactly is the structure of sentences of that form? Aristotle wrestled with the question, but he was obliged to leave it unanswered—and it cannot be answered within his doctrine of the proposition.

The logical system which Aristotle develops in the *Prior Analytics* is based upon his doctrine of the proposition. The arguments he considers all consist of two premises and a single conclusion, each of their three components being a simple proposition. Logic is a general discipline, and Aristotle wanted to deal generally with *all* possible arguments. But there are indefinitely many arguments, and no treatise could possibly deal individually with all of them. In order to treat generally that indefinitely immense multiplicity, Aristotle introduced a simple device. Instead of employing particular terms—'man', 'horse', 'swan'—in his discussions, he used letters—A, B, C. Instead of such sentences as 'Every octopus has eight tentacles' we find quasi-sentences or sentence-schemata such as 'Every A is B.' That use of letters and schemata allows Aristotle to speak with full generality; for what holds true of a schema, holds true of *every* particular instance of that schema. If, for example, Aristotle shows that when 'Some A is B' is true so also is 'Some B is A', then he has implicitly shown that *every* particular affirmative proposition 'converts' in this way: if some sea-creatures are mammals, some mammals are sea-creatures; if some men are

Greeks, some Greeks are men; if some democracies are illiberal, some illiberal regimes are democratic; and so on, for all the indefinitely many sentences of the form 'Some A is B.'

Aristotle invented the use of schematic letters. Logicians are now so familiar with his invention, and employ it so unthinkingly, that they may forget how crucial a device it was: without the use of such letters logic cannot become a general science of argument. The *Prior Analytics* makes constant use of schematic letters. Thus the very first argument-pattern which Aristotle discusses runs like this: 'If A is predicated of every B, and B of every C, necessarily A is predicated of every C.' In arguments of this form, all three propositions are universal, affirmative and assertoric. An instance might be: 'Every animal that breathes possesses lungs; every viviparous animal breathes; therefore every viviparous animal possesses lungs.'

In the course of the first part of the *Prior Analytics* Aristotle considers all possible pairings of simple propositions, and determines from which pairs a third simple proposition may correctly be inferred as conclusion, and from which pairs no conclusion can correctly be inferred. He divides the pairings into three groups or 'figures', and his discussion proceeds in a rigorous and orderly fashion. The pairings are taken according to a fixed pattern, and for each pair Aristotle states, and proves formally, what conclusion, if any, may correctly be inferred. The whole account is recognised as the first essay in the science of formal logic.

The logical theory of the *Prior Analytics* is known as 'Aristotle's syllogistic'. The Greek word '*sullogismos*' is explained by Aristotle as follows: 'A *sullogismos* is an argument in which, certain things being assumed, something different from the things assumed follows from necessity by the fact that they hold'. The theory of the *Prior Analytics* is a theory of the *sullogismos*—a theory, as we might put it, of deductive inference.

Aristotle makes great claims for his theory: 'every proof and every deductive inference (*sullogismos*) must come about through the three figures that we have described'; in other words, every possible deductive inference can be shown to consist of a chain of one or more arguments of the type Aristotle has analysed. Aristotle is, in effect, claiming that he has produced a complete and perfect logic. The claim is audacious, and it is false; for there are in fact innumerably many inferences that Aristotle's theory cannot analyse. The reason is simple: Aristotle's theory of inference is based upon his theory of propositions, and the deficiencies of the latter produce deficiencies in the former. Yet those deficiencies are not readily seen, and later thinkers were so impressed by the power and elegance of Aristotle's syllogistic that for two millennia the *Analytics* were taught as though they constituted the sum of logical truth.

The *Prior Analytics* is indeed a work of outstanding genius. There are internal difficulties within Aristotle's system (notably in his account of deductions involving problematic propositions), and the text contains some errors and obscurities. But those are minor flaws: by and large, the *Analytics* is a paradigm of logical thought. It is elegant and systematic; its arguments are orderly, lucid and rigorous; it achieves a remarkable level of generality. If it can no longer be regarded as a complete logic, it can still be admired as a nearly perfect fragment of logic.

8 *Knowledge*

The logic of the *Prior Analytics* serves to derive the theorems of a science from its axioms. The *Posterior Analytics* is primarily concerned to study the nature of the axioms themselves, and hence the general form of an axiomatised science. To a surprisingly large extent, the *Posterior Analytics* is independent of the particular logical doctrine of the *Prior Analytics*: the deficiencies in Aristotle's theory of inference do not infect the theory of axiomatisation, nor do they render the *Posterior Analytics* invalid as an account of scientific form.

Aristotle's account of the axioms is based upon his conception of the nature of knowledge; for a science is meant to systematise our *knowledge* of its subject-matter, and its component axioms and theorems must therefore be propositions which are known and which satisfy the conditions set upon knowledge. According to Aristotle, 'we think we know a thing (in the unqualified sense, and not in the sophistical sense or accidentally) when we think we know both the cause because of which a thing is (and know that it is its cause) and also that it is not possible for it to be otherwise'. A zoologist, then, will *know* that cows have four stomachs if, first, he knows *why* they do (if he knows that they have four stomachs *because* of such-and-such a fact) and, secondly, he knows that cows *must* have four stomachs (that it does not merely *happen* to be the case that they do). Those two conditions set upon knowledge govern Aristotle's whole approach to axiomatic science in the *Posterior Analytics*.

The first condition set upon knowledge is a condition of causality. The word 'cause' must be taken in a broad sense: it translates the Greek '*aitia*', which some people prefer to render by 'explanation'. To *explain* something is to say why it is so; and to say why something is so is to cite its *cause*. There is thus the closest of connections between explanation and cause, in the broad sense.

The condition of causality is linked to a number of other requirements which the axioms of any science must satisfy.

> If knowing is what we have laid it down to be, demonstrative knowledge must be based upon things which are true and primary and immediate, and more known than and prior to and causes of the conclusion; for thus the principles will be appropriate to what is being proved. There can be an inference without these conditions, but there cannot be a proof; for it will not yield knowledge.

The principles or starting-points of demonstrative knowledge are the axioms on which the science is based; and Aristotle's general point is that those principles or axioms must satisfy certain requirements if the system they ground is to be a science, a system of *knowledge*.

Clearly, the axioms must be true. Otherwise they could neither be known themselves nor ground our knowledge of the theorems. Equally clearly, they must be 'immediate and primary'. Otherwise there will be truths prior to them from which they can be derived—and thus they will not after all be axioms or first principles. Again, in so far as our knowledge of the theorems depends upon the axioms, it is reasonable to say that the axioms must be 'more known' than the theorems.

It is the final condition in Aristotle's list, that the axioms be 'prior to and causes of the conclusion', which is linked most directly to his account of what knowledge is. Our knowledge of the theorems rests upon the axioms, and knowledge involves a grasp of causes; hence the axioms must state the ultimate causes which account for the facts expressed by the theorems. A man who reads through an axiomatised science, starting from the axioms and proceeding through the successive theorems, will in effect be reading off a list of causally connected facts.

At first glance, the causality condition seems odd. Why should we suppose that knowing something requires knowing its cause? Surely we know large numbers of facts about whose causes we are quite in the dark? (We know *that* inflation occurs; but economists cannot tell us *why* it does. We know *that* the Second World War broke out in 1939; but historians dispute among themselves about the *causes* of the war.) And does not the causality condition threaten an infinite regress? Suppose I know X; then according to Aristotle I know the cause of X. Call that Y. Then it seems to follow that I must know the cause of Y too; and so on *ad infinitum*.

The second of those problems was explicitly discussed by Aristotle. He held that there are some facts which are causally primary, or which have no causes apart from themselves; and he sometimes expresses this by saying that they are self-caused or self-explanatory. Why do cows have horns? Because they are deficient in teeth (so that the matter which would have formed teeth goes to make horns). Why are they deficient in teeth? Because they have four stomachs (and so can digest their food unchewed). Why do they have four stomachs? Because they are ruminants. Why, then, are cows ruminants? Simply because they are *cows*—there is no *further* feature, apart from their being cows, which explains why cows are ruminants; the cause of a cow's being a ruminant is just its being a cow.

That cows are ruminants is self-explanatory. Aristotle usually says that such self-explanatory facts are definitions, or parts of definitions; so that the axioms of the sciences will for the most part consist of definitions. A definition, in Aristotle's sense, is not a statement of what some word means. (It is no part of the meaning of the word 'cow' that cows are ruminants; for we all know what 'cow' means long before we know that cows are ruminants.) Rather, definitions state the essence of a thing, what it is to be that thing. (It is part of the essential nature of a cow that it is a ruminant; what it is to be a cow is to be a ruminant animal of a certain kind.) Some modern philosophers have rejected—and ridiculed—Aristotle's talk of essences. But in fact Aristotle grasped an important part of the scientific endeavour: from the fundamental natures of substances and stuffs—from their essences—the scientist seeks to explain their other, non-essential, properties. Aristotle's axiomatic sciences will start from essences and successively explain derivative properties. The theorems of animal biology, say, will express the derived properties of animals, and the deduction of the theorems from the axioms will show how those properties are dependent upon the relevant essences.

But must *all* knowledge be causal or explanatory in this way? Although Aristotle's official view is that 'we know each thing only when we know its cause', he often uses the word 'know'— just as we do—in cases where the cause escapes us. And indeed Aristotle is surely mistaken in asserting that knowledge is always causal. But it would be wrong simply to lament the mistake and pass on. Aristotle, like Plato before him, was primarily concerned with a special type of knowledge—with what we may call scientific understanding; and it is plausible to claim that scientific understanding involves knowledge of causes. Although we may know quite well that inflation occurs without being able to say why it does, we cannot claim to understand the phenomenon of inflation until we have a grasp of its causes, and the science of economics is imperfect until it can supply that causal understanding. Taken as a piece of lexicography, Aristotle's definition of 'knowledge' is false; construed as a remark about the nature of the scientific enterprise, it expresses an important truth.

So much for the condition of causality. The second condition in Aristotle's account of knowledge is that what is known must be the case of necessity: if you know something, that thing *cannot* be otherwise. In the *Posterior Analytics* Aristotle elaborates the point. He connects it with the thesis that only universal propositions can be known. He infers that 'the conclusion of such a proof must be eternal—therefore there is no proof or knowledge about things which can be destroyed'.

The necessity condition with its two corollaries seems no less strange than the causality condition. Surely we do have knowledge of contingent facts (for example, that the population of the world is increasing), and of particular facts (for example, that Aristotle was born in 384 BC). Moreover, many of the sciences seem to countenance such knowledge. Astronomy, for example, deals with the sun and the moon and the stars; and the case is similar with geography, which Aristotle studied in his *Meteorology*, and, most obviously, with history. Aristotle, it is true, thinks that the objects of astronomy are not perishable but eternal. He also holds that 'poetry is more philosophical and more serious than history—for poetry tends to describe what is universal, history what is particular'. (History, in other words, is not granted full scientific status.) But that does not alter the fact that some sciences deal unequivocally with particulars.

Furthermore, Aristotle believed (as we shall shortly see) that the basic entities of the world are perishable particulars. And it would be absurdly paradoxical if he were driven to the view that there is no scientific knowledge of those fundamental objects. In fact, Aristotle is wrong to infer from the necessity condition that knowledge must be about eternal objects. It is a universal and perhaps a necessary truth that humans have human parents ('a man', as Aristotle puts it, 'generates a man'); and that truth is, in a sense, eternal—at least, it is *always* true. But it is not a truth *about* eternal objects—it is a truth about mortal, perishable men. Aristotle himself concludes, at the end of a tangled argument, that 'to say that all knowledge is universal . . . is in a way true and in a way not true . . . It is clear that knowledge is in a way universal and in a way not.' Thus he allows that there is, 'in a way', knowledge of particulars; and we must dismiss the second corollary of the necessity condition as a mistake.

As for the first corollary I have already remarked that in Aristotle's opinion the theorems of science do not always hold universally and of necessity: some of them hold only 'for the most part', and what holds 'for the most part' is explicitly distinguished from what holds always. 'All knowledge deals either with what holds always or with what holds for the most part (how else could one either learn it or teach it to someone else?); for it must be determined either by what holds always or by what holds for the most part—for example, that honey-water for the most part benefits the feverish.' Aristotle's assertion that scientific propositions must be universal is an exaggeration, on his own admission; and the same must be said for the necessity condition itself.

Science strives for generality; in order to understand particular occurrences we must see them as part of some general pattern. Aristotle's view that knowledge is of what cannot be otherwise is a reflection of that important fact. But it is a distorted reflection, and the necessity condition laid down in the *Posterior Analytics* is too stringent.

9 *Ideal and achievement*

Aristotle has emerged thus far as a profoundly systematic thinker. The various sciences are autonomous but systematically interrelated. Each individual science is to be developed and presented in the form of an axiomatic system—'in the geometrical manner', as later philosophers put it. Moreover, the set of concepts within which Aristotle's notion of science finds its place was itself systematically examined and ordered. Perhaps none of that is surprising. Philosophy, after all, is nothing if not systematic, and Aristotle's system—his 'world picture'—has for centuries been held up for admiration and praise.

Some scholars, however, have disputed that view. They have denied that Aristotle was a system-builder. Themselves distrusting the grandiose claims of systematic philosophy, they find Aristotle's virtues to lie elsewhere. For them, Aristotle's philosophy is essentially 'aporetic': he poses masses of particular problems or *aporiai*, and seeks particular solutions to them. His thought is tentative, flexible, changing. He does not sketch a grand design and then fill in the details, each neatly and elegantly fitting its assigned position; rather, his methods, his modes of argument and his conceptual wardrobe all alter from time to time and from topic to topic, being individually tailored to suit individual problems. Aristotle works piecemeal.

That anti-systematic interpretation of Aristotle's thought is now widely accepted. It has something to be said in its favour. Book III of the *Metaphysics*, for example, consists of a long catalogue of problems or *aporiai*, and much of the remainder of the *Metaphysics* is given over to their solution. Or consider the following passage: 'here, as elsewhere, we must set down the phenomena and first go through the puzzles; then we must prove the reputable opinions about these matters—if possible, all of them, if not, the majority and the most important'. First, set down prevailing views on the matter ('the phenomena', that is 'what seems to be the case', are the reputable opinions on the subject); then go through the puzzles those views raise (because they are obscure, perhaps, or mutually inconsistent); finally, prove all or most of the views to be true. That is hardly a recipe for system-building; yet it is a recipe Aristotle commends and himself sometimes follows.

Moreover, the aporetic interpretation at first sight seems to do justice to an aspect of Aristotle's work which on the traditional interpretation must seem puzzling. Aristotle's scientific treatises are never presented in an axiomatic fashion. The prescriptions of the *Posterior Analytics* are not followed in, say, the *Meteorology* or the *Parts of Animals*. Those treatises do not lay down axioms and then proceed to deduce theorems; rather, they present, and attempt to answer, a connected sequence of problems. On the traditional view, the treatises must seem—to put it paradoxically—wholly un-Aristotelian: the trumpeted system is simply not apparent in their pages. On the aporetic interpretation, the treatises represent the essence of Aristotle's philosophy: his occasional reflections on systematisation are not to be taken too seriously—they are ritual gestures towards a Platonic notion of science, evidence of Aristotle's own fundamental convictions.

It is undeniable that many of Aristotle's treatises are, in large part, aporetic in style—they do discuss problems, and discuss them piecemeal. It is also undeniable that the treatises contain little or nothing in the way of axiomatised development. It is right to stress those points. But it is wrong to infer that Aristotle was not at bottom a systematic thinker. The theory expounded in the *Posterior Analytics* cannot be dismissed as an irrelevant archaism, a mere genuflection to Plato's ghost. There are so many hints and intimations of systematisation in the treatises that the solution of *aporiai* cannot be regarded as the be-all and end-all of Aristotle's scientific and philosophical enquiries; and—a point worth underlining—even the piecemeal discussions of individual problems are given an intellectual unity by the common conceptual framework within which they are examined and answered. Systematisation is not achieved in the treatises; but it is an ideal, ever present in the background.

What, then, are we to say of the unsystematic features of Aristotle's works? First, not all of Aristotle's treatises are works *of* science: many are works *about* science. The *Posterior Analytics* is a case in point. That treatise is not presented axiomatically; but then it is a treatise *about* the axiomatic method—it is concerned not to develop a science but rather to examine the way in which a science should be developed. Again, many parts of the *Physics* and the *Metaphysics* are essays on what we might call the foundations of science. We should not expect writings about the structure and grounds of science to exhibit themselves the features which they demand of writings within the sciences.

But what of the aporetic aspects of Aristotle's properly scientific works? Why are the *Meteorology* and the *Parts of Animals*, say, not presented axiomatically? The answer is disconcertingly simple. Aristotle's system is a grand design for finished or completed sciences. The *Posterior Analytics* does not describe the activities of the scientific researcher—it determines the form in which the researcher's results are to be systematically organised and displayed. Aristotle had not discovered everything. He may, indeed, have had his optimistic moments: Cicero reports that 'Aristotle, accusing the old philosophers who thought that philosophy had been perfected by their own efforts, says that they were either very stupid or very vain; but that he himself could see that, since great advances had been made in so few years, philosophy would be completely finished in a short time.' We know that such optimism on Aristotle's part would itself have been 'either very stupid or very vain'; and in fact Aristotle does not ever, in his treatises, boast of having completed any branch of knowledge. His achievement, great though it was, inevitably fell short of his ideal; and the Aristotelian system was designed with the ideal in mind.

Aristotle says quite enough to enable us to see how, in a perfect world, he would have presented and organised the scientific knowledge he had industriously amassed. But his systematic plans are plans for a completed science, and he himself did not live long enough to discover everything. Since the treatises are not the final presentations of an achieved science, we should not expect to find in them an orderly succession of axioms and deductions. Since the treatises are intended, in the end, to convey a systematic science, we should expect them to indicate how that system is to be achieved. And that is exactly what we do find: Aristotle was a systematic thinker; his surviving treatises present a partial and unfinished sketch of his system.

---

10 *Reality*

Science is about real things. That is what makes it knowledge rather than fantasy. But what things are real? What are the fundamental items with which science must concern itself? That is the question of ontology, and a question to which Aristotle devoted much attention. One of his ontological essays, the *Categories*, is relatively clear; but most of his ontological thought is to be found in the *Metaphysics*, and in some of the most obscure parts of that perplexing work.

'Now the question which, both now and in the past, is continually posed and continually puzzled over is this: What is being? That is, what is substance?' Before sketching Aristotle's answer to that question we must ask about the question itself: What is Aristotle after? What does he mean by 'substance'? And *that* question is best approached by a somewhat circuitous route.

The *Categories* is concerned with classifying types of predicate ('*katēgoria*' is Aristotle's word for 'predicate'). Consider a particular subject, say Aristotle himself. We can ask various types of question about him: *What* is he?—a man, an animal etc. What are his *qualities*?—he is pale, intelligent etc. *How large* is he?— five feet ten, ten stone eight. How is he *related* to other things?— he is Nicomachus' son, Pythias' husband. *Where* is he?—in the Lyceum. These different types of question are answered appropriately by way of different types of predicate. The question 'How large?' attracts predicates of *quantity*, the question 'How related?' attracts predicates of *relation*, and so on. Aristotle thinks that there are ten such classes of predicate, and that each class can be individually characterised. For example, 'what is really peculiar to quantities is that they can be called equal and unequal'; or 'in respect of qualities alone are things called like and unlike'. Not all of Aristotle's classes are equally clearly delineated, and his discussion of what belongs to what class contains some puzzles. Again it is not clear why Aristotle settles for *ten* classes. (He rarely makes use, outside the *Categories*, of all ten classes; and he was probably not firmly committed to that precise number.) But the general point is plain enough: predicates fall into different classes.

Aristotle's classes of predicates are themselves now called 'categories', the term 'category' having been transferred from the things classified to the things into which they are classified, so that it is normal to talk of 'Aristotle's ten categories'. More importantly, the categories are generally referred to as categories *of being*; and Aristotle himself will sometimes refer to them as 'the classes of the things that exist'. Why the move from classes of predicates to classes of *beings*, of things that are or exist? Suppose that the predicates 'man' and 'healthy' are true of Aristotle: then there must *be* such as thing as man, and there must *be* such a thing as health. In general, there must be something corresponding to every predicate which is true of anything; and the things corresponding in this way to predicates will themselves be classified in a manner corresponding to the classification of the predicates. Indeed, in a sense there is only one classification here. In classifying predicates, we thereby classify things. In saying that the predicate applied to Aristotle in the sentence 'Aristotle is in the Lyceum' is a predicate of place, we are saying that the Lyceum is the place. Things, like predicates, come in different sorts; and if there are ten classes or categories of predicate, there are ten classes or categories of things. The classification of predicates is, as it were, merely a reflection in language of the underlying classification of things.

Predicates which answer the question 'What is so-and-so?' fall into the category which Aristotle calls 'substance', and the things which belong to the category are substances. The class of substances is peculiarly important; for it is *primary*. In order to understand the primacy of substance we must turn briefly to a notion of central significance to Aristotle's whole thought.

Aristotle noticed that certain Greek terms are ambiguous. 'Sharp', for example, in Greek as in English, can be applied to sounds as well as to knives; and it is plain that it is one thing for a sound to be sharp and quite another for a knife to be sharp. Many ambiguities are easily detected, like that of 'sharp'; they may provide material for puns, but they do not cause serious puzzlement. But ambiguity is sometimes more subtle, and it sometimes infects terms of philosophical importance; indeed, Aristotle thought that most of the key terms in philosophy were ambiguous. In the *Sophistical Refutations* he spends some time in expounding and solving sophistical puzzles that are based on ambiguity, and Book V of the *Metaphysics*, sometimes called Aristotle's 'philosophical lexicon', is a set of short essays on the different senses of a number of philosophical terms. 'Something is called a cause in one way if . . ., in another if . . .'; 'something is said to be necessary if . . . , or if . . .'. And so on, for many of the terms central to Aristotle's own philosophical system.

One of the terms which Aristotle recognises as ambiguous is the term 'being' or 'existent'. Chapter 7 of Book V of the *Metaphysics* is given over to 'being'; and Book VII begins by observing that 'things are said to be in many senses, as we described earlier in our remarks on ambiguity; for being signifies what a thing is, that is, this so-and-so, and quality or quantity or each of the other things predicated in this way'. There are at least as many senses of 'being', then, as there are categories of beings.

Some ambiguities are merely 'chance homonymies'—as with the Greek word '*kleis*', which means both 'bolt' and 'collar-bone'. Of course it is not a matter of chance that '*kleis*' was applied to collar-bones as well as to bolts: what Aristotle means is that there is no connection of meaning between the two uses of the term—you could be perfectly capable of using the word in one of its senses without having an inkling of the other. But not all ambiguities are like that, and in particular the word 'be' or 'exist' is not an example of chance homonymy: 'things are said to exist in many ways, but with reference to one thing and to some single nature, and not homonymously' ('not homonymously' here means 'not by *chance* homonymy'). Aristotle first illustrates what he has in mind by two non-philosophical examples:

> Everything that is healthy is so called with reference to health—some things by preserving it, some by producing it, some by being signs of health, some because they are receptive of it; and things are called medical with reference to the art of medicine—for some things are called medical by possessing the art of medicine, others by being well adapted to it, others by being instruments of the art of medicine. And we shall find other things called in a similar manner to these.

The term 'healthy' is ambiguous. We call men, complexions, resorts, diets and other things healthy. But George V, Bognor Regis and All Bran are not healthy in the same sense. Yet those different senses are all interconnected, and their connection is ensured by the fact that all refer to some one thing, namely health. For George V to be healthy is for him to *possess* health; for Bognor to be healthy is for it to *produce* health; for All Bran to be healthy is for it to *preserve* health; and so on. 'Some single nature' enters into the explanation of what it is for each of these diverse things to be diversely healthy. Healthiness thus possesses unity in diversity.

And so it is with being or existence.

> Thus things are said to exist also in many ways, but all with reference to one starting-point. For some are said to exist because they are substances, others because they are affections of substances, others because they are paths to substance or destructions or privations or qualities or producers or creators of substances or of things said to exist by reference to substance, or are negations of these or of substance.

Just as everything called healthy is so called with reference to health, so everything said to be or exist is so said with reference to substance. There exist colours and sizes, changes and destructions, places and times. But for a colour to exist is for some *substance* to be coloured, for a size to exist is for some *substance* to have it, for a movement to exist is for some *substance* to move. Non-substances exist, but they exist only as modifications or affections of substances. For a non-substance to exist is for an existing substance to be modified in some way or other. But the existence of substances is not thus parasitic: substances exist in a primary sense; for a substance to exist is *not* for something else—something non-substantial—to be as it were substantified.

Existence, like healthiness, possesses unity in diversity; and substance is the focal point of existence as health is of healthiness. That is the chief way in which the class of substances is primary in relation to the other categories of being.

Then what is it to be substance? Substance-predicates are those which provide possible answers to the question 'What is it?'; but that question is too vague to give any secure guidance. In Book V of the *Metaphysics* Aristotle offers more precise assistance: 'things are called substances in two ways: whatever is the ultimate subject, which is no longer said of anything else; and whatever, being this so-and-so, is also separable'. The second way in which things are called substances couples two notions frequently employed by Aristotle in his reflections on the question: a substance is 'this so-and-so', and it is also 'separable'.

'This so-and-so' translates the Greek '*tode ti*', an unorthodox phrase which Aristotle nowhere explains. What he seems to have in mind can perhaps be expressed in the following way. Substances are things to which we can refer by use of a demonstrative phrase of the form '*this* so-and-so'; they are things that can be picked out, identified, individuated. Socrates, for instance, is an example of a 'this so-and-so'; for he is *this man*—an individual whom we can pick out and identify.

But what about, say, Socrates' complexion, his paleness? Can we not refer to that by the phrase 'this paleness'? Is this paleness not something which we can identify and reidentify? Aristotle says that 'the particular pale is in a subject, namely the body (for all colour is in a body)', and by 'the particular pale' he appears to mean 'this paleness', an individual instance of the quality of being pale. But if this paleness is an *individual* thing, it does not follow that it is a *substance*: substances are not just cases of 'this so-and-so'; they are also 'separable'. What is separability here?

Plainly, Socrates may exist without his paleness (for he may get a sun-tan and cease to be pallid); but Socrates' paleness cannot exist without Socrates. Socrates is separable from his paleness. Socrates' paleness is not separable from Socrates. That is surely part of what Aristotle means by separability; but it is probably not a complete account. For one thing, Socrates cannot exist devoid of *all* coloration—he may cease to be pale, but he cannot cease to be coloured; he may be separable from this paleness, but he is in danger of being *in*separable from colour as such.

We need to refer again to Aristotle's account of the ambiguity of being. Some things, we saw, are parasitic upon others: for them to exist is for some *other* existent to be somehow related to them. We may usefully connect parasitism and separation in the following way: a thing is separable if it is *not* thus parasitic. Socrates, then, will be separable—not merely separable from his paleness, but absolutely separable—because for Socrates to exist is not for his paleness—or anything else whatsoever—to be modified in a certain way; Socrates' paleness is not separable, not merely because it cannot exist unless Socrates does, but because for it to exist is for some *other* thing—Socrates—to be pale.

We can now offer the following account of what it is to be a substance: a thing is a substance if it is *both* an individual (a 'this so-and-so', something capable of being designated by a demonstrative phrase), *and also* a separable item (something non-parasitic, a thing whose existence is not a matter of some *other* thing's being modified in some way or other).

We can now at last return to Aristotle's eternal question: What things in fact *are* substances? We should not expect a simple and authoritative answer from Aristotle (after all, he says that the question is perpetually puzzling), and his own attempts at an answer are in fact hesitant and difficult to understand. But one or two things do emerge fairly clearly. Aristotle's predecessors had, he thought, implicitly offered a number of different answers to the question. Some had held that *stuffs*—gold, flesh, earth, water—were substances (he is thinking primarily of the earliest Greek philosophers, who focused their attention on the material constituents of things). Others had held that the ultimate *parts* of ordinary things were substances (Aristotle is thinking of the ancient atomists, whose basic entities were microscopical corpuscles). Yet other thinkers had proposed that *numbers* were substances (the Pythagoreans and certain of Plato's followers fall into this camp). Finally, some had chosen to regard abstract entities or *universals* as substances (Plato's doctrine of Forms is the outstanding example of such a theory).

Aristotle rejected all these views. 'It is plain that of the things that are thought to be substances, most are powers—both the parts of animals . . . and earth and fire and air.' For earth to exist, we might say, is for certain substances to have certain powers (in Aristotle's view, for them to have the power or tendency to move downwards); and for fire to exist is for substances to burn and heat and have a tendency to rise. As for the parts of animals, 'all these are defined by their functions; for each is truly such if it can perform its own function—for example, an eye, if it can see—and what cannot do so is an eye only homonymously (for example, a dead one or one made of stone)'. An eye is something that can see; for eyes to exist is for animals to be capable of seeing.

Numbers are plainly non-substantial. The number three exists just in so far as there are groups of three things. Numbers are essentially numbers of things, and although the number ten is not identical with any or every group of ten items, still the existence of the number ten consists precisely in there being such groups or sets of ten substances.

Aristotle devotes most of his polemical attention to the fourth view of substance. Plato's theory of Forms was by far the most elaborate ontological theory with which Aristotle was acquainted, and it was a theory to which, in his years in the Academy, he was perpetually exposed. Aristotle's arguments against the Platonic theory were first set out in a special treatise *On the Ideas*, which survives only in fragments. He returned to the attack again and again, and produced a vast and varied array of considerations against the theory. In addition, he offered a group of more general arguments against any view that takes universals to be substances.

Aristotle held that for whiteness to exist is for certain substances to be white. Plato, on the contrary, held that for a substance to be white is for it to share in whiteness. In Aristotle's opinion, white *things* are prior to *whiteness*, for the existence of whiteness is simply a matter of there being white things. In Plato's opinion, *whiteness* is prior to white *things*, for the existence of white things is simply a matter of their sharing in whiteness. Aristotle's arguments against Platonism demand close inspection; many of them are powerful, but it is only fair to say that they have not convinced determined Platonists.

If Platonism goes, what remains? What are Aristotelian substances? The answer is a robustly commonsensical one. The first and plainest examples of substances are animals and plants; to those we may add other natural bodies (the sun, the moon and stars, for example), and perhaps also artefacts (tables and chairs, pots and pans). In general, perceptible things—middle-sized material objects—are the primary furniture of Aristotle's world; and it is significant that he often poses his ontological question by asking if there are any substances *apart* from perceptible substances. Such, in Aristotle's view, are the basic realities, and the things with which science principally concerns itself.

11 *Change*

Can we say anything more, in general philosophical terms, about those middle-sized material objects which are the chief substances in Aristotle's world? One of their most important features is that they *change*. Unlike Plato's Forms, which exist for ever and never alter, Aristotle's substances are for the most part temporary things which undergo a variety of alterations. There are, in Aristotle's view, four types of change: a thing can change in respect of substance, of quality, of quantity and of place. Change in respect of substance is coming-into-being and going-out-of-existence, generation and destruction; such a change occurs when a man is born and when he dies, when a statue is made and when it is smashed. Change in respect of quality is alteration: a plant alters when it grows green in the sunlight or pale in the dark; a candle alters when it grows soft in the heat or hardens in the cold. Change in respect of quantity is growth and diminution; and natural objects typically begin by growing and end by diminishing. Finally, change in respect of place is motion.

Most of the *Physics* is devoted to a study of change in its different forms. For the *Physics* studies the philosophical back-ground to natural science; and 'nature is a principle of motion and change', so that 'things have a nature if they possess such a principle'. The subject-matter of natural science consists of moving and changing things. Aristotle's predecessors had been puzzled by the phenomena of change: Heraclitus had thought that change was perpetual and essential to the real world; Parmenides had denied the very possibility of coming-into-being, and hence of any sort of change; Plato had argued that the ordinary changing world could not be a subject of scientific knowledge.

In the first books of the *Physics* Aristotle argues that every change involves three things. There is the state *from* which the change proceeds, the state *to* which the change proceeds, and the *object* which persists through the change. In Book V the account is embellished slightly: 'there is something which initi-ates the change, and something which is changing, and again something in which the change takes place (the time); and apart from those, something from which and something to which. For all change is from something to something; for the thing chang-ing is different from that *to* which it is changing and from that *from* which—for example, the log, the hot, the cold'. When a log becomes hot, it changes *from* a state of coldness; it changes *to* a state of hotness; and the log itself persists through the change.

That in every change there is an initial state and an end state may be granted; and the states must be distinct, or else no change will have occurred. (An object may change from white to black, and then back to white again. But if its colour is the same *throughout* a given period, then it has not changed colour during that period.) And in the cases of qualitative change, quantitative change and locomotion, it is plain that there must be a subject that persists through the change. 'There is no change apart from the things that change', or 'all change is a change of something'; and for a thing to change it must retain its identity while altering in some aspect—in size, in quality, in position. But what of change in respect of substance? How does that fit Aristotle's analysis?

It is natural to suggest that the two end-states in generation and destruction are non-existence and existence. When Socrates came into being, he changed *from* a state of non-existence *to* a state of existence, and he persisted through the change. (In cases of destruction the two end-states occur in reverse order.) But a moment's reflection shows the absurdity of that idea. Socrates does not *persist through* his generation, nor does he *persist through* his destruction. For these two changes mark the beginning and the ending of Socrates' existence.

At this point Aristotle observes that substances—material bodies—are in a sense *composite*. A house, for example, consists of bricks and timbers arranged in a certain structure; a statue consists of marble or bronze carved or cast into a certain shape; an animal consists of tissues (flesh, blood and the rest) organised on certain principles. All substances thus consist of two 'parts', stuff and structure, which Aristotle habitually calls 'matter' and 'form'. Matter and form are not physical components of substances: you cannot cut up a bronze statue into two separate bits, its bronze and its shape. Rather, matter and form are *logical* parts of substances: an account of what substances are requires mention both of their stuff and of their structure. Nor should we imagine the matter as the physical aspect of a substance and the form as a sort of non-physical additive: both stuff and structure are aspects of the unitary physical object.

We can now see that 'whatever comes into being must always be divisible, and be part *thus* and part *thus*—I mean part matter and part form'. And

> it becomes clear . . . that substances . . . come into being from some underlying subject; for there must always be something that underlies, from which what comes into being comes into being—for example, plants and animals from seed. And the things that come into being do so in some cases by change of shape (for example, statues), in some by addition (for example, growing things), in some by subtraction (for example, a marble Hermes), in some by putting together (for example, a house) . . .

When a statue comes into being or is made, the persisting object is not the statue itself but the matter of the statue, the bronze or the marble; and the end-states are those of being shapeless and being shaped. When a man comes into being, what persists is the stuff, not the man; and the stuff is first (in the seed) non-human and then human.

That account of the nature of change had the great merit of allowing Aristotle to overcome many of the difficulties about change which his predecessors had raised. But it is not wholly compelling. Thomas Aquinas, one of Aristotle's most sympathetic critics, observed that the theory rules out the possibility of creation. Aquinas's God had created the world *out of nothing*; the world came into being, and that was a substantial change—but no pre-existing matter had a form imposed upon it, for there was no pre-existing matter there. If you reflect solely on the sublunary world, Aquinas says, you may be inclined to accept Aristotle's analysis of change. But if you look higher you will see that not *all* change will fit the analysis. Whether or not we agree with Aquinas's theory, we may agree with his logic; for we surely do not want to rule out, on purely logical grounds, the very possibility of creation. (The modern cosmologists' theory of the constant creation of particles is not *logically* mistaken.) But if Aristotle's account of change is too restrictive, that is of no great moment for his theory of science; for that theory is primarily concerned with ordinary, sublunary, changing things.

Strictly speaking, what I have described so far is not Aristotle's account of change itself, but rather his account of the pre-conditions for change. At any rate, in Book III of the *Physics* he poses the question 'What is change?', and gives an answer which is meant to complement the discussion of the first book. His answer is this: 'Change is the actuality of the potential *qua* such.' (That sentence is often cited as Aristotle's definition of *motion*. The word 'motion' in English usually means 'change of place', 'locomotion'. Aristotle's word here is '*kinēsis*': though the word is sometimes restricted to locomotion, it usually means 'change' in general, and in Book III of the *Physics* it has that usual meaning.) Aristotle's critics have pounced upon that sentence as an example of pompous obscurantism. It merits a brief commentary.

The terms 'actuality' and 'potentiality' form a constant refrain in Aristotle's treatises. They serve to mark the difference between something which is actually so-and-so and something which is potentially so-and-so; between, say, a builder who is slapping mortar on bricks, and one who is not doing so but still has the skills and capacities required to do so. It is one thing to have a capacity, another to exercise it; one thing to possess potential, another to actualise it. Aristotle makes a number of claims about the distinction between actuality and potentiality, some of them acute, some dubious. He holds, for example, that 'actuality is in all cases prior to potentiality both in definition and in substance; and in time it is in a way prior and in a way not'. The first point is true: in defining a potentiality we must specify what it is a potentiality *for*, and in doing that we name an actuality. (To be a builder is to be capable *of building*, to be visible is to be able *to be seen*.) Since the reverse is not true (actuality does not in the same way presuppose potentiality), an actuality is prior in definition to its correlative potentiality. But the claim that actuality is prior to potentiality in time is less plausible. Aristotle means that before there can be any potential so-and-sos, there must be actual so-and-sos—before there can be any potential men (that is any stuff that may become human), there must be actual men. For, he says, 'in all cases what is actually so-and-so comes into being from what is potentially so-and-so by the agency of something actually so-and-so—for example, men from men, a musical person by the agency of a musical person—there always being something that initiates the change and what initiates the change being itself actually so-and-so'. The underlying thought seems to be that causing something to be so-and-so is a matter of transmitting a certain character to it—and you can only transmit what you possess yourself. If someone comes to be musical he must have been *made* musical by someone; that agent, since he transmitted musicality, must himself have been actually musical. The argument is ingenious; but in fact causation need not be—and usually is not—a matter of transmission.

Aristotle's account of change calls upon actuality and potentiality. Actuality and potentiality for what? The answer emerges in the course of Aristotle's argument: it is the potentiality *to be changing*. In place of Aristotle's obscure sentence, 'Change is the actuality of the potential *qua* such', we may therefore write

'Change is the actuality of the changeable *qua* changeable.' Now that is supposed to explain what it is for something to be changing: if we replace the abstract nouns 'change' and 'actuality' by verbs, we may paraphrase Aristotle as follows: 'Something is in the process of changing whenever it possesses a capacity to change and is exercising that capacity.' That paraphrase reduces the obscurity of Aristotle's analysis, but it seems to make the analysis platitudinous. Perhaps, however, Aristotle does not intend to give an illuminating definition of change but rather to make an interesting point about the sort of actuality involved in change. For he thinks that some actualities are incompatible with their correlative potentialities. What *is* white cannot *become* white. If a surface is *actually* white, it is not *potentially* white. Before being painted white, a ceiling is potentially but not yet actually white; after being painted, it is actually but no longer potentially white. Other actualities are different: being actually so-and-so is quite compatible with still being potentially so-and-so. When I am actually smoking a pipe, I am still capable of smoking a pipe (otherwise I could not go on). When a steeplechaser is actually galloping over the course, he is still capable of galloping (otherwise he would never reach the end). The point of Aristotle's definition of change is that changes are actualities of the latter sort: while it is actually changing, the object is still capable of changing; for if it ceased to be capable of changing, it would thereby cease to be actually changing.

Aristotle has much more than that to say about change. Change takes place in time and space, and the *Physics* offers intricate theories about the nature of time, of place and of empty space. Since space and time are infinitely divisible, Aristotle analyses the notion of infinity. He also discusses a number of particular problems concerning the relation of motion to time, including a brief treatment of Zeno's celebrated paradoxes of motion.

The different essays which make up the *Physics* are among the more finished of Aristotle's surviving works: although their subject-matter is thorny and sometimes produces difficult passages of argument, their general structure and purport are always clear. The *Physics*, in my own view, is one of the best places to start reading Aristotle.

12 *Causes*

Material objects change, and their changes are caused. The scientist's world is full of causes, and scientific knowledge, as we have already seen, requires the capacity to state causes and to give explanations. We should expect Aristotle's scientific treatises to be filled with causal pronouncements and explanations, and we should want his philosophical essays to include some account of the nature of causation and explanation. Neither expectation is disappointed.

The core of Aristotle's account of explanation is his doctrine of 'the four causes'. Here is his brief exposition of that doctrine:

> A thing is called a cause *in one way* if it is a constituent from which something comes to be (for example, bronze of the statue, silver of the goblet, and their genera); *in another way* if it is the form and pattern, that is, the formula of its essence, and the genera of this (for example, 2:1, and in general number, of the octave), and the parts present in the account; *again*, if it is the source of the first principle of change or rest (for example, the man who deliberates is a cause, and the father of the child, and in general the maker of what is being made and the changer of what is changing); *again*, if it is as a goal—that is, that for the sake of which (for example, health of walking—Why is he walking?—we say: 'In order to be healthy', and in so saying we think we have stated the cause); and also those things which, when something else has changed it, stand between the changer and the goal—for example, slimming or purging or drugs or instruments of health; for all these are for the sake of the goal, and they differ from one another in being some instruments and others actions.

Aristotle tells us that things are called 'causes' in four different ways, but his illustrations are brief and enigmatic. Consider the

first example: 'bronze of the statue'. Aristotle can hardly mean
that bronze explains, or is the cause of, the statue, since that
makes no sense at all. But what *does* he mean? The first point to
observe is that, in Aristotle's view, to ask for a cause is to seek
'the because-of-which': it is to ask *why* something is the case. A
question 'Why?' requires an answer 'Because'; so explanatory
sentences which cite causes can always be expressed in the form
'X because Y.'

Secondly, Aristotle says that 'the because-of-which is always
sought in this way: Because of what does one thing belong to
another? . . . for example, Because of what does it thunder?
Because of what does noise occur in the clouds? For in this way
one thing is being sought of another. Again, Because of what
are these things, namely bricks and timbers, a house?' Whenever
we seek a cause, we ask why *this is that*, why so-and-so is such-
and-such. That is to say, the fact we are trying to explain can be
expressed in a simple subject–predicate sentence: S is P. The
question we ask is: Why is S P? And the answer can be put in
the form S is P because Y. (We can of course ask not only why
wading-birds have webbed feet, but why there are any wading-
birds at all; and if the former question asks 'Because of what
does one thing belong to another?', the latter question seems to
be concerned with *one* thing only, namely wading-birds. Aristotle answers that point by appealing to his analysis of substances
into matter and form: to ask why there are wading-birds is to
ask why animal tissues sometimes have such-and-such a form—
and that is to ask 'Because of what does one thing belong to
another?')

Finally, Aristotle says that 'the cause is the middle term': to
ask why S is P is, as it were, to look for a link joining S to P; and
that link will constitute a 'middle term' between S and P. 'Why
is S P?'—'Because of M.' More fully: 'S is P, because S is M, and
M is P.' Why do cows have several stomachs? Because cows are
ruminants and ruminants have several stomachs. Not all
explanations need actually have that specific form; but Aristotle
holds that all explanations *can* be couched in that form, and that
the form exhibits the nature of causal connections most
perspicuously.

That account of explanatory sentences enables us to see how
Aristotle's notion of explanation is integrated with his logic, and

how the causes which are the prime objects of the scientist's search may be expressed within the axiomatic system which presents his finished product. (Every deduction within that system will be, roughly speaking, of the form: S is M; M is P; so S is P. It will thus mirror perfectly the structure of explanatory sentences.) Moreover, we are now better equipped to understand the doctrine of the 'four causes'.

'The constituent from which something comes to be', Aristotle's first type of cause, is usually called 'cause as matter' by him and 'the material cause' by his commentators. The illustration, 'bronze of the statue', is elliptical for something of the form 'The statue is so-and-so because the statue is made of bronze and bronze things are so-and-so.' (Insert 'malleable', 'brown', 'heavy', 'covered in verdigris' etc. in place of 'so-and-so'.) The middle term, 'made of bronze', expresses the cause of the statue's being, for example, malleable; and because bronze is the constituent stuff of the statue the cause here is the 'material' cause.

Aristotle's second sort of cause, 'the form and pattern', is normally referred to as the 'formal' cause. The illustration is again obscure. Consider instead the following example: 'what it is and why it is are the same. What is an eclipse?—Privation of light from the moon by the earth's screening. Why is there an eclipse? or: Why is the moon eclipsed?—Because the light leaves it when the earth screens it.' The moon is eclipsed because the moon is deprived of light by being screened and things deprived of light by being screened are eclipsed. Here the middle term, 'deprived of light by being screened', explains why the eclipse occurs; and it states the form or essence of an eclipse—it says what an eclipse actually is.

We ourselves tend to associate the notion of causation most readily with the action of one thing on another—with pushings and pullings. Modern readers may feel most at home with Aristotle's third type of cause, which is usually called the 'efficient' or 'motive' cause. At least, Aristotle's illustrations of the efficient cause have features which we now associate closely with the idea of causation. Thus the examples seem to suggest that efficient causes are *distinct* from the objects they operate upon (the father is distinct from the son, whereas the bronze is not distinct from the statue), and that causes *precede* their effects (the man who deliberates does so before he acts, whereas the screening does not occur before the eclipse).

Aristotle, however, does not regard efficient causes as radically different from material and formal causes. Moreover, he holds that efficient causes do not always precede their effects—indeed, he treats simultaneity of cause and effect as the norm. His illustration, 'the father of the child', might be expanded as follows: 'The child is snub-nosed because the child has a snub-nosed father and children with snub-nosed fathers are snub-nosed.' Here the cause, *having a snub-nosed father*, does not precede the effect. Elsewhere we find examples of antecedent causes: 'Why did the Persian War come upon the Athenians? What was the cause of the Athenians' being warred upon?—Because they attacked Sardis with the Eretrians; for that initiated the change.'

Aristotle refers to his fourth cause as 'that for the sake of which' and 'the goal'. It is usually known as the 'final' cause ('*finis*' is the Latin word for 'end' or 'goal'). The normal way of expressing final causes, as Aristotle's example indicates, is by using the connective 'in order to': 'He is walking in order to be healthy.' Final causes are odd, in various ways: first, they are not readily expressed in terms of 'the because-of-which'—'in order to' does not easily translate into 'because'. Secondly, they seem to be appropriate only to a very small number of cases, namely, human intentional actions (for 'in order to' expresses an intention, and only human actions are intentional). Thirdly, they appear to post-date their effects (health, which allegedly causes the walking, comes about *after* the walking). Fourthly, they may be effective without even existing (health may cause the man to walk and yet never exist—he may be too dissipated ever to become healthy, or he may be run over by a bus in the course of his perambulations).

The third and fourth oddities are the least troublesome. Aristotle explicitly recognises that final causes follow their effects, and he implicitly acknowledges cases in which a final cause is effective but non-existent—neither point struck him as strange. The second oddity is more important. Aristotle does not think that final causes are appropriate only to intentional behaviour; on the contrary, the primary arena within which final causes exert themselves is that of nature—of the animal and vegetable world. I shall return to this in a later chapter. The first oddity demands a comment here.

How do final causes fit Aristotle's account of the structure of explanatory sentences? One favourite example of a final cause is expressed concisely thus: 'Why is there a house?—In order to preserve a man's belongings.' We might expand the explanation as follows: houses are roofed because houses are shelters for belongings and shelters for belongings are roofed. Here 'shelter for belongings' is the middle term, and it expresses the final cause of houses—it states the goal of having a house. But that gloss on Aristotle's illustration takes us some way from his text, and it is very difficult to provide a similar gloss for the example of the man who jogs for the sake of his health.

The fact is that final causes do not fit easily into the tight structure we are using, and we should perhaps relax things somewhat. 'Why is S P? Because of M.' In some cases, the relation of M to S and P will be, as before, that S is M and M is P. In other cases it may be more complex. In the case of final causes M will explain why S is P inasmuch as M is both a goal for S and something achievable by way of P. 'Why does he walk?—For health': health is his goal; and health is achievable by walking. 'Why do ducks have webbed feet?—For swimming': swimming is a goal for ducks (that is, it is good for ducks to swim); and swimming is made easier by having webbed feet.

Aristotle's treatment of explanation contains much more than the distinction among four types of cause. I shall mention two further points. 'Since things are called causes in many ways, it happens that the same thing has many causes non-incidentally; for example, both the art of statue-making and the bronze are causes of the statue—not in virtue of something else, but *qua* statue—but not in the same way: one is cause in the sense of matter, the other in the sense of origin of change.' The same thing may have several different causes. It is tempting to construe 'the same thing' in a weak sense: the statue is heavy, say, because it is made of bronze; the statue is life-size because the sculptor made it so. The two causes are causes not of the very same *feature* of the statue, but rather of features of the very same *statue*. But that is not Aristotle's meaning; rather, he holds that one and the same *feature* of the statue may receive two distinct explanations, according to two different modes of causality. Thus he says that thunder occurs 'both because when fire is extinguished it necessarily sizzles and makes a noise and—if things are as the Pythagoreans say—in order to threaten and frighten those in Hell'. And in the biological works he regularly looks for double causes in nature.

That is puzzling. Surely if Y explains X, then there is no room for supposing that, in addition, Z explains X; if Y accounts for X, X is accounted for, and there is no accounting left for Z to do. It hardly makes any difference if Y and Z are different types of cause. If we think we can give an adequate explanation of, say, the behaviour of a dog purely in mechanical terms (by a set of material and efficient causes), then we shall reject any further putative explanation in terms of the animal's goals or ends— such an attempt can explain nothing, since everything is already explained.

It is possible that Aristotle means something a little different from what he says: bronze may, in a way, be a cause of the statue's being heavy; but it is not by itself fully adequate to account for the weight of the statue—we need to add a reference to the sculptor, for he could quite well have fashioned a *light* statue out of bronze. The point, then, is not that X can be adequately explained by Y and also adequately explained by some different Z; but rather that an adequate explanation of X may require mention both of Y and of Z. That is a true observation; but it is not quite the observation Aristotle seems to be making.

Finally, a word about chance. Some of Aristotle's predecessors had ascribed many natural phenomena to chance. Aristotle rejects their view. But did he himself leave any room for chance in nature? He certainly believes that in nature some things happen not invariably but only for the most part; and he identifies 'the accidental' with the exceptions to what happens for the most part. For the most part, men go grey; if Socrates does not go grey, then that is accidental, and may have occurred by chance. 'And that there is no knowledge of the accidental is clear; for all knowledge deals either with what holds always or with what holds for the most part (for how else could one either learn it or teach it to someone else?).'

Thus, in Aristotle's view, there *are* accidental phenomena in nature, but they are not subject to knowledge—that is to say, they cannot form part of any developed science. Does Aristotle infer that the world is to some extent indeterminate, that not all events are bound together by the nexus of causation? He does not do so explicitly; indeed, he tends to say that the exceptions to natural regularities occur because of, and can be explained in terms of, peculiarities in the matter of the thing in question. Thus accidental phenomena do, or at least may, have causes. Aristotle does not, or need not, admit random or causeless events into his world. But he does allow that not all events are amenable to scientific understanding, for not everything exhibits the sort of regularity which science requires.

13 *Empiricism*

How are we to acquire the knowledge which is to be packaged in neat Euclidean sciences? How do we get in touch with the substances which constitute the real world? How do we chart their changes? How do we hit upon their causes and uncover their explanations? Deductive logic is not the means of discovering facts about the world: Aristotle's syllogistic provides a system within which knowledge can be articulated, but logic is not, save incidentally, a device for discovery.

The ultimate source of knowledge is, in Aristotle's view, perception. Aristotle was a thoroughgoing empiricist in two senses of that term. First, he held that the notions or concepts with which we seek to grasp reality are all ultimately derived from perception, 'and for that reason, if we did not perceive anything, we would not learn or understand anything, and whenever we think of anything we must at the same time think of an idea'. Secondly, he thought that the science or knowledge in which our grasp of reality consists is ultimately grounded on perceptual observations. That is hardly surprising: as a biologist, Aristotle's primary research tool was sense-perception, his own or that of others; as an ontologist, Aristotle's primary substances were ordinary perceptible objects. Plato, having given abstract Forms the leading role in his ontology, was led to regard the intellect rather than perception as the searchlight which illuminated reality. Aristotle, placing sensible particulars at the centre of the stage, took sense-perception as his torch.

Perception is the source of knowledge, but it is not knowledge itself. How, then, are the facts given in perception transformed into scientific knowledge? Aristotle describes the process as follows.

> All animals . . . have an innate capacity to make discriminations, which is called perception; and if perception is present in them, in some animals the percept is retained and in others it is not. Now for those in which it is not retained . . . there is no knowledge outside perception. But for some perceivers it is possible to hold the percept in their minds; and when many such things have come about, there is a further difference, and some, from the retention of such things, come to have a general account, while others do not. Thus from perception there comes memory, as we call it; and from memory (when it occurs often in connection with the same thing) experience—for memories that are many in number form a single experience. And from experience, or from the whole universal that has come to rest in the mind . . . there comes a principle of skill and of knowledge.

We perceive particular facts—that this thing, here and now, is thus-and-so (that Socrates, say, is now going grey). Many of the facts we perceive are similar—it is not just Socrates, but Callias and Plato and Nicomachus and the rest who are seen to go grey. Those percepts stick in the mind and become memories. When we possess a mass of similar memories we have what Aristotle terms 'experience'; and 'experience' is turned into something close to knowledge when the multitude of particular facts are, as it were, compressed into a single general fact—the fact that, for the most part, all men go grey. (I say 'something close to knowledge': knowledge itself only arrives when we grasp the cause of greying—when we learn that men go grey because, say, the sources of pigmentation dry up.) Knowledge, in sum, is bred by generalisation out of perception.

That story may seem open to criticism. First of all, it is quite clear that most of our knowledge is *not* acquired in the way Aristotle suggests. We do not normally require a mass of similar observations before we jump to a universal judgement—I doubt if Aristotle observed hectocotylisation in more than one or two octopuses, and he surely dissected very few prawns before giving his general description of their internal parts. The story he tells of the growth of general knowledge from particular observations may be correct at bottom, but its plot must be made considerably more sophisticated if it is to be an adequate account of our actual procedures.

Secondly, Aristotle's story will meet a philosophical challenge. Is sense-perception really reliable? If so, how can we tell that it is? How can we distinguish illusion from genuine perception? Or again, are we really justified in moving from particular observations to general truths? How can we know if we have made enough observations or if our actual observations are a fair sample of the field of possible observations? Questions of that sort have been asked by sceptically-minded philosophers for centuries, and they render dubious Aristotle's reliance on perception and generalisation.

Aristotle was well aware of the dangers of hasty generalisation; for example, 'the cause of the ignorance of those who take that view is that, while the differences among animals with regard to copulation and procreation are manifold and unobvious, those people observe a few cases and think that things must be the same in all cases'. But Aristotle has nothing to say on a more general level about the problems raised by generalisation: those problems—problems of 'induction' as they were later called—did not receive detailed philosophical attention until long after Aristotle's death.

Aristotle has a little more to say about the problems of perception. In his psychological treatise *On the Soul* he remarks in passing that the reliability of the senses varies according to the objects they are directed towards. If our eyes tell us 'That is white' they are most unlikely to be wrong; if they say 'That white thing is a daisy' they have a greater chance of erring. And Book IV of the *Metaphysics* considers and dismisses a number of sceptical positions. But the remarks in *On the Soul* are not backed by argument, and Aristotle's reply to the sceptics is (in the part which concerns us here) little more than a brusque dismissal.

He thinks that their views are not seriously held: 'it is evident that no one—neither those who state the thesis nor anyone else—is actually in that condition. For why does anyone walk to Megara rather than stay where he is when he thinks he should walk there? Why doesn't he walk into a well or over a cliff in the morning if there is one about?' And he asks, scornfully, if 'they are really puzzled as to whether sizes and colours are such as they seem to those at a distance or to those who are near, to the healthy or to the sick; whether what seems heavy to the weak or to the strong really is heavy; whether what seems to be the case to men awake or to men asleep really is true'.

The fact is that Aristotle did not take sceptical doubts about perception very seriously, and he did not pay any attention to sceptical doubts about generalisation. One great service of later Greek philosophy was to make up for Aristotle's omission: epistemological question became the focus of attention for Stoics, Epicureans and Sceptics.

---

14 *Aristotle's world-picture*

Aristotle was an industrious collector who amassed a prodigious quantity of detailed information on a vast variety of topics. He was also an abstract thinker, whose philosophical ideas ranged wide. Those two parts of his thought were not kept in distinct compartments. On the contrary, Aristotle's scientific work and his philosophical investigations together formed a unified intellectual outlook. Aristotle was a remarkable scientist and a profound philosopher, but it is as a philosopher-scientist that he excels. He was, according to an ancient aphorism, 'a scribe of Nature who dipped his pen in Thought'.

His main philosophico-scientific writings are *On Generation and Destruction, On the Heavens, Meteorology, On the Soul*, the collection of short psychological treatises known collectively as the *Parva Naturalia*, the *Parts of Animals*, and the *Generation of*

Animals. All those treatises are scientific, in the sense that they are based on empirical research, and attempt to organise and explain the observed phenomena. They are all philosophical, in the sense that they are acutely self-conscious, reflective and systematically structured attempts to arrive at the truth of things.

Aristotle himself indicates the general plan of his work at the beginning of the *Meteorology*.

> I have already dealt with the first causes of nature and with all natural motion [in the *Physics*], and also with the heavenly bodies, arranged in their upper paths [in *On the Heavens*], and with the number and nature of the material elements, with their mutual transformations, and with generation and destruction in general [in *On Generation and Corruption*]. The part of this enquiry remaining to be considered is what all the earlier thinkers called meteorology . . . When we have dealt with these subjects, let us see if we can give some account, on the lines we have laid down, of animals and plants, both in general and in particular; for when we have done that, we shall perhaps have arrived at the completion of the plan we set ourselves at the beginning.

Aristotle offers a clear view of the nature of reality. The basic constituent stuffs of the sublunary world are four: earth, air, fire and water. Each element is defined by its possession of two of the four primary powers or qualities—wetness, dryness, coldness, hotness. The elements have each a natural movement and a natural place. Fire, if left to itself, will move upwards and will find its place at the outermost edges of the universe; earth naturally moves downwards, to the centre of the universe; air and water find their places in between. The elements can act upon and change into one another; such elemental interactions are discussed in *On Generation and Destruction*, and something approximating to chemistry may be found in Book IV of the *Meteorology*.

Earth tends downwards, and our earth is naturally at the centre of the universe. Beyond the earth and its atmosphere come the moon, the sun, the planets and the fixed stars. Aristotle's geocentric astronomy, which attaches the heavenly bodies to a series of concentric spheres, was not his own creation. He was not a professional astronomer but relied upon the work of his contemporaries, Eudoxus and Callippus. The treatise *On the Heavens* is concerned with abstract astronomy. Aristotle's main contention is that the physical universe is spatially finite but temporally infinite—it is a vast but bounded sphere which has existed without beginning and will exist without end.

Around the earth is its atmosphere. The events in the sublunary sphere had occupied much of the attention of the early Greek scientists, and Aristotle follows their lead. The *Meteorology* studies 'ta meteōra', literally 'the things suspended in mid-air': the phrase referred originally to such phenomena as clouds, thunder, rain, snow, frost, dew—roughly speaking, to the weather; but it was easily extended to include matters which we should classify under astronomy (meteors, comets, the milky way, for example) or under geography (rivers, the sea, mountains, etc.). Aristotle's *Meteorology* contains his own explanations of these various phenomena. The work has a strong empirical base, but it is firmly governed by theory. The unity it possesses derives largely from the dominance of one notion, that of 'exhalation'. Aristotle holds that 'exhalations' or evaporations are continuously being given off by the earth. They are of two sorts, wet or steamy, and dry or smoky. Their action can explain, in a uniform fashion, most of the events that take place in the atmosphere.

On the earth itself the most remarkable objects of study are living things and their parts. 'Of the parts in animals, some are incomposite, namely those which divide into uniform pieces (for example, flesh into flesh), others are composite, namely those which divide into non-uniform pieces (for example, a hand does not divide into hands, nor a face into faces) . . . All the non-uniform parts are composed from the uniform parts, for example, hands from flesh and sinews and bones.' There is no sharp boundary between non-living and living things; and although living things can be arranged in a hierarchy—a 'ladder of nature' of ascending worth and complexity—the grades in the hierarchy are not rigorously separated. Plants blend into the lowest of animals; and from those to man, who naturally stands at the top of the scale, there is a continuous progression. Such is the natural world. It continues for ever, exhibiting constant regularity in continuous change.

Circular motion, that is, the motion of the heavens, has been seen . . . to be eternal, because its motions and those determined by it come into being and will exist from necessity. For if that which moves in a circle is always moving something else, the motion of those things too must be circular—for example, since the upper movement is circular, the sun moves in this way; and since this is so, the seasons for that reason come into being in a circle and return upon themselves; and since they come into being in this way, so again do the things governed by them.

And how is the world run? Are there gods to keep it going? Outwardly Aristotle was a conventional polytheist; at least, in his will he ordered statues to be dedicated at Stagira to Zeus and to Athena. But such performances did not mirror his beliefs:

> Our remote ancestors have handed down remnants to their posterity in mythical form to the effect that these [sc. the heavenly bodies] are gods and that the divine encompasses the whole of nature. But the rest has been added by way of myth to persuade the vulgar and for the use of the laws and of expediency. For they say that they are anthropomorphic and like some of the other animals—and other things consequent upon and similar to that; but if you were to separate what they say and accept only the first part, that they thought the primary substances to be gods, you would think they had spoken divinely.

Zeus and Athena, the anthropomorphic gods of the Olympian pantheon, are mere myths; but 'our remote ancestors' were not purveyors of unmixed superstition. They rightly saw, or half saw, first that the 'primary substances' are divine ('god seems to everyone to be among the causes and a sort of first principle'), and secondly that the primary substances should be sought in the heavens.

The heavenly bodies, which Aristotle often refers to as 'the divine bodies', are made of a special stuff, a fifth element or 'quintessence'; for 'there is some other body, separate from those here about us, whose nature is more honourable in that it is further removed from the world below'. Now 'it is the function of what is most divine to think and to use its intellect', so that the heavenly bodies, being divine, must therefore be alive and intelligent. For although 'we tend to think of them as though they were simply bodies—units exhibiting order but quite without life—we must suppose that they partake in action and in life . . . We must think that the actions of the stars are just like those of animals and plants.'

In Book VII of the *Physics* Aristotle argues for the existence of a changeless source of change—an 'unmoved mover' as it is normally called. If there is to be any change in the universe, there must, he holds, be some original source which imparts change to other things without changing itself. The unmoved mover is outside the universe: 'must there be something unchanging and at rest outside what is changing and no part of it, or not? And must this be true of the universe too? It would presumably seem absurd if the principle of change were *inside* it.' The external mover 'initiates change as an object of love; and other things initiate change by changing themselves'. The concentric celestial spheres, and the celestial bodies they carry, are all quintessential and divine; but they are moving divinities. Beyond them, incorporeal and outside the universe, is the primary divinity, the changeless originator of all change.

What are we to make of all this? Some scholars take Aristotle's words at what seems to be their face value, and find living gods scattered throughout his writings—he thus becomes a profoundly religious scientist. Other scholars dismiss Aristotle's use of the words 'god' and 'divine' as a mere *façon de parler*: the primary substances are divine only in the sense that other things are dependent upon them—and Aristotle becomes a wholly secular thinker.

Neither of those two views is plausible. There is too much about gods in the treatises to permit us to discount Aristotle's theologising as empty word-play; and, on the other hand, Aristotle's gods are too abstract, remote and impersonal to be regarded as the objects of a religious man's worship. Rather, we might connect Aristotle's remarks about the divinity of the universe with the sense of wonderment which nature and its works produced in him. 'It is because of wonderment that men, both now and at first, start to study philosophy'; and that study, properly conducted, does not diminish the initial admiration. For Aristotle was impressed by a deep reverence for the value and excellence of the universe about him:

In what way does the nature of the world contain what is good and what is best—as something separate and independent, or as its own orderliness? Rather, in both ways, as an army does. For the excellence of an army resides both in its orderliness and in its general, and especially in the latter. For he does not depend on the orderliness but it does depend on him. And all things—fish and birds and plants—are ordered in a way, yet not in the same way; and it is not the case that there is no connection between one thing and another—there is a connection.

15 *Psychology*

There is a fundamental distinction within the natural world: some natural substances are alive, others are inanimate. What marks off the former from the latter is their possession of *psuchē*. The word '*psuchē* (from which our word 'psychology' derives) is usually translated as 'soul', and under the heading of *psuchē* Aristotle does indeed include those features of the higher animals which later thinkers tend to associate with the soul. But 'soul' is a misleading translation. It is a truism that all living things—prawns and pansies no less than men and gods—possess a *psuchē*; but it sounds bizarre to suggest that a prawn has a soul. Since a *psuchē* is what animates, or gives life to, a living thing, the word 'animator' (despite its overtones of Disneyland) might be used. (I shall generally keep to the conventional 'soul', but I shall also occasionally use 'animator'.)

Souls or animators come in varying degrees of complexity.

Some things possess all the powers of the soul, others some of them, others one only. The powers we mentioned were those of nutrition, of perception, of appetition, of change in place, of thought. Plants possess only the nutritive power. Other things possess both that and the power of perception.

And if the power of perception, then that of appetition too. For appetition consists of desire, inclination and wish; all animals possess at least one of the senses, namely touch; everything which has perception also experiences pleasure and pain, the pleasant and the painful; and everything which experiences those also possesses desire (for desire is appetition for the pleasant) . . . Some things possess in addition to these the power of locomotion; and others also possess the power of thought and intelligence.

Thought, in Aristotle's view, requires imagination and hence perception; so that any thinking creature must be capable of perceiving. And perception never exists apart from the first principle of animation, that of nutrition and reproduction. Thus the various powers or faculties of the soul form a hierarchical system.

What is a soul or animator? And how do living creatures acquire one?

In his treatise *On the Soul* Aristotle offers a general account of what a soul is. He first argues to the conclusion that 'if we are to state something common to every type of soul, it will be that it is the first fulfilment of a natural body that has organs'. He later observes that such an account is not particularly illuminating, and suggests, as an improvement, that 'a soul is a principle of the aforesaid powers and is defined by them, namely by nutrition, perception, thought, movement'. Aristotle himself advises us not to spend too much time over these generalities but rather to concentrate on the different functions of the soul.

Yet the generalities contain something of great importance. Aristotle's first general account of the soul amounts to this: for a thing to have a soul is for it to be a natural organic body actually capable of functioning. The second general account simply explains what those functions are. Thus Aristotle's souls are not *pieces* of living things; they are not bits of spiritual stuff placed inside the living body; rather, they are sets of powers, capacities or faculties. Possessing a soul is like possessing a skill. A skilled man's skill is not some part of him, responsible for his skilled acts; similarly, a living creature's animator or life-force is not some part of it, responsible for its living activities.

That view of the soul has certain consequences, which Aristotle was quick to draw. First, 'one should not ask if the soul and the body are one, any more than one should ask of the wax and the shape or in general of the matter of anything and that of which it is the matter'. There is no problem of the 'unity' of soul and body, or of how soul and body can act upon each other. Descartes later wondered how on earth two things so different as body and soul could coexist and work together; for Aristotle such issues do not arise.

Secondly, 'that the soul—or certain parts of it, if it is divisible into parts—is not separable from the body is not unclear'. Fulfilments cannot exist apart from the things that are fulfilled. Souls are fulfilments of bodies. Hence souls cannot exist apart from bodies, any more than skills can exist apart from skilled men. Plato had held that souls pre-existed the birth and survived the death of those bodies they animated. Aristotle thought that that was impossible. A soul is simply not the *sort* of thing that could survive. How could my skills, my temper or my character survive me?

Aristotle's general view of the nature of souls is elaborated in his detailed accounts of the different life-functions: nutrition, reproduction, perception, movement, thought. Such functions or faculties are functions or faculties *of the body*, and Aristotle's psychological investigations can take a biological turn without, as it were, changing the subject. Thus imagination, for example, is described as 'a motion coming about by the agency of an act of perception': an act of perception is a physiological change, and it may cause a further physiological change, which constitutes an imagination. Some may object that Aristotle ignores the psychological aspect of imagination by concentrating on its physiological manifestations. But Aristotle holds that the physiology *is* the psychology, that souls and their parts are *physical* capacities.

On the Soul and the *Parva Naturalia* are governed by that biological attitude towards animation. In the *Generation of Animals* Aristotle asks where the soul or animator comes from: how do creatures begin to live? A popular view, accepted by Plato, had it that life begins when the soul enters the body. Aristotle comments: 'clearly, those principles whose actuality is corporeal cannot exist without a body—for example, walking without feet; hence they cannot come in from outside—for they can come in neither alone (for they are inseparable), nor in some body (for the semen is a residue of food that is undergoing change).' The 'principles' or powers of the soul are corporeal principles—to be animated is to be a *body* with certain capacities. Hence to suppose that those capacities could exist outside any body is as absurd as to imagine that walking could take place apart from any legs. The soul cannot simply drift into the foetus from outside. (In principle, it could arrive 'in some body', that is, in the semen; but in fact the semen is the wrong sort of stuff to carry or transmit those capacities.)

Aristotle's accounts of nutrition, reproduction, perception, desire and movement are all consistently biological. But consistency is threatened when he turns to the highest psychological faculty, that of thought. In the *Generation of Animals*, immediately after the sentences just quoted, Aristotle continues: 'Hence it remains that thought alone comes in from outside, and that it alone is divine; for corporeal actuality has no connection at all with the actuality of thought.' Thought, it seems, *can* exist apart from body. The treatise *On the Soul* speaks of thought with special caution, hinting that it *may* be separable from body. In what is perhaps the most perplexing paragraph he ever wrote, Aristotle distinguishes between two sorts of thought (later known as 'active intellect' and 'passive intellect'). Of the first of these he says: 'this thought is separable and impassive and unmixed, being essentially actuality . . . And when separated it is just what it is, and it alone is immortal and eternal.'

The special status of thought depends upon the view that thinking does not involve any corporeal activity. But how can Aristotle hold that view? His general account of the soul makes it plain that thinking is something done by 'natural organic bodies', and his particular analysis of the nature of thought makes thinking dependent upon imagination and hence upon perception. Even if thinking is not itself a corporeal activity, it requires other corporeal activities in order to take place.

Aristotle's treatment of thought is both obscure in itself and hard to reconcile with the rest of his psychology. But neither that fact, nor the various errors and inexactitudes in his physiology, should dim the light of his work on psychology: it rests on a subtle insight into the nature of souls or animators, and it is persistently scientific in its approach to psychological questions.

16 *Evidence and theory*

Aristotle's general account of the world is wholly exploded. Most of his explanations are now seen to be false. Many of the concepts he operated with appear crude and inadequate. Some of his ideas seem quite absurd. The chief reason for Aristotle's downfall is simple: in the sixteenth and seventeenth centuries, scientists applied quantitative methods to the study of inanimate nature, and chemistry and physics came to assume a dominating role. Those two sciences seemed to be fundamental in a way in which biology was not: they examined the same stuffs as biology, but from a closer, and a mathematical, viewpoint—a biology unsupported by physics and chemistry lacked all foundation. Aristotle's physics and chemistry are hopelessly inadequate when compared to the work of the new scientists. A new 'world picture', based on the new sciences, replaced the Aristotelian view, and if Aristotle's biology survived for a further century or so, it survived as a limb torn from the body, as a fragment of a colossal statue.

Why did Aristotle not develop a decent chemistry or an adequate physics? His failing must be set down in large part to a certain conceptual poverty. He did not have our concepts of mass, force, velocity, temperature, and he thus lacked the most powerful tools of the physical sciences. In some cases he had a rough and primitive form of the concept—after all, he knew what speed was, and he could weigh things. But his notion of speed is in a sense non-quantitative. He did not *measure* velocity; he had no notion of miles per hour. Or again, consider temperature. Heat is a central notion in Aristotelian science. The hot and the cold are two of the four primary powers, and heat is vital to animal life. Aristotle's predecessors had disagreed among themselves over what objects were hot and what cold. 'If there is so much dispute over the hot and the cold,' Aristotle remarks, 'what must we think about the rest?—for these are the clearest of the things we perceive'. He suspects that the disputes occur 'because the term "hotter" is used in several ways', and he conducts a long analysis of the different criteria we use for calling things hot. The analysis is subtle, but—to our eyes—it suffers from a glaring deficiency: it does not mention *measurement*. For Aristotle, hotness is a matter of degree, but not of *measurable* degree. To that extent he lacked the notion of temperature.

Conceptual poverty is closely tied to technological poverty. Aristotle had no proper clocks, and no thermometers. Measuring devices and a quantitative conceptual apparatus go together. The former are inconceivable without the latter, the latter are useless without the former. Lacking one, Aristotle lacked both. In an earlier chapter I suggested that Aristotle's zoological researches did not suffer from his non-quantitative approach. The case is different with the natural sciences: chemistry without laboratory equipment and physics without mathematics are bad chemistry and bad physics.

It would be absurd to blame Aristotle for his conceptual poverty: poverty is a lack, not a failing. But many students of Aristotle's science are inclined to impute two serious failings to him, one methodological and the other substantial. It is alleged, first, that Aristotle regularly subordinated fact to theory, that he would start from theory, and then twist the facts to fit it; and secondly, that his natural science was permeated by a childlike determination to find plans and purposes in the world of nature. Let us take the methodological accusation first.

Consider the following passage:

> we might say that plants belong to earth, aquatic animals to water, land-animals to air . . . The fourth kind must not be looked for in these regions; yet there *should* be a kind corresponding to the position of fire—for this is reckoned the fourth of the bodies . . . But such a kind must be sought on the moon; for that evidently shares in the fourth remove—but that is matter for another treatise.

The passage comes in the middle of a sophisticated and informed discussion of certain questions of generation. It would be charitable to regard it as a joke, but it is not jocular in tone—Aristotle convinces himself, by a feeble analogy, that there are kinds of animals corresponding to three of his elements; he infers that there must be a kind corresponding to the fourth element; and, failing to find such things on the earth, he places them on the moon. What could be more absurd? What less scientific?

Well, the passage *is* absurd; and there are one or two others to match it. But all scientists are capable of idiocy: there are remarkably few idiotic passages in Aristotle's writings, and the judicious reader will not make much of them. Rather, he will find other passages more characteristic of the man. Speaking of the motions of the heavenly bodies, Aristotle writes:

> as to how many there are, let us now say what some of the mathematicians say, in order to get some idea of the matter and so that our mind will have some definite number to grasp hold of. As to the future, we must make enquiries ourselves and discuss the matter with other enquirers, and if those who study these matters have views different from those now expressed, we must love both parties but listen to the more accurate.

Again: 'to judge by argument and by the facts which seem to hold about them, the generation of bees takes place in that manner. But we have not yet acquired an adequate grasp of the facts: if we ever do acquire such a grasp, we must then rely on perception rather than on arguments—and on arguments if what they prove is in agreement with the phenomena'. Aristotle has just given a long and careful account of the generation of bees. The account is based primarily on observations, but it is also speculative, relying to some extent on theoretical considerations. Aristotle explicitly recognises this speculative aspect of his account, and he explicitly holds that speculation is subordinate to observation. Theory is indispensable when the facts are as yet insufficiently known, but observation always has priority over theory.

Aristotle elsewhere makes the same point in more general terms: 'we must first grasp the differences between animals and the facts about them all. After that, we must try to discover their causes. For that is the natural method of procedure, once the research about each of them is done; for from that will become apparent the subjects about which and the principles from which our proofs must be conducted.' Again:

empirical science must pass down the principles—I mean, for example, empirical astronomy must supply those of the science of astronomy; for when the phenomena were sufficiently grasped, the astronomical proofs were discovered. And similarly in every other art and science whatsoever. Thus if the facts in each case are grasped, it will then be our task to give a ready supply of proofs. For if none of the true facts of the case is missing, we shall be able to discover the proof of everything of which there is proof and to construct a proof—and to make plain where proof is not possible.

Aristotle frequently criticises his predecessors for putting theory before the facts. Thus, of Plato and his school:

speaking of the phenomena, they say things that do not agree with the phenomena ... They are so fond of their first principles that they seem to behave like those who defend these in dialectical arguments; for they accept any consequence, thinking that they have true principles—as though principles should not be judged by their consequences, and especially by their goal. And the goal in productive science is the product, but in natural science it is whatever properly appears to perception.

Nothing could be clearer. Empirical research precedes theory. The facts must be collected before the causes are sought. The construction of an axiomatic science (of 'proofs') depends upon the presence of 'all the true facts of the case'. Of course, Aristotle never had a grasp of *all* the facts; he often thought he had facts when he only had falsehoods; and he sometimes jumped precipitately into theorising. Moreover, theory should to some extent control the collection of facts: undisciplined amassing of facts is an unscientific exercise; and it may be, as some philosophers both ancient and modern have argued, that there is no such thing as a 'pure' fact uncontaminated by theory. But despite all this, two things are perfectly plain: Aristotle had a clear view of the primacy of observation, and his scientific treatises—in particular, his works on biology—regularly remain true to that view.

In the next chapter I turn to the accusation that Aristotle

childishly makes the natural world a stage on which plans and purposes are acted out.

17 *Teleology*

We see more than one kind of cause concerned with natural generation—namely that for the sake of which, and the source of the principle of change. Thus we must determine which of these comes first and which second. It seems that the first is the one we call 'for the sake of something'; for this is the account of the thing, and the account is a principle in the same way both in the products of skill and in those of nature. For, either by thought or by perception, the doctor determines on health and the builder on a house; and then they give accounts and causes of everything they do, and explain why it should be done in this way. Now that for the sake of which, or the good, is more prevalent in the works of nature than in those of skill.

Here, in the introductory chapter of the *Parts of Animals*, Aristotle sets out what is called his teleological view of nature. Final causes occur in the works of nature no less than in the products of human skill, and in order to explain natural phenomena we must appeal to 'that for the sake of which'. Explanation in terms of final causes is explanation in terms of 'the good', for if ducks have webbed feet *for the sake of* swimming, then it is *good*—that is, good for *ducks*—to have webbed feet. Final causes are primary because they are identified with 'the account of the thing': being a swimmer is part of a duck's essence, and a proper account of what it is to be a duck will require reference to swimming. Final causes are not imposed on nature by theoretical considerations; they are observed in nature: '*we see* more than one kind of cause'. (The term 'teleology' is connected with the Greek '*telos*', which is Aristotle's

word for 'goal': a teleological explanation is one which appeals
to goals or final causes.

Throughout his biological works Aristotle constantly looks for
final causes. Why do teeth, unlike the other hard parts of animal
structure, continue to grow?

> The cause of that growth in the sense of that for the sake of
> which is to be found in their function. For they would soon be
> worn away if there were no accretion to them—as it is, in
> certain old animals which are gross feeders but possess small
> teeth, the teeth are completely worn away, for they are
> destroyed more quickly than they grow. That is why here too
> nature has produced an excellent contrivance to fit the case;
> for she makes loss of the teeth coincide with old age and
> death. If life lasted for ten thousand or one thousand years,
> the teeth would have had to be enormous at first and to grow
> up often; for even if they grew continuously, they would
> nevertheless be smoothed down and so become useless for
> their work. So much for that for the sake of which they grow.

Why do men have hands?

> Anaxagoras says that men are the most intelligent of animals
> because they possess hands; but it is reasonable to think that
> they have got hands because they are most intelligent. For
> hands are a tool, and nature, like an intelligent man, always
> assigns each thing to something that can use it (it is better to
> give a flute to someone who is actually a flute-player than to
> provide a man who owns a flute with the skill of flute-
> playing); for she has provided the greater and superior thing
> with that which is less, and not the less with that which is
> more honourable and greater. Thus if this is better, and if
> nature does what is the best in the circumstances, man is not
> most intelligent because of his hands but has hands because
> he is the most intelligent of animals.

Often final causes are contrasted with 'necessity', and in
particular with the constraints imposed by the material nature of
the animals or animal parts in question. But even where necessity is invoked to explain the phenomena, there is still room for
explanation in terms of final causes. Why do water-birds have
webbed feet?

For these causes, they have them from necessity; and because of what is better they have such feet for the sake of life, so that, living in the water where their wings are useless, they may have feet that are useful for swimming. For they are like oars to oarsmen or fins to fish; hence if in fish the fins are destroyed or in water-birds the webbing between the feet, they no longer swim.

Aristotle's teleology is sometimes summed up in the slogan 'Nature does nothing in vain', and he himself frequently uses aphorisms of that tenor. But although Aristotle holds that final causes are to be found throughout the natural world, they are not to be found literally everywhere. 'The bile in the liver is a residue, and is not for the sake of anything—like the sediment in the stomach and in the intestines. Now nature sometimes uses even residues for some advantageous purpose; but that is no reason for seeking a final cause in all cases.' Book V of the *Generation of Animals* is entirely devoted to such non-purposeful parts of animals.

Natural behaviour and natural structure usually have final causes—for nature does nothing in vain. But the final causes are constrained by necessity—nature does the best she can 'in the circumstances'; and sometimes there is no final cause to be discovered at all.

The *Physics* contains a number of arguments in support of natural teleology. Some of them rest upon the characteristically Aristotelian notion that 'art imitates nature' or 'the arts are imitations of nature': if we can see final causes in the products of skill, all the more so can we see them in the products of nature. Another argument enlarges upon the assertion in the *Parts of Animals* that 'we see' final causes in nature.

It is particularly clear in the case of the other animals which act neither by skill nor after enquiry nor after deliberation (hence some people wonder whether spiders, ants and the like perform their tasks by reason or by something else). And if you proceed little by little in this way, it becomes apparent that in plants too there occurs what is conducive to the goal—for example, leaves for the sake of sheltering the fruit. So that if the swallow builds its nest and the spider its web by nature and for the sake of something, and if plants too produce leaves for the sake of the fruit and grow their roots downwards rather than upwards for the sake of nutrition, it is plain that there are causes of this sort in the things that come to be and are by nature.

But *do* we 'see' final causes in nature? And what exactly are we supposed to see? The phrases 'in order to' and 'for the sake of' seem to be primarily of service in explaining the intentional actions of conscious agents. Then is Aristotle ascribing agency and intentionality to natural phenomena? He is surely not attributing intentions to animals and plants or saying that the final causes of their activities are what *they* purpose; for it is evident that ducks do not plan to have webbed feet or plants contrive their leaves. Aristotle's teleology does not consist in a puerile ascription of intentions to vegetables.

Is Aristotle attributing intentions not to natural creatures but to Nature herself? There are several passages in which Aristotle does speak of Nature as the intelligent artificer of the natural world. 'Like a good housekeeper, Nature does not waste anything which might be put to good use.' Such passages should not be lightly dismissed. But Nature the Artificer cannot be all that there is to Aristotle's teleology; for in the detailed teleological explanations which fill his biological writings he rarely adverts to the plans of Nature or the purposes of a grand Designer.

But if we are not to interpret Aristotle's teleology in terms of intentional planning, how are to interpret it? Consider the following passage.

> Snakes copulate by twining around one another; and they have no testicles and no penis, as I have already observed— no penis because they have no legs, no testicles . . . because of their length. For because they are naturally elongated, if there were further delay in the region of the testicles, the semen would grow cool because of its slow passage. (This happens in the case of men who have large penises: they are less fertile than those with moderate penises because cold semen is not fertile and semen that is carried a long way cools.)

If the snake's semen had to wind its way through a pair of testicles after travelling the length of the snake's body, it would become cold and infertile—and *that* is why snakes have no testicles. (They have no penis because the penis is naturally located between the legs, and snakes have no legs.) In order to procreate successfully, snakes must lack testicles: they would not survive if they did not procreate, and they could not procreate if they had testicles. That explains their lack of testicles. The explanation is fantastical in its content, but it is an explanation of a perfectly respectable type.

In general, most structural features and behavioural traits of animals and plants have a function. That is to say, they serve the performance of some activity which is essential, or at least useful, to the organism—if the organism did not perform that activity it would not survive at all, or would only survive with difficulty. If we are seeking an understanding of animal life, we must grasp the functions associated with the creature's parts and behaviour. If you know that ducks have webbed feet and also know that they swim, you are not yet in possession of full understanding—you need to grasp in addition that the webbing *helps* ducks to swim, and that swimming is an essential part of the duck's life.

Aristotle expresses this by saying that one answer to the question 'Why do ducks have webbed feet?' is 'In order to swim.' His 'in order to' sounds odd to us only because *we* associate 'in order to' primarily with intentional action. Aristotle associates it primarily with function, and he sees function in nature. He is surely right. Natural objects do contain functional parts and do exhibit functional behaviour; the scientist who is unaware of such functions is ignorant of a major part of his subject-matter.

'Nature does nothing in vain' is a regulative principle for scientific enquiry. Aristotle knows that some aspects of nature are functionless. But he recognises that a grasp of function is crucial to an understanding of nature. His slogans about the prudence of Nature are not pieces of childish superstition, but reminders of a central task of the natural scientist.

18 *Practical philosophy*

The preceding chapters have been concerned with the theoretical sciences. Aristotle himself devoted most of his time to that great branch of knowledge, but he did not ignore the practical sciences. Indeed, two of his most celebrated treatises, the *Politics* and the *Nicomachean Ethics*, belong to the practical branch of philosophy. Those works are not practical in the sense of being manuals. On the contrary, they are full of analysis and argument, and they rest upon much historical and scientific research. They are works of practical *philosophy*, practical in the sense that their purpose or aim is not merely to purvey truth but also to affect action: 'the present treatise is not, like the others, undertaken for the sake of understanding—for we are conducting the enquiry not in order to know what goodness is but in order to become good men'.

Aristotle wrote two *Ethics*, the *Nicomachean* and the *Eudemian*. The title '*Ethics*' is slightly misleading, and so too are the standard English translations of two key terms in Aristotle's practical philosophy—'*aretē*', normally rendered 'virtue', and '*eudaimonia*', normally rendered 'happiness'. A few remarks on these words are in order.

Aristotle himself refers to his treatises as the '*ēthika*', and the transliteration of that Greek word gives us the title '*Ethics*'. But the Greek term means 'matters to do with character', and a better title would be *On Matters of Character*. As for '*aretē*', the word means something like 'goodness' or 'excellence'. Aristotle can talk of the *aretē* of an argument or of an axe as well as of a man. Human *aretē* is human excellence—what it is to be a good human being—and it has only an indirect connection with what we think of as virtue. Finally, '*eudaimonia*' does not refer to a mental state of euphoria, as 'happiness' tends to in English: to be *eudaimōn* is to flourish, to make a success of life, and the connection between *eudaimonia* and happiness is again indirect.

What, then, is Aristotle's 'ethical' philosophy? 'It seems no doubt uncontroversial to say that *eudaimonia* is the best thing, but we need to say more clearly what it is'. Each of us wants to flourish or do well, and all our actions, in so far as they are rational, are directed to that ultimate goal. The primary question for practical philosophy, then, is this: How are we to achieve *eudaimonia*? In what does flourishing consist? What is it to be a successful human being? Aristotle is not asking what makes us happy, and he is not concerned with the question of how we *ought* to lead our lives, if that question is construed as a moral one. He wants to instruct us in how to make a success of our lives.

Aristotle's answer depends upon a philosophical analysis of the nature of *eudaimonia*. *Eudaimonia*, he argues, is 'an activity of the soul in accordance with excellence'. To say that *eudaimonia* is an 'activity' is to say that to flourish involves *doing* things as opposed to being in a certain state. (Being happy—like, say, being in love—is a state of mind: flourishing is not a state but an activity or set of activities.) To say that *eudaimonia* concerns the soul (or the animator) is to say that human flourishing requires the exercise of certain of the faculties by which life is defined; in particular, a person cannot be said to flourish as a human being unless he is exercising distinctively human faculties. Finally, *eudaimonia* is an activity 'in accordance with excellence'. To flourish is to do certain things excellently or well. A man who exercises his faculties but does so inefficiently or badly cannot be said to be making a success of his life.

Then what are the excellences in accordance with which we should act? Aristotle distinguishes between excellences of character and excellences of intellect. The former include both what we think of as moral virtues—courage, generosity, fair-mindedness and so on—and also such dispositions as a proper self-respect, an appropriate degree of ostentation, and wit; the latter include such things as knowledge, good judgement, 'practical wisdom'. In addition, Aristotle spends some time in discussing the quasi-excellence of friendship.

Men are marked off from other animals by possessing reason and the power of thought. Men 'contain something divine—what we call the intellect is divine', and our intellect is 'the divine within us'. Indeed, 'each of us actually *is* intellect, since that is our sovereign and best element'. The excellences most properly human, then, are the intellectual excellences, and *eudaimonia* consists primarily in activity in accordance with those excellences—it is a form of intellectual activity. 'Thus any choice or possession of the natural goods—of the body, wealth, friends or any other good—which will best produce contemplation by the god [that is, by our intellect, the god within us], is best and is the finest standard; and any which, either because of deficiency or because of excess, prevents us from cultivating the god and from contemplating, is bad.' To flourish, to make a success of life, requires engagement in intellectual pursuits. Aristotle thought that such pursuits were immensely enjoyable, and that the intellectual life offered an unparalleled happiness; but his main thesis in the *Ethics* is not that happiness consists in intellectual activity, but that excellent intellectual activity constitutes success or flourishing for men. The intellectual giants of history may not all have been happy men, but they were all successful men—they all flourished and achieved *eudaimonia*.

Intellectual activity is not enough. Men are not isolated individuals, and the human excellences cannot be practised by solitary hermits. 'Man', Aristotle says, 'is by nature a social animal' (the word I translate as 'social' is usually rendered by 'political'). That remark is no casual aphorism, but a piece of biological theory. 'Social animals are those which have some single activity common to them all (which is not true of all gregarious animals); such are men, bees, wasps, ants, cranes.' 'What is peculiar to men, compared to the other animals, is that they alone can perceive the good and bad, the just and the unjust, and the rest—and it is partnership in these things which makes a household and a State.' Society and the State are not artificial trappings imposed upon natural man: they are manifestations of human nature itself.

Societies appear in different forms. The first thing to be stressed in connection with Aristotle's idea of a State is its size. 'A State cannot be made from ten men—and from 100,000 it is no longer a State.' The Greek city-states whose histories formed the factual background to Aristotle's political theory were, most of them, of pygmy proportions. They were frequently torn by faction, and their independence was ultimately destroyed by the advance of Macedonian power. Aristotle was familiar with the evils of faction (Book V of the *Politics* is given over to an analysis of the causes of civil strife), and he was intimate with the Macedonian court; yet he never lost his conviction that the small city-state was the right—the natural—form of civil society.

A State is a collection of citizens, and a citizen, in Aristotle's view, 'is defined by nothing else so well as by participation in judicial functions and in political office'. The affairs of a State are run directly by its citizens. Each citizen will be a member of the assembly or deliberative body of the nation, he will be eligible for the various offices of State, which include financial and military appointments, and he will be a part of the judiciary (for under Greek legal procedure the functions of judge and jury were not distinguished).

How much political power a citizen possessed would depend on the type of constitution which his State enjoyed, different constitutions entrusting to different persons or institutions the authority to pass legislation and to determine public policy. Aristotle produced a complex taxonomy of constitutions, the three main types of which are monarchy, aristocracy and democracy. In certain circumstances Aristotle favoured monarchy. 'When either a whole family or an individual is so remarkable in point of excellence that his excellence exceeds that of everyone else, then it is just that that family or that individual should be king and sovereign over all matters.' But such circumstances are rare, and in practice Aristotle preferred democracy. 'The view that the multitude, rather than a few good men, should be sovereign . . . would seem perhaps to be true. For although each member of the multitude is not a good man, still it is possible that, when they come together, they should be better—not as individuals but collectively, just as communal dinners are better than those supplied at one man's expense.'

A State, however constituted, must be self-sufficient, and it must achieve the goal or end for which States exist.

It is evident that a State is not a sharing of locality for the purpose of preventing mutual harm and promoting trade. Those things must necessarily be present if a State is to exist; but even if they are all present a State does not thereby exist. Rather, a State is a sharing by households and families in a good life, for the purpose of a complete and self-sufficient life.

The 'good life', which is the goal of the State, is identified with *eudaimonia*, which is the goal of individuals. States are natural entities, and like other natural objects they have a goal or end. Teleology is a feature of Aristotle's political theory no less than of his biology.

That notion of the goal of the State is linked to another high ideal. 'A fundamental principle of democratic constitutions is liberty . . . One form of liberty is to rule and be ruled turn and turn about . . . Another form is to live as one wishes; for men say that that is the aim of liberty, since to live not as one wishes is the mark of a slave.' Liberty at home is complemented by a pacific external policy; for Aristotelian States, although armed for defence, will have no imperialist ambitions. (But Aristotle is said to have urged Alexander the Great to 'deal with Greeks in the manner of a leader, with foreigners in that of a master, caring for the former as friends and relatives, treating the latter as animals or plants'.)

But liberty is severely restricted in Aristotle's State. It is the prerogative of citizens, and a large majority of the population does not possess citizenship. Women have no liberty. And there are slaves. Some men, according to Aristotle, are slaves by nature, and it is therefore permissible to make them slaves in fact. 'Someone who, being a man, belongs by nature not to himself but to someone else, is a slave by nature. He belongs to someone else if, being a man, he is an article of property—and an article of property is an instrument which aids the actions of and is separable from its owner.' Slaves may enjoy a good life— they may have kind masters. But they have no liberty and no rights.

The citizens own slaves, and they own other forms of property too. Aristotle argues at length against communism. 'Evidently', he concludes, 'it is better that property should be private, but that men should make it common in use.' But he immediately adds that 'it is the task of the legislator to see that the citizens become like that'. Aristotle's State will not own the means of production, nor will it direct the economy; but the legislature will ensure that the citizens' economic behaviour is properly governed.

The voice of the State, muted in economic affairs, is strident in social matters. The State intervenes before birth: 'since the legislator must from the start consider how the children who are reared are to have the best physique, he must first pay attention to sexual union, determining when and between what sort of people marital relations may exist'. Interference continues during childhood, especially in connection with education.

> No one would dispute that the legislator must busy himself especially about the education of the young . . . Since the whole city has one goal, it is evident that there must also be one and the same education for everyone, and that the superintendence of this should be public and not private . . . Public matters should be publicly managed; and we should not think that each of the citizens belongs to himself, but that they all belong to the State.

Aristotle describes in considerable detail the various ways in which the State should regulate the lives of its citizens. Each regulation, however benevolent in purpose, is a curtailment of liberty—and in Aristotle's claim that the citizens 'all belong to the State' the reader may detect the infant voice of totalitarianism. If Aristotle loved liberty, he did not love it enough. His State is highly authoritarian.

What has gone wrong? Some may suspect that Aristotle erred at the very first step. He confidently assigns a positive function to the State, supposing that its goal is the promotion of the good life. Given that, it is easy to imagine that the State, eager to ameliorate the human condition, may properly intervene in any aspect of human life and may compel its subjects to do whatever will make them happy. Those who see the State as a promoter of Good often end up as advocates of repression. Lovers of liberty will prefer to assign a negative function to the State and to regard it rather as a defence and protection against Evil.

19 The arts

Aristotle is often accused of presenting a narrowly intellectual view of the good life: Homer and Phidias—or Rembrandt and Bach—will not, in his opinion, serve as examples of success or as illustrations of *eudaimonia*. That accusation may well be unjust, for the ideal of 'contemplation' advanced in the *Ethics* is perhaps large enough to encompass a life of artistic or literary genius. But however that may be, Aristotle did in practice have the greatest veneration for such genius: that is apparent from every page of his treatise on the arts, the *Poetics*.

The *Poetics* is short, and it survives only in a curtailed form. It contains an interesting essay on language and linguistics, which may be supplemented by the treatment of style in Book III of the *Rhetoric*. It says a little about the emotions, on which Aristotle writes at length and with great subtlety in Book II of the *Rhetoric*. But it consists largely of what most commentators have seen as literary theory or literary criticism. That, however, is not how Aristotle saw his tract: the *Poetics* is a contribution to 'productive' science—its aim is to tell us not how to judge a work of art, but how to produce one.

Art, Aristotle thinks, is a matter of representation or 'imitation'. 'Epics, and tragic poetry, and also comedy and dithyrambs and most flute- and harp-music, are all by and large imitations.' Art imitates or represents human life, and in particular human actions. Human actions differ in character, 'and it is this difference which distinguishes tragedy from comedy; for the latter is supposed to imitate men who are worse, the former men who are better, than those of today'. Much of the *Poetics* is devoted to tragedy. The discussion starts from a celebrated definition. 'Tragedy is an imitation of an action which is serious and complete, and which has a certain magnitude. Its language is well seasoned, with each of the kinds of seasoning used separately in its different parts. It is in dramatic, not narrative, form.

And through pity and fear it accomplishes a purgation of emotions of that sort'.

Of the six elements of tragedy which Aristotle distinguishes— plot, character, language, thought, spectacle, song—the plot is the most important. It is in virtue of its lot that a tragedy will be 'complete' or unitary, and it is through its plot that a tragedy will perform its purgative function: 'the chief means by which a tragedy works on the emotions are parts of the plot, namely discoveries and reversals'. The plot revolves about a central figure, the 'tragic hero' as he was later called, who must be a man 'neither pre-eminent in excellence and goodness nor falling into misfortune through badness and villainy, but rather through some mistake—a man of high reputation and good fortune, like Oedipus or Thyestes or famous men from such families'. The protagonist of a tragedy enjoys great success (Oedipus was King of Thebes). He has made some 'mistake' (Oedipus unwittingly killed his father and married his mother). The mistake is discovered, and a 'reversal' occurs (Oedipus' mother commits suicide, he blinds himself and is banished from Thebes). By its organic unity, and its implicit universality, the story works upon the feelings of the audience.

Aristotle's conception of tragedy, which had a profound effect upon the later history of European drama, may seem blinkered. His definition hardly fits the great tragedies of Shakespeare, not to mention the works of modern playwrights whose heroes, or anti-heroes, possess neither the social standing nor the grand history of an Oedipus. But Aristotle was not attempting to produce a 'theory' of tragedy which would hold good for all time. He was telling his contemporaries, who worked within the conventions of the Greek stage, how to write a play. (His advice is based upon a mass of empirical research into the history of Greek drama.)

Again, Aristotle's notion of the goal of tragedy may appear odd. He stresses the effect which tragedy has on the feelings and passions of an audience. But do tragedies always purge an audience of pity and fear? And if they do, is it plausible to regard emotional purgation as the primary function of tragedy? No doubt tragedy has an emotional aspect; but it also has aesthetic and intellectual aspects.

Aristotle was well aware of those aspects, even if they do not feature prominently in his definition of tragedy. Much of the *Poetics* deals implicitly with aesthetic matters, inasmuch as it discusses the 'well-seasoned language' and the rhythms which tragedy requires. Of the intellectual aspect of art Aristotle has this to say:

> everyone enjoys imitation. A sign of that is what happens in actual cases; for we enjoy looking at very accurate likenesses of things which in themselves are painful to see—for example, the forms of the foulest animals, and corpses. The reason for this is that learning is most pleasant not only to philosophers but also to other men, even if they share the pleasure briefly. That is why we enjoy seeing likenesses—as we look, we learn and infer what each thing is, saying 'That's him.'

The pleasure of learning is thus an important ingredient in the productive sciences. Contemplation or the actuality of knowing is the prime component of *eudaimonia*, which is the goal of the practical sciences. Truth and knowledge are the direct aim of the theoretical sciences. The desire for knowledge, which Aristotle thought to be part of every man's nature and which was patently the dominant aspect of his own personality, informs and unifies the tripartite structure of Aristotelian philosophy.

20 *Afterlife*

On Aristotle's death, his friend and pupil Theophrastus assumed his mantle, and under him the Lyceum remained a bright focus of scientific and philosophical study. But in the third century BC the light of Aristotelianism dimmed. Other schools of thought—the Stoics, the Epicureans, the Sceptics—dominated the philosophical stage, and the sciences developed separately from philosophy and became the domain of specialists.

Yet Aristotle was never forgotten, and his work enjoyed more than one renaissance. From the first to the sixth century AD, a sequence of scholarly commentators preserved his writings and revivified his thought. There was a second renewal of interest in Byzantium in the eighth century. Later, in the twelfth century, Aristotle came to Western Europe, where his texts were read by learned men and translated into Latin, and copies were widely disseminated and widely read. Aristotle was known, magisterially, as 'the Philosopher'. His thought was all-pervasive, and the half-hearted attempts by the Church to suppress his writings only confirmed their authority. For some four centuries Aristotle's philosophy and Aristotle's science ruled the West with virtually unchallenged sway.

An account of Aristotle's intellectual afterlife would be little less than a history of European thought. In part his influence was simple and direct: Aristotle's various doctrines and beliefs were purveyed as received truths, and his ideas, or their reflection, can be seen in the pages of philosophers and scientists, of historians and theologians, of poets and playwrights. But the influence also took a subtler form. The structure as well as the content of Aristotle's thought impressed itself upon posterity. The concepts and the terminology of the Lyceum provided the medium within which philosophy and science developed, so that even those radical thinkers who determined to reject Aristotelian views found themselves doing so in Aristotelian language. When today we talk of matter and form, of species and genera, of energy and potentiality, of substance and quality, of accident and essence, we unwittingly speak the language of Aristotle and think in terms and concepts which were forged in Greece two millennia ago.

It is worth adding that our modern notion of scientific method is thoroughly Aristotelian. Scientific empiricism—the idea that abstract argument must be subordinate to factual evidence, that theory is to be judged before the strict tribunal of observation—now seems a commonplace; but it was not always so, and it is largely due to Aristotle that we understand science to be an empirical pursuit. The point needs emphasising, if only because Aristotle's most celebrated English critics, Francis Bacon and John Locke, were both staunch empiricists who thought that they were thereby breaking with the Aristotelian tradition. Aristotle was charged with preferring flimsy theories and sterile syllogisms to the solid, fertile facts. But that charge is unjust; and indeed it could only have been brought by men who did not read Aristotle's own works with proper attention and who criticised him for the faults of his successors.

Aristotle undoubtedly had influence. But influence and greatness are not the same thing, and we might yet ask what makes Aristotle a Master—'the master of those who know', as Dante called him—and why he is still worth reading. His greatest single achievement was surely his biology. By the work recorded in the *Researches*, the *Parts of Animals*, and the *Generation of Animals*, he founded the science of biology, set it on a sure empirical and philosophical basis, and gave it the shape it would retain until the nineteenth century. Second only to his biology is his logic. Here too Aristotle founded a new science, and Aristotle's logic remained until the end of the last century the logic of European thought. Few men have founded one science; Aristotle apart, none has founded more than one.

But in biology and in logic Aristotle is outdated. If we want to learn biology or logic, we no longer turn to Aristotle's treatises: they are now of historical interest only. The same is not true of Aristotle's more philosophical writings. The essays in the *Physics*, the *Metaphysics* and the *Ethics* are less sure, less perfect, less scientific than the logic and the biology; but they are, paradoxically, more alive. For here Aristotle has not yet been overtaken. The *Ethics*, for example, can indeed be read as a historical document—as evidence for the state of practical philosophy in the fourth century BC. But it can also be read as a contribution to current debate, and modern philosophers still treat Aristotle as a brilliant colleague. The philosophical treatises are rich, difficult, exciting: they are still studied as urgent commentary on matters of permanent concern.

Finally, Aristotle set before us, explicitly in his writings and implicitly in his life, an ideal of human excellence. Aristotelian man may not be the sole paragon or the unique ideal, but he is surely an admirable specimen, emulation of whom is no low ambition. I end with a passage from the *Parts of Animals* which expresses some of the best in Aristotelian man.

Of natural substances, some we hold to be for ever free from generation and destruction, others to partake in generation and destruction. The former are worthy and divine, but our studies of them are less adequate; for there is remarkably little evidence available to perception from which we might make enquiries about them and about the things we long to know. But about perishable substances—plants and animals— we are much better off with regard to knowledge, because we are brought up among them; for anyone who is willing to take enough trouble may learn much of the truth about each kind. Each of the groups gives pleasure: even if our grasp of the former is slight, nevertheless because of their worth knowledge of them is more pleasant than knowing everything here about us (just as it is more pleasant to see any small part of the things we love than to see accurately many other large things); and since of the latter we have better and greater knowledge, our grasp of them has the superiority—and again, because they are nearer to us and more akin to our nature, they gain somewhat compared to philosophical study of things divine.

Since we have treated the latter and set down our views, we must now speak of animal nature, as far as is possible omitting nothing whether of less or greater worth. For even in the case of those that are not pleasing to the senses, the nature which fashioned them nevertheless gives immeasurable pleasures to the student who can discern the causes of things and is naturally of a philosophical turn. For it would be irrational and absurd if, while we take pleasure in contemplating the likenesses of those things because we contemplate at the same time the skill of the painter or the sculptor who fashioned them, we should yet fail to enjoy more the contemplation of the natural things themselves, particularly if we can discern their causes. Thus we should not childishly complain against the enquiry into the less worthy animals; for in everything natural there is something marvellous.

Heraclitus is reported to have said to some visitors who wished to meet him and who hesitated when they saw him warming himself at the stove: 'Come in, be bold: there are gods here too.' In the same way we should approach the study of every animal without shame; for in all of them there is something natural and something beautiful.

Chronological table

384 BC	Aristotle born at Stagira
367	A. migrates to Athens and joins Plato's Academy
356	Birth of Alexander the Great
347	Death of Plato; A. leaves Athens for the court of Hermias at Atarneus, and settles at Assos
345	A. moves to Mytilene on Lesbos (and later returns to Stagira)
343	Philip of Macedon invites A. to Mieza to tutor Alexander
341	Death of Hermias
336	Philip killed; Alexander crowned
335	A. Returns to Athens and begins teaching in the Lyceum
323	Death of Alexander
322	A. leaves Athens for Chalcis, where he dies

Further reading

All of Aristotle's works are available in English in the 'Oxford Translation': J. A. Smith and W. D. Ross (eds), *The Works of Aristotle Translated into English*, 12 volumes (Oxford, 1912–52).

A revised version of the Oxford Translation is about to be published by the Princeton University Press. Good English translations, with facing Greek text, can be found in the volumes of the Loeb Classical Library. Some of Aristotle's works are published in Penguin and other paperback series. The Clarendon Aristotle (general editor J. L. Ackrill) provides close translations and philosophical commentaries on several of Aristotle's works.

The classic edition of the Greek text by Immanuel Bekker (Berlin, 1831) is now out of date: modern texts are to be found in such collections as the Oxford Classical Texts, the Loeb Classical Library, the Teubner Library and the Budé series.

Of the many general books on Aristotle, I mention: W. D. Ross, *Aristotle* (London, 1923) G. E. R. Lloyd, *Aristotle* (Cambridge, 1968) J. L. Ackrill, *Aristotle the Philosopher* (Oxford, 1981) W. K. C. Guthrie, *A History of Greek Philosophy*, vol. 6: *Aristotle: An Encounter* (Cambridge, 1981). Perhaps the most influential work written on Aristotle this century is: W. W. Jaeger, *Aristotle* (Oxford, 1948; 1st German ed., Berlin, 1923).

Most scholarly studies of Aristotle have taken the form either of editions and commentaries on individual treatises or of papers and articles in the learned journals. There is an anthology of articles, designed to cover most aspects of Aristotle's thought, in: J. Barnes, M. Schofield and R. Sorabji (eds), *Articles on Aristotle*, 4 volumes (London, 1975–9). Each volume contains a full bibliography.

The evidence bearing on Aristotle's life has been assembled and discussed in: I. Düring, *Aristotle in the Ancient Biographical Tradition* (Göteborg, 1957). Some idea of what life in the Lyceum was like may be got from: J. P. Lynch, *Aristotle's School* (Berkeley, 1972).

There is a comprehensive account of Aristotle's scientific views in: F. Solmsen, *Aristotle's System of the Physical World* (Ithaca, New York, 1960). On zoology and biology it is still worth reading: G. H. Lewes, *Aristotle — a Chapter from the History of Science* (London, 1865) W. d'A Thompson, *On Aristotle as a Biologist* (London, 1912). For Aristotle's method in science and philosophy see: G. E. L. Owen, 'Tithenai ta Phainomena', in

S. Mansion (ed.), *Aristote et les problèmes de méthode* (Louvain, 1961), reprinted in *Articles on Aristotle*, vol. 1. There is a recent full-length study of psychology: E. Hartman, *Substance, Body, and Soul* (Princeton, New Jersey, 1977). On Aristotle's teleology, on his notion of causation, and on numerous related issues see: R. Sorabji, *Necessity, Cause and Blame* (London, 1980).

The standard work on Aristotle's logic is: G. Patzig, *Aristotle's Theory of the Syllogism* (Dordrecht, 1968; 1st German ed., Göttingen, 1959) and there is further material in: K. J. J. Hintikka, *Time and Necessity* (Oxford, 1973).

Many of the problems raised by Aristotle's metaphysical speculations are discussed in: J. Owens, *The Doctrine of Being in the Aristotelian Metaphysics* (3rd ed., Toronto, 1978) and there are three important papers by Owen: G. E. L. Owen, 'Logic and Metaphysics in Some Earlier Works of Aristotle', in I. Düring and G. E. L. Owen (eds), *Aristotle and Plato in the Mid-Fourth Century* (Göteborg, 1960), reprinted in *Articles on Aristotle*, vol. 3; 'The Platonism of Aristotle', *Proceedings of the British Academy* 50 (1965), 125–50, reprinted in *Articles on Aristotle*, vol. 1; 'Aristotle on the Snares of Ontology', in R. Bambrough (ed.), *New Essays on Plato and Aristotle* (London, 1965).

As for practical philosophy, there is a helpful guide to the *Ethics*: W. F. R. Hardie, *Aristotle's Ethical Theory* (2nd ed., Oxford, 1980) and a collection of papers: A. O. Rorty (ed.), *Essays on Aristotle's Ethics* (Berkeley and London, 1980).

For an introductory account of Aristotle's views on the State see: R. G. Mulgan, *Aristotle's Political Theory* (Oxford, 1977).

References

All works cited are by Aristotle unless otherwise stated. References to Aristotle's writings normally consist of an abbreviated title, a book number (in Roman numerals), a chapter number (Arabic), and a specification of page, column and line in the standard edition of the Greek text by Immanuel Bekker. (Most subsequent editions of the Greek and most English translations print Bekker references in their margins at regular intervals.) Thus Mr II 9, 369a31, refers to line 31 of column a on page 369 of Bekker's edition, a line which occurs in the ninth chapter of the second book of Aristotle's *Meteorology*.

Abbreviations

C	*Categories*	PA	*Parts of Animals*
EE	*Eudemian Ethics*	Ph	*Physics*
GA	*Generation of Animals*	Pl	*Politics*
GC	*On Generation and*	Po	*Poetics*
	Corruption	PoA	*Posterior Analytics*
H	*On the Heavens*	PrA	*Prior Analytics*
HA	*History of Animals*	Pro	*Protrepticus*
I	*On Interpretation*	R	*Rhetoric*
M	*Metaphysics*	S	*On the Soul*
MA	*Movement of Animals*	SR	*Sophistical Refutations*
Mr	*Meteorology*	T	*Topics*
NE	*Nicomachean Ethics*		

Page

90. *All men*: M I 1, 980a22

    the activity: M XII 7, 1072b27

    the acquisition: Pro fragment 53 Rose=B 56 Düring, quokted by Iamblichus, Pro 40.20–41.2

    we must not: NE X 7, 1177b31–5

    he wrote: Diogenes Laertius, *Lives of the Philosophers* V 21

91. *In every form*: R III 1, 1404a8–12

92. *he surrounds*: Atticus, fragment 7 (p. 28 ed. Baudry), quoted by Eusebius, *Preparation for the Gospel* XV ix 14, 810D

94. *he did not want*: Aelian, *Varia historia* III 36

    an inscription: Ibn Abi Usaibia, *Life of Aristotle* 18, printed in I. Düring,

Aristotle in the Ancient Biographical Tradition (Göteborg, 1957), p. 215

95. *they drew up*: W. Dittenberger (ed.), *Sylloge inscriptionum Graecarum* (3rd ed., Leipzig, 1915), no. 275.

as for what: *Letters*, fragment 9 (in M. Plezia (ed.), *Aristoteles: Privatorum scriptorum fragmenta* (Leipzig, 1977), quoted by Aelian, *Varia historia* XIV 1

96. *the city of Assos*: S. Mekler (ed.), *Academicorum philosophorum index Herculanensis* (Berlin, 1902), p. 23

98. *First, let us*: HA I 6, 491a19–21

The octopus: HA IV 1, 524a3–20

99. *this is plain*: HA V 8, 542a2–6

100. *it defends itself*: HA IX 45, 630b8–11

are generated: HA V 19, 551a1–7

101. *an experiment*: HA VI 3, 561a6–562a20

102. *the so-called teuthoi*: HA IV 1, 524a25–8

inflamed: Pliny, *Natural History* VIII xvi 44

103. *Their error*: GA III 5, 756a31–4

he worked: anon., *Vita Aristotelis Marciana* 6 (in Düring, op.cit., p. 98)

he is the first: Strabo, *Geography* XIII I 54

one should make: T I 14, 105b12–15

104. *we have given*: M I 3, 983a33–b6

in the case: SR 34, 184a9–b9

105. *for if the difficulties*: NE VII 1, 1145b6–7

In all cases: SR 34, 183b18–27

106. *Investigation*: M II 1, 993a30–b5; b11–19

107. *why did he*: Philodemus, *On Rhetoric* col. LIII 41–2, vol. II, pp. 57–8 Sudhaus

108. *at once gave up*: *Nerinthus*, fragment 64 Rose, quoted by Themistius, *Oration* XXXIII 295D

In the gymnasium: Epicrates, fragment 11 Kock, quoted by Athenaeus, *Deipnosophists* 59D

110. *whom it is not right*: *Poems*, fragment 3 (in Plezia, op.cit.), quoted by Olympiodorus, *Commentary on the Gorgias* 41.9

Plato used: Aelian, *Varia historia* IV 9

113. *The causes*: M XII 4, 1070a31–3

all thought: M VI 1, 1025b25

there are three: M VI 1, 1026a18–19

114. *If there are*: M VI 1, 1026a26–30 *the theoretical*: M VI 1, 1026a22–3

139. *change is*: Ph III 1, 201a10–11

140. *actuality is*: M IX 8, 1049b10–12

    in all cases: M IX 8, 1049b24–7

142. *A thing is called*: Ph II 3, 194b23–195a3

143. *the because-of-which*: M VII 17, 1041a23–7

    the cause is: PoA II 2, 90a7

144. *what it is*: PoA II 2, 90a15–18

145. *Why did*: PoA II 11, 94a36–b2

146. *Why is there*: PoA II 11, 94b9

    Since things: Ph II 3, 195a4–8

147. *both because*: PoA II 11, 94b32–4

    And that there is: M VI 2, 1027a20–2

148. *and for that*: S III 8, 432a7–9

149. *All animals*: PoA II 19, 99b35–100a9

150. *the cause*: GA III 5, 756a2–6

    reliability of the senses: S III 3, 428b18–25

151. *it is evident*: M IV 4, 1008b12–16

    they are really: M IV 5, 1010b4–9

    . *a scribe*: Suda, s.v. Aristoteles

152. *I have already*: Mr I 1, 338a20–7; 339a7–9

153. *Of the parts*: HA I 1, 486a5–8; 13–14

154. *Circular motion*: GC II 11, 338a18–b6

    Our remote: M XII 8, 1074b1–10

    god seems: M I 2, 983a8–9

    . *there is some other*: H I 2, 269b14–16

    it is the function: PA IV 10, 686a29

155. *we tend*: H II 12, 292a19–22; b1–2

    must there be: MA 4, 699b31–5

    initiates change: M XII 7, 1072b3–4

    It is because: M I 2, 982b12–13

156. *In what way*: M XII 10, 1075a11–18

    Some things: S II 3, 414a29–b6; b16–18

157. *if we are to state*: S II 1, 412b4–6

    a soul is: S II 2, 413b11–13

158. *one should not*: S II 1, 412b6–8

    that the soul: S II 1, 413a3–5

    a motion: S III 3, 429a1–2

    clearly, those: GA II 3, 736b22–7

159. *Hence it remains*: GA II 3, 736b27–9

    this thought: S III 5, 430a17–18; 22–3

160. *if there is so much*: PA II 2, 648a33–b1

161. *we might say*: GA III 11, 761b13–23

162. *as to how many*: M XII 8, 1073b10–17

     to judge: GA III 10, 760b28–33

     we must first: HA I 6, 491a10–14

163. *empirical science*: PrA I 30, 46a17–27

     speaking of: H III 7, 306a6–7; 12–18

164. *We see more*: PA I 1, 639b12–21

165. *The cause of*: GA II 6, 745a27–b3

     . *Anaxagoras*: PA IV 10, 687a8–18

166. *For these causes*: PA IV 12, 694b6–12 *aphorisms*: e.g. H I 4, 271a33

     The bile: PA IV 2, 677a14–18

     art imitates: Mr IV 3, 381b6; Pro fragment B 23 Düring, quoted by Iamblichus, Pro 34.8–9

     It is particularly: Ph II 8, 199a20–30

167. *like a good*: GA II 6, 744b16–17

     Snakes copulate: GA I 7, 718a18–25

169. *the present treatise*: NE II 2, 1103b26–8

170. *It seems*: NE I 7, 1097b22–3

     an activity: NE I 7, 1098a16

     contain something: GA II 3, 737a10–11

     the divine: EE VIII 2, 1248a27; NE X 7, 1178a2–3

171. *Thus any choice*: EE VIII 3, 1249b16–21

     Man is: Pl I 1, 1253a2

     Social animals: HA I 1, 488a8–10

     What is peculiar: Pl I 1, 1253a15–18

172. *A State*: NE IX 10, 1170b31–2

     is defined by: Pl III 1, 1275a22–3

     When either: Pl III 17, 1288a15–19

     . *The view that*: Pl III 11, 1281a40–b3

     It is evident: Pl III 9, 1280b29–34

173. *A fundamental*: Pl VI 1, 1317a40; b2–3; 11–13

     deal with Greeks: Letters, fragment 6a (in Plezie, op.cit.), quoted by Plutarch, *On the Fortune of Alexander* 329B

     Someone who: Pl I 4, 1254a14–17

     Evidently: Pl II 5, 1263a38–40

     Since the legislator: Pl VII 16, 1334b29–32

174. *No one would*: Pl VIII 1, 1337a11–12; 21–4; 26–9

175. *Epics*: Pl 1, 1447a13–16

     and it is this: Po 2, 1448a16–18

     tragedy is: Po 6, 1449b24–8

176. *the chief means*: Po 6,
1450a33–5

neither pre-eminent: Po 13,
1453a8–12

177. *everyone enjoys*: Po 4,
1448b8–17

178. *Of natural substances*: PA I 5,
644b22–645a23

AUGUSTINE

HENRY CHADWICK

Contents

NOTE: This book uses material from the Larkin Stuart Lectures, Toronto 1980, and the Sarum Lectures, Oxford 1982–3.

Abbreviations

Ac	*Contra Academicos*
B	*De baptismo*
BC	*De bono conjugali*
BV	*De beata vita*
C	*Confessiones*
CD	*De civitate Dei*
CE	*De consensu evangelistarum*
CG	*De correptione et gratia*
CR	*De catechizandis rudibus*
DDC	*De doctrina christiana*
DEP	*Contra duas epistulas Pelagianorum*
DP	*De dono perseverantiae*
E	*Epistulae*
EJo	*In epistulam Johannis*
EP	*Contra Epistulam Parmeniani*
F	*Contra Faustum Manichaeum*
GC	*De gratia Christi et de peccato originali*
GL	*De Genesi ad litteram*
J	*Contra Julianum Pelagianum*
Jo	*Tractatus in Evangelium Johannis*
LA	*De libero arbitrio*
M	*De moribus ecclesiae catholicae et de moribus Manichaeorum*
N	*De natura et gratia*
O	*De ordine*
P	*Enarrationes in Psalmos*
PM	*De peccatorum meritis*
QA	*De quantitate animae*
QH	*Quaestiones de Heptateucho*
QS	*De diversis quaestionibus ad Simplicianum*
R	*Retractationes*
S	*Sermones*
SL	*De spiritu et littera*
Sol	*Soliloquia*
T	*De Trinitate*
VR	*De vera religione*

1 *The formation of Augustine's mind: Cicero, Mani, Plato, Christ*

A short introduction to Augustine's thought cannot also offer biography. Partly because he wrote the most famous and influential of all ancient autobiographies, the psychology and personality of the man have naturally attracted concentrated attention. Among ancient men he had an unsurpassed power to articulate feelings. His writings are also a major source for the social history of his age. This book cannot be about that side of him, but concerns the making of his mind. That making was a drawn-out process; for he changed his mind on some points and developed his position on others. He described himself as 'a man who writes as he progresses and who progresses as he writes' (E 143). The shifts were closely related to the pressure of successive controversies in which he played a part, and reference to the historical setting is therefore essential for understanding. But beyond this we are not here concerned with his 'life and times'.

Aurelius Augustinus was born in AD 354 and died in 430. He lived all but five years of his life in Roman North Africa, and for the last thirty-four years was bishop of a busy seaport, Hippo, now Annaba in Algeria. At Hippo only bishop Augustine had books, and his own family background was not one of high culture. That culture he acquired through education. By his writings, the surviving bulk of which exceeds that of any other ancient author, he came to exercise pervasive influence not only on contemporaries but also on the West since his time. The extent of that influence can be summarized, in telegraphic style, by listing the debates which have been part of this man's legacy:

1. The theology and philosophy of the medieval schoolmen and of the creators of medieval universities were rooted in Augustinian ideas of the relation between faith and reason.

When Peter Lombard compiled his *Sentences* (1155) to provide a basic textbook of theology, a very high proportion was drawn from Augustine. So too his contemporary Gratian cited many texts from him in making the West's principal handbook of canon law.

2. The aspirations of all western mystics have never escaped his influence, above all because of the centrality of the love of God in his thinking. He first saw the paradox that love, which is in quest of personal happiness, necessarily implies some self-renunciation and the pain of being made what one is not.

3. The Reformation found its mainspring in criticizing medieval Catholic piety as resting more on human effort than on divine grace. The Counter-Reformation replied that one can affirm the sovereignty of God's grace without also denying the freedom of the will and the moral value ('merit') of good conduct. Both sides in the controversy appealed on a huge scale to texts of Augustine.

4. The eighteenth century found itself passionately divided between those who asserted the perfectibility of man and those who saw human nature as held down by a dead weight of personal and collective egotism; in other words by what Augustine called 'original sin'. The men of the Enlightenment thought the actual perfecting of man hindered by belief in original sin and disliked Augustine very much. They were displeased when the philosopher Kant, who had so eloquently proclaimed the Enlightenment principle that one must dare to think for oneself, decisively assented to the belief that human nature is distorted by a pervasive radical evil.

5. In reaction against the Enlightenment the Romantic movement identified the heart of religion with feeling rather than with the conclusions of intellectual arguments. Augustine was not in the least anti-intellectual, but he did not think that intellect had the last word and he pioneered a highly positive evaluation of human feelings. We owe to him our use of the word 'heart' in this sense.

6. He was the most acute of Christian Platonists and did much to lay the foundations for the synthesis between Christianity and classical theism stemming from Plato and Aristotle. Plotinus in the third century AD deeply influenced him by his systematization of the Platonic tradition, but Augustine also became one

of the most penetrating of all critics of this philosophical tradition to which he himself owed so much.

7. He saw more clearly than anyone before him (or for a long time after him) that issues of supreme importance are raised by the problem of the relation of words to the reality they attempt to describe. He was a pioneer in the critical study of non-verbal communication.

Anselm, Aquinas, Petrarch (never without a pocket copy of the *Confessions*), Luther, Bellarmine, Pascal, and Kierkegaard all stand in the shade of his broad oak. His writings were among the favourite books of Wittgenstein. He was the *bête noire* of Nietzsche. His psychological analysis anticipated parts of Freud: he first discovered the existence of the 'sub-conscious'.

He was 'the first modern man' in the sense that with him the reader feels himself addressed at a level of extraordinary psychological depth and confronted by a coherent system of thought, large parts of which still make potent claims to attention and respect. He affected the way in which the West has subsequently thought about the nature of man and what we mean by the word 'God'. Although as a follower of Plato he was little concerned with the natural physical environment, and wrote with fear of scientific investigations conducted without reverence and in indifference to ethical considerations, yet the modern scientist's assumption that mathematical order and rationality are the supreme features of the world had no more eloquent advocate in antiquity than he. He therefore contributed something substantial to the attitude towards the created order which would make the emergence of modern science possible. On the other hand, he cannot be fairly read if he is treated as other than what he was, a man of the ancient world, whose mind and culture were altogether shaped by the literature and philosophy of Greece and Rome and whose conversion to Christianity set him in some degree at odds with the classical past. In relation to that past he stood as both critic and transmitter to the medieval and modern worlds.

Just as the Greeks assumed with some reason that no one had written poetry to surpass Homer, or history in a way that rivalled Herodotus and Thucydides, or philosophy which was not a series of footnotes to Plato, Aristotle, the Stoics, and

Epicurus, so also the Romans attributed the status of a classical model to their own past masters—Cicero for prose and oratory, Virgil and Horace for poetry. In Augustine's time there were educated people who knew entire orations of Cicero, and the whole of Virgil, by heart. Because the invention of printing has made books relatively inexpensive compared with manuscripts, such feats of memory appear needless and almost incredible to us today, but in the ancient and medieval worlds much school education consisted of learning by rote at an impressionable age. Cicero's prose and Virgil's poetry were so profoundly stamped on Augustine's mind that he could seldom write many pages without some reminiscence or verbal allusion. In youth he also read with deep admiration Sallust's sombre histories of the Roman Republic and the comedies of Terence. These too were part of the literary air he naturally breathed, and into his prose he would frequently work some turn of phrase taken from classical Latin literature. Many such allusions have been identified only comparatively recently, and it is certain that there are more yet to be located.

Augustine was not unique in his age in possessing this high literary culture. His cultural background was that of Roman Africa, rich colonial provinces which had long enjoyed peace and prosperity with highly educated people who adorned their villas with noble mosaic and sculpture such as one can see in the Bardo Museum at Tunis. Since the Muslim conquest of the region more than 200 years after Augustine's death, the north and south sides of the Mediterranean have belonged to separate cultural if not commercial worlds, and have spoken different languages except during the relatively brief period of French domination in modern times. In Augustine's age both north and south belonged to a single world, and wrote and spoke a good Latin which the Africans pronounced with a marked regional accent. North Africa supplied Italy with much of its grain. A summer voyage from Carthage or Hippo to Puteoli (Pozzuoli) or Ostia was a short sea journey made by several ships every week, and contact with Italy was frequent and easy. The wealth of Roman Africa often exceeded that found in Italy even among well-to-do families, and the African provinces had a strong sense of being independent and of wanting to make their own decisions.

Roman Africa had produced distinguished writers: in the first century, Manilius wrote a verse handbook on astrology; in the second century there was Fronto, tutor to the emperor Marcus Aurelius; Apuleius of Madaura, best-selling author not only of the 'Golden Ass' (*Metamorphoses*) with its characteristic mixture of magic, religion, and sex, but also of long influential hand-books on Platonic philosophy; Aulus Gellius, author of the 'Attic Nights'—a kind of reader's digest guide to effective dinner-party conversation. In Augustine's age there was Macrobius, whose commentary on Scipio's Dream (the last book of Cicero's *Republic*) became a major source of information about Neoplatonic philosophy for the medieval West; also the self-consciously pagan Martianus Capella, who, probably after Augustine's life-time, composed 'The Marriage of Philology and Mercury' to teach his readers the elements of the seven liberal arts and to show how their study can lead one up to heaven.

During the second century a vigorious Christian mission in North Africa established a large number of congregations for whose use the Greek Bible was translated into Latin. The converts included brilliant figures such as Tertullian at the end of the second century, creator of the vocabulary of western theology and master of witty polemic against pagan critics or dangerous heretics; and Cyprian, elected bishop of Carthage soon after his baptism, martyred ten years later in 258, insistent on upholding the ritual purity of the Catholic Church and on the juridical authority of the apostolic ministry. In the age of Constantine the Great early in the fourth century two African Christians wrote defences of their faith against philosophical critics; Arnobius and Lactantius were partly indebted to Greek Christian writers before them.

The population of Roman Africa was very mixed. On the farms the peasants were Berber and Phoenician, speaking Punic. At the seaports like Carthage and Hippo many of the traders were Greek-speaking with close links to Sicily and South Italy, at that age (and long afterwards) a largely Greek-speaking region. But Latin was the language of the educated and the army and the administration. The culture of Augustine's home and school was wholly Latin, though his mother Monica bore a Berber name.

Late Roman Carthage was a successful trading city. Its population had a taste not only for animal and gladiatorial fights in the amphitheatre but also for less bloody occasions such as poetry competitions and good plays at the theatre. The city possessed well-qualified jurists, physicians, and teachers of literature—'grammarians' as they were called. Augustine was not born and raised in this urban world. He was a provincial country boy, born at an inland hill town called Thagaste in the province of Numidia Consularis, a cross-roads and market in what is now eastern Algeria at Souk-Ahras. There his father Patrick owned a few acres and one or two slavegirls, but was far from being rich. Patrick died when Augustine was a teenager with a lot of adolescent problems. Augustine also had a brother and a sister, but whether he was the eldest or the second or the third child is a matter on which there is no evidence. Education at the local school at Thagaste, as at all such small towns, was in the hands of a single teacher. Augustine found the man more effective with the cane than in inspiring his pupils with interest in their studies. Soon he passed on to another teacher at nearby Madaura. After Patrick's death he went on to Carthage, financed by a wealthy neighbour, Romanianus.

Augustine later looked back on his school days as a miserable experience, valuable only as a training for the conflicts, injustices, and disappointments of adult life. A highly sensitive and bookish boy, he felt he had largely educated himself by his reading in great authors. The punishments endured by children, however deserved, actually benefited only those disposed to be benefited, and left others merely resentful and even more anti-social than before. He never wrote with admiration or gratitude about any of his teachers.

As a schoolboy at Thagaste he began to learn Greek. Although he disliked the toil of learning the language, he was soon able to use a Greek book whenever necessary, and in his maturity he was competent to make his own translation of quite technical philosophical texts. But he never dreamed of acquiring a mastery of Homer and Greek literature, as a number of late Roman aristocrats did. He shared a feeling not uncommon in the Latin West of late antiquity that the West ought by now to have intellectual self-respect. It needed to stand on its own two feet and should do more than merely adapt Greek masterpieces for inferior Latin speakers. People did not then know or wish to notice that their hero Virgil owed a vast amount to Homer. They were, however, aware that in philosophy the Greeks were and remained the supreme masters. Cicero and Seneca had composed dialogues and 'letters' adapting Greek philosophical debates for the instruction of the Romans. Cicero's philosophical dialogues were a mine of clearly set out information about the debates between the different schools, and in his twenties Augustine came to know their content very well.

Though not ignorant of Greek, Augustine was always more comfortable with a Latin version if that happened to be available. He was familiar with the *Categories* of Aristotle, which were available to him in Latin, and with his investigations of the laws of valid inference. The knotty problem of 'future contingents' discussed in the notorious ninth chapter of Aristotle's tract on *Interpretation* was familiar to him also. In agreement with the Neoplatonists of his time he used language about the uncertainties of the future which was more determinist than the followers of Aristotle liked; he wanted to say that events which to us are 'contingent' (i.e. they would not have occurred unless something happened to cause them) are not uncertain to God (F 26. 4–5). In other words, though we have minds too limited to see it, the future is as unalterable as the past. Augustine was particularly interested in Stoic logic and ethical assertions. He was fascinated by the question of how far language communicates meaning about reality. He was capable of acute analysis of the problems contained in Epicurus' hedonist contention that by 'right' and 'wrong' we really mean 'pleasing' and 'displeasing'.

Paradoxically, the Greek thinker whose work most deeply entered his bloodstream was Plato, of whose works singularly little was available in Latin. Cicero had translated about half the *Timaeus*, and on this dialogue Calcidius in the fourth century had composed an elaborate commentary which Augustine could have known (but probably did not). It would not have been difficult for him to find Greek copies of Platonic dialogues at either Carthage or Rome, where he taught for a time. Both cities had citizens who knew the language. But he never seems to have made any direct study of the original text.

The form of Platonic philosophy which eventually (when he was 31) captured his mind was the 'modern' Platonism which we now call Neoplatonism, taught a century earlier by Plotinus

(205–270) to an esoteric circle, and then vigorously presented to the public by his acute pupil, editor, and biographer Porphyry of Tyre (*c.*250–*c.*305). Though Plotinus did his teaching at Rome and Porphyry lived part of his life in Sicily, both men wrote exclusively in Greek. Despite the abstraction and complexity of the ideas, Plotinus and Porphyry came to have enormous influence, in the Latin West quite as much as in the Greek East. In Plotinus, during the flush of his first enthusiasm for Platonism, Augustine declared he saw 'Plato come to life again' (Ac. 3.41), a phrase which accurately refects what Plotinus himself set out to do, for he regarded Plato as more than a man with great independent powers of thought. Plato ranked for him as an authority.

Absorbing the principal doctrines of Stoic ethics and, in Porphyry's hands, much Aristotelian logic as well, Neoplatonism became altogether dominant over all other philosophical positions in late antiquity. Works by both Plotinus and Porphyry were translated into Latin by Marius Victorinus, an African who taught rhetoric and philosophy in Rome and at the height of his reputation, about the time that Augustine was born, had startled a largely pagan aristocracy by being baptized. Victorinus also translated some logical works by Aristotle and Porphyry, notably the *Introduction* to Aristotle's logic composed by Porphyry with such clarity and terse precision that the book became a standard handbook for a millennium.

Cicero

The most potent initial influence guiding the young Augustine in philosophical matters came from Cicero's dialogues. Of the many works of Cicero which Augustine knew intimately, one dialogue called *Hortensius*, vindicating the necessity of philosophical thinking for any critical judgement even for someone engaged in public and political life, exercised an extraordinary, catalytic effect. In the works of his old age he was still to be quoting phrases from this book which he first read as a nineteen-year-old student at Carthage. Cicero partly adapted for the Roman world an exhortation to study philosophy written by no less than Aristotle himself. Cicero's ideal was personal self-sufficiency and an awareness that happiness, which everyone seeks, is not found in a self-indulgent life of pleasure, which merely destroys both self-respect and true friendships. Contemplating the paradox that everyone sets out to be happy and the majority are thoroughly wretched, Cicero concluded with the pregnant suggestion that man's misery may be a kind of judgement of providence, and our life now may even be an atonement for sins in a prior incarnation. The *Hortensius* also included a warning that the pursuit of bodily pleasure in food, drink, and sex, is distracting for the mind in pursuit of higher things.

Augustine was never a glutton or a drinker; but his sexual drive was strong. At the age of seventeen to eighteen at Carthage he had already taken to his bed a girl-friend of servile or low social class, a steady relationship which put an end to adolescent adventures. For over thirteen years Augustine lived with her entirely faithfully. She soon produced an initially unwanted but in the event much loved son, whom they called Adeodatus or 'God's gift', equivalent to Theodore or Jonathan or its Punic cognate form. The boy turned out very clever, but died at the age of seventeen.

The immediate effect of reading *Hortensius* was to make Augustine think seriously about ethical and religious issues. His father had been a pagan, baptized only on his deathbed. He was hot-tempered and not always faithful to his wife; Augustine betrays no sign of having felt close to him. His mother, on the other hand, was devout in Christian faith and practice, daily at prayers in her local church, often guided by dreams and visions. She had made him a catechumen in infancy. As a sceptical teenager he used occasionally to attend church services with her, but found himself mainly engaged in catching the eye of the girls on the other side of the basilica. At Carthage aged nineteen he found that the seriousness of the questions raised by Cicero, especially about the quest for happiness, moved him to pick up a Latin Bible. He was repelled by the obscurity of its content and the barbarous style of the rather primitive version made by half-educated missionaries in the second century. The Old Latin Bible (the reconstruction of which by modern scholars has been a remarkable critical operation) was not a book to impress a man whose mind was full of elegant Ciceronian diction and Virgilian turns of phrase, and who enjoyed good plays at the theatre. In disgust Augustine turned away from what seemed a naïve myth about Adam and Eve and from the doubtful morality of the Israelite patriarchs. To any prospect of his returning to the Church of his mother, the incompatibility between the two genealogies of Jesus in Matthew and Luke gave the final *coup de grâce* (S 51.6).

So Augustine looked elsewhere for help. He was drawn to astrology, which seemed to offer a guide to live by without looking too like religion, and then to the occult theosophy taught more than a century earlier by Mani (AD 216–77).

Mani

The religion of Mani, or Manicheism, expressed in poetic form a revulsion from the material world, and became the rationale for an ultra-ascetic morality. The Manichees regarded 'the lower half of the body' as the disgusting work of the devil, the very prince of darkness. Sex and the dark were intimately associated in Mani's mind, and the Dark was the very essence of evil. One would not expect such a religion to have attractions for a young man to whom sex was important (unless it were that one could attribute all one's lower impulses to the powers of darkness and disown personal responsibility). However, the Manichee community consisted of two classes or grades of adherent. Absolute celibacy was required only of the higher grade, the Elect. Mere Hearers, of whom Augustine became one, were allowed sexual relations at 'safe' periods of the month, and were expected to take steps to avoid conceiving a child; but if a child arrived, that was not a ground for expulsion from the society. Hearers therefore were allowed to live with wives or, as in Augustine's case, concubines, but were not encouraged to think of sexuality in any positive light. It was the devil's invention.

Mani denied any authority to the Old Testament with its presupposition of the goodness of the material order of things and of its Maker. He deleted as interpolations all texts in the New Testament which assumed either the order and goodness of matter or the inspiration and authority of the Old Testament scriptures. Otherwise he thought his expurgated New Testament a sound book. He generously acknowledged truth in all religious systems, and rejected orthodox catholic Christianity for being too exclusive and negative towards other religious myths and forms of worship. Yet he wanted to be considered Christian, while asserting that his revelation founded 'a distinct religion'. He was a 'heretic' in the strict sense of a person wanting to stay within the community while reinterpreting its fundamental documents and beliefs in ways unacceptable to the main body, and persisting therein when asked to correct himself. He employed some biblical themes and terms, and allowed a redemptive role to Jesus—only he understood Jesus as a symbol of the plight of all humanity rather than as a historical person who walked the earth and was crucified. A quasi-divine redeemer could not in truth have been physically born or killed (an opinion anticipating Islamic doctrine); the crucifixion was no kind of actuality but a mere symbol for the suffering which is the universal human condition.

Mani interpreted everything he took from Christianity within a dualistic and pantheistic framework: this is seen in the immensely complex and elaborate mythology in which he cast his doctrine. The central question for him was the origin of evil. He explained evil as resulting from a primeval and still continuing cosmic conflict between Light and Dark, these terms being both symbol and physical reality. The forces of good and evil in the world have strengths and weaknesses such that neither side can vanquish the other. In consequence of the damage inflicted by the powers of Dark on the realm of Light, little fragments of God, or Soul, have become scattered throughout the world in all living things, including animals and plants. Melons and cucumbers were deemed to contain a particularly large ingredient of divinity, and were therefore prominent in the diet of Manichee elect. Food laws for the Elect were elaborate, and wine strictly forbidden. Manichee teachers and missionaries liked to recruit from members of the Church. The infiltration of Manichee notions could be detected when Christians at the eucharist accepted the host but not the chalice. Church people could be specially impressed by the fine parchment and calligraphy of Manichee sacred books and by the special solemnity of their music.

Although Mani accorded a high place in his myth to Jesus, supreme and infallible teaching office was located for his community not in Jesus nor in old Jewish books but in Mani himself, the Apostle of God, the very Paraclete foretold by Jesus as coming along later to reveal truths for which the altogether too

Jewish disciples were unprepared. Mani had no place whatever for the particularity which the Church inherited from its Jewish matrix. By a bizarre twist he presented his lush, partly erotic mythology with the claim that it was a rational, coherent account of revealed truth, in strong contrast to the simple faith of orthodox Christians who believed on mere authority. Manichee propoganda devoted much attention to onslaughts upon the morality and historical accuracy of the Old Testament and those parts of the New Testament which seemed too Jewish for Manichee taste. Above all, the Manichees urged that they had the only satisfactory answer to the problem of evil: it was an ineradicable force inherent in the physicality of the material world. No one could plausibly hold that the ultimate author of so uncomfortable a world could be both omnipotent and truly good. If the argument was to be coherent, either the omnipotence or the goodness must be sacrificed. Manichee teachers took it for granted that everyone knew without further definition or inquiry just what is meant by 'evil'.

During a full ten years, in teaching posts first at Carthage and then at Rome, Augustine remained associated with the Manichees. A combative critic of Catholic orthodoxy and conscious of his own intellectual superiority to members of the Church, whose bishops he held in contempt for their lack of education and critical inquiry, he converted many friends to share his Manichee beliefs. But during his twenties he was not only teaching Latin literature and the arts of rhetoric. He was also reflecting on philosophical issues and logical problems to which studies in rhetoric naturally led. Mounting doubts came to beset him. Was Mani right when he asserted that the supremely good Light-power was weak and impotent in conflict with the Dark? How could one properly worship a deity so powerless and humiliated? Moreover, the Manichees myth gave a large role to the two great and good lights of sun and moon and held a dogmatic position about the explanation of eclipses, namely that sun and moon are then using special veils to shut out the distressing sight of cosmic battles. Augustine was disturbed to find that the Manichee account was at variance with that of the best astronomers. One might demythologize orthodox Christianity and still have something of great importance left; Augustine felt that this was not true of Manicheism, where the myth was of the essence. Growing disillusion with the sect reached a climax when he put his doubts before a teacher held in high regard by the Manichees, Faustus. He found the man's eloquence greater than his capacity for thought. Further, the moral life of the Elect, who claimed sinless perfection, turned out to be less celibate than he had supposed.

He began to look about for alternatives to Manicheism. Already he had developed an interest in combining Manichee beliefs about the balance of good and evil with Neopythagorean ideas about proportion as an element in the beauty of the whole, about the good 'monad' (one is one and all alone and evermore shall be so) in contrast to the evil of infinite plurality. In his mid twenties he even wrote a book on this subject which in later retrospect he scorned as a half-baked piece of ill-digested stuff (C iv.20–7). Increasingly his doubts plunged him into suspense of judgement. He became intensely interested in the theory of knowledge: how do we know anything? How can we be absolutely sure? How do we communicate with each other when words can be misleading, or construed in a sense quite different from that intended by the speaker? Is everyday language, so frequently defying the rules of logic, a source of light or fog?

In this hesitant state of mind Augustine devoured books by sceptical philosophers, dogmatically assertive about the uncertainty and inconclusiveness of all received opinions, of sense-perception, and of the power of words to tell one anything important that one does not really know already.

This was his mind when he arrived at Milan in 384 as the city's new professor of rhetoric but with hopes of rising higher still. Milan was the imperial residence. If, despite Italian smiles at his African vowels, he could speak so eloquently as to attract favourable attention at court, and if he could gain the support of influential officials, perhaps he might aspire to be nominated as governor of a province (C vi.19). Admittedly there were obstacles to the ambition. He was a middle-class provincial without the recommendation of personal wealth to back him. Moreover, he still had living with him his 'common-law wife', his Carthaginian girlfriend, Adeodatus' mother. What would raise no eyebrow when done by a city professor of rhetoric might not be acceptable at government house. His widowed mother Monica, who had devotedly pursued him to Milan, saw that her son's much loved but uneducated partner in bed and board was a fatal hindrance to his secular desire for distinction and honour. Eventually the woman was sent back to Carthage. The parting was with great pain on both sides. Augustine was then engaged to marry a youthful heiress, whose dowry would facilitate the realization of his hopes. Until she was old enough to marry, Augustine turned for consolation to a temporary mate; she had no deep significance for him. His feelings were numb.

At Milan Augustine met, for the first time in his life, a Christian intellectual with ability not far short of his own: Ambrose the bishop, a man of high education, who also knew his way about the corridors of power at the court. He received Augustine kindly, and Monica held him in deep respect as a pastor. Before becoming bishop in 374, he had been provinical governor of that part of nothern Italy. His education in an aristocratic and Christian household had made him fluent in Greek. For his sermons he drew ideas and inspiration not only from Greek Christian theologians like Basil of Caesarea and the Jewish theologian Philo, elder contemporary of St Paul, but also from Plotinus. Ambrose's debt to Plotinus was combined with caution about pagan philosophy as a guide to truth.

Another Christian intellectual at Milan who influenced Augustine was an older man named Simplicianus, through whom he became drawn into a group of laymen of high education and social standing, who met to read Plotinus and Porphyry. They much admired Marius Victorinus, whose last years had been devoted to the deployment of Neoplatonic logic in defence of orthodox Trinitarian belief. Augustine was never greatly influenced by the obscure theological writings of Victorinus. But his readings in Plotinus and Porphyry, translated by Victorinus, set his mind on fire. That may seem surprising to the modern reader, for whom Neoplatonism can easily seem intricate and esoteric. The Neoplatonic philosophy of Being has presuppositions or axioms very different from those of modern scientific method: its starting point is mind, not matter.

Plotinus and Porphyry

Porphyry's biography of Plotinus portrays the awe in which the great philosopher was held, at least in his inner circle of pupils.

Porphyry wrote the biography to accompany his edition of Plotinus, partly because he wanted everyone to know how right his hero had been to entrust him with the publication of his treatises; how profoundly Plotinus had admired his pupil's critical mind and capacity for composing inspired ecstatic verses; and how at the age of 68 Porphyry himself had on one blissful occasion attained mystical union with the One, an experience which came only four times in life even to the divinely illuminated Plotinus. Plotinus is represented as a man of unique genius, whose guardian spirit was no inferior power, and whose mind never relaxed its concentration on the highest peaks of the intellect.

Like his elder Christian contemporary Origen, Plotinus lived an ascetic life of minimal food and sleep, given to vegetarianism and no baths. 'He always seemed ashamed of being in the body', and never celebrated his birthday. To his numerous male and female pupils Plotinus became a father figure, consulted on major and minor decisions of life. He had a preternatural discernment of mendacity and, like Christian bishops, was asked to arbitrate in disputes. He successfully dissuaded the highly-strung Porphyry from suicide.

In his philosophical system Plotinus set out to paint a kind of word-picture of the entire structure of things on the assumption that there is intimate correspondence between reality and the process of human thought. He attached high importance to the dialectic of Plato's dialogues, *Parmenides* and *Sophist*, especially Plato's analysis of identity and difference. That is, if we say x and y are 'the same', we imply distinction between them if the assertion of identity is to be interesting. Conversely, to point out that x and y are different implies an underlying bond of identity between them. So, beyond the multiplicity and the differences perceived and experienced in this world, there lies a unity and a permanence. Likewise the world of perceived appearances is one of perpetual change; but change presupposes a substratum which remains permanent.

Plato attributed changelessness to the higher world of Being grasped by the mind, in contrast to the ever-changing flux of Becoming discerned by the bodily senses. Hence Plato's theory of Forms (or Ideas), eternal absolutes: whatever in this world we call just or good or beautiful or true, is so in so far as it derives from the respective absolute. The Forms are the objective, constant, and universally valid reality. Moreover, these universals are perceived not by the five bodily senses, but by an austerely mathematical process of pure mental abstraction. Bloodless as these abstractions may appear, Platonism understands these universals as highly causative: individual existents cannot be accounted for in isolation, but only as members of a prior class. Therefore, for a Platonist, the universal is more real than any particular instance—a doctrine countered by Aristotle with the criticism that universals are mental classifications with reality only as they are embodied in particular existents. In his 'Introduction' Porphyry pursued his theme of reconciling Plato and Aristotle by juxtaposing these two opinions and carefully abstaining from giving a verdict between them.

Aristotle had been interested in self-consciousness, in which the knower and the object known are identical. Plotinus took this observation a stage further to form a theology, many themes of which came to seem self-evident axioms to Augustine. At the summit of the hierarchy of being is the One, God, the unknowable and Absolute, yet apprehended by the soul as a presence transcending all knowing. In the great chain or continuum of being which Plotinus identified as the structure of things, the higher level is cause of whatever is immediately lower. Plotinus spoke of the evolution or development of the hierarchy of being as 'emanation', a strongly physical image. In the process of emanation there is gradual loss; for every effect is slightly inferior to its cause. Nevertheless the imperfection inherent in its inferiority can be overcome as it returns towards its cause. And the cause itself is always undiminished by its timeless giving of existence to the inferior effect.

This way of thinking of causative emanation in the great chain of being enabled Plotinus to achieve several things at once. On the one hand it solved the problem of how to keep the transcendent One and the world from losing all relation to each other, without the Absolute ceasing to be Absolute, and without the world logically dropping out of existence altogether. It expressed a kind of redemption by 'conversion' to the source of being. On the other hand, it alleviated a problem which caused acute mental gymnastics for all Platonists, namely answering the question how evil could ever have entered into the continuum of things, when that was an overflow of supreme goodness and power.

Plotinus taught that at the apex of the hierarchy are three divine existences: the One, Mind, and Soul. The One is supremely Good, and therefore all lower levels of the hierarchy below the One must be also distinct from the Good; in short, less than perfectly good. Even Mind has some inferiority about it, some delusions about its own grandeur. Soul, still further down the scale, has the power to produce matter. Matter, being at the opposite extremity of the hierarchy from the good One, is in cosmic terms utter evil, formless non-being.

The Neoplatonists cordially hated theosophy, and its Manichee form more than all. Plotinus' treatise 'Against the Gnostics' (ii.9) inaugurated a series of Neoplatonic essays in polemic against Manicheism. By seeing the cosmos as a great chain of being, Plotinus could declare that evil is no more than a defect of being-and-goodness, inherent in the mere fact of an inferior level. But two other explanations of evil were also prominent in his thinking. Of these the first answer looked towards the consequence of misused free choice grounded in a potentiality for weakness in the soul. The second answer looked towards matter. Weakness in the soul tended to make it absorbed in external and material things. Thereby the cosmic, non-moral evil of defect of being inherent in matter becomes a root of moral evil in the soul. 'Without matter there can be no moral evil' (Plotinus i.8,14). The presence of matter to the soul brings out its weakness and causes its fall. At the same time, Plotinus wished to speak of the coming forth and descent of the soul as necessary for the fulfilment of its potential powers and for the service that soul has to render to the inferior world of the senses (iv.8,4–5). It is fair to deduce that even Plotinus failed to achieve a clear and consistent position. After his conversion Augustine sought to correct Plotinus' mistakes.

The doctrines of Porphyry were similar to those of his master Plotinus. In the Neoplatonic school there was disagreement about the cult of the gods. Plotinus and Porphyry felt reserve towards participation in sacrifices to propitiate the spirits. Porphyry wrote a treatise *On the Soul's Return* (that is, to God), to Augustine profoundly exciting reading; this presented a compromise position. He allowed that good philosophy could be extracted at shrines from inspired oracles uttered by Apollo through his prophetesses. But he wrote critically of fellow-pagans who supposed that the soul could be purified directly through participation in temple sacrifices or external ritual acts. Animal sacrifices were too earth-bound. Moreover, the custom of eating the meat afterwards was not congenial to vegetarian principles. So Porphyry urged that the soul's purging could be achieved only by 'flight from the body', to which it had become united by a chapter of sad accidents. By abstinence from meat and from sexual activity, the soul could be gradually emancipated from its bodily fetters.

Porphyry taught that happiness consists in wisdom, which is found by obeying the ancient command of Delphi, 'Know yourself'. Admittedly, wickedness in the soul makes man impotent to practise continual intellectual contemplation, so that at best such moments are transitory. But 'exercise yourself to return to yourself; gather from the body all the spiritual elements dispersed and reduced to a mass of bits and pieces'. 'The soul is thrust into poverty, the more that its ties to the flesh are strengthened. But it can become truly rich by discovering its true self, which is intellect.' 'Our end is to attain the contemplation of Being.' 'He who knows God has God present to him. He who does not know is absent from God who is everywhere present.' Augustine's *Confessions* echo this language.

Porphyry taught that God contains all things but is contained by nothing. The One is present to all that participates in the existence flowing from its source in God. Goodness must be self-diffusive. But all plurality depends upon and seeks to return to higher and prior unity. In the hierarchy of being it is axiomatic that it is good to exist, and that degrees of being are also degrees of goodness. Porphyry wrote that 'everything which has being is good in so far as it has being; even the body has its own beauty and unity'. (Augustine says the same, VR40.) Between material things and the higher realms of intelligible reality, the soul occupies a median position. By neglect and an inexplicable act of self-assertive defiance it is capable of sinking to pride, envy, and carnal things. But by ascetic restraint and by introspective contemplation, the soul can ascend to its true fulfilment. This fulfilment is 'the enjoyment of God'. This last phrase Augustine was to make his own.

Porphyry drew from Plotinus the concept that at the apex of the chain of being there lies, beyond the reach of our five senses, a divine Triad of being, life, and intelligence, all reciprocal, defined as a unity within which one can discern distinctions. The structure of things is that of a rhythmic procession out from the ultimate principle of being, from potentiality to actuality, from abstract to concrete, from identity to that otherness which is also a diminution in the level of being. The destiny of eternal souls is to return whence they have come. Souls are inherently immortal. The doctrine of return or conversion is the meaning of Plato's doctrine of Reminiscence, i.e. that all knowledge is a recalling to mind of what one once knew (in a previous existence) but had forgotten. This doctrine the Neoplatonists, and Augustine after them, largely replaced by the notion of divine illumination directly shining within the soul.

Near the end of his life Porphyry (who is reported by some Christian writers to have been a Christian in his youth and then to have apostatized) composed a lengthy and bitter attack on Christian beliefs and on the historical trustworthiness of the biblical books. His book against the Christians was not known to Augustine. Porphyry's works, however, may fairly be described as offering an alternative religious philosophy, designed, whether consciously or unconsciously, to provide a rival and antidote to Christianity.

The Milan group of Platonists gripped their new professor of rhetoric with Victorinus' translations of tracts by Plotinus and Porphyry. The language Augustine found there about the problem of evil and about mystical experience of the immaterial transcendent realm had an immense impact. The Neoplatonists were telling him that the soul has an immediate and inherent power of self-knowledge; moreover, that this power can be realized only as and when the perceptions of the five senses are set aside and the mind undergoes a purification, by dialectic, which purges it of physical images and elevates it to the beatific vision of which Plato spoke. They believed this to be a natural power of the soul, realized as it gradually opens itself to divine light and truth.

Augustine was later to describe, in the seventh book of the *Confessions*, how at Milan he attempted deep meditation on the Neoplatonic method. Platonism liberated him from the Manichee notion of God as subtle luminous matter. By introspection in solitude and by practising the way of dialectical regress from external to internal, from inferior and physical to superior and mental, he briefly attained a vision of eternal truth and unchanging beauty. He was disappointed by the extreme transience of an experience so profound, and by the fact that afterwards he found himself as consumed with pride and lust as before. Nevertheless, he knew that in that 'flash of a trembling glance' he had attained a dazzling glimpse of the immutable and eternal Being, an immaterial reality wholly transcending his own all too changeable mind (C vii.23). There is no hint of a suggestion in his later retrospect written as a Christian that this preconversion experience was anything less than authentic. Later in the *Confessions* (xi.11) he would use almost identical language about the union of love and dread, the dread induced by the contemplation of the unapproachable Other so distant and 'unlike', the love by the awareness of the Other who is so similar and so near; the dread corresponding to negative and impersonal attributes, the love asking to be expressed in frankly personal terms.

At the heart of the experience he described lay the conviction that the finite creature has an insatiable longing for a fulfilment that can be found only in what lies beyond itself, and indeed beyond human capacity for definition or description.

Neoplatonic exhortations to suppress the passions and the physical senses took Augustine back to Cicero's warning that sexual indulgence does not make for mental clarity. Porphyry's tract on vegetarianism taught that, 'just as priests at temples must abstain from sexual intercourse in order to be ritually pure at the time of offering sacrifice, so also the individual soul needs to be equally pure to attain to the vision of God.' Augustine knew himself to be 'dragged down by the weight of carnal life'. He was not a Christian; yet it was through Christians like Simplicianus of Milan that he had discovered an experience of deep psychological importance to him, giving him both a sense of total certitude and also an awareness of his own impermanence in contrast to the eternal Being of the One. He found himself torn in a struggle between a meditative philosophy which called his soul to higher things than the body, and his habit of sexual activity, by which he felt himself bound and in which he had long found a source of physical, if not psychological, satisfaction. He began to hope and pray that he would eventually attain continence, 'but not yet' (C viii.16). It was both a comfort and a stimulus that Cicero's *Hortensius* had taught that 'the mere search for higher happiness, not merely its actual attainment, is a prize beyond all human wealth or honour or physical pleasure'.

Towards conversion

If the paradoxical effect of Cicero's *Hortensius* when he was nineteen had been to drive him to Manicheism, the effect of his Platonic readings when he was thirty-one was to impel him towards Porphyry's greatest object of hatred, the Church. The Neoplatonic circle at Milan was specially interested in parts of the New Testament, such as the prologue to St John's Gospel or St Paul's strongly Platonizing language in 2 Corinthians 3–4, which offered a biblical foundation for a Christian Platonism. The Christians in this group were concerned to interpret St Paul's epistle to the Romans in a way that averted Manichee determinism and dualism. As a Manichee Augustine had interpreted the apostle as being inconsistent not only with the Old Testament but also with himself. Pauline language about the conflict of flesh and spirit (Galatians 5 and Romans 7) was taken by the Manichees as a charter for their belief that the body's sexual impulses are at the root of all evil. The Milan Neoplatonists took a slightly less pessimistic view. Soon Augustine was convinced that from Plato to Christ was hardly more than a short and simple step, and that the teaching of the Church was in effect 'Platonism for the multitude', a pictorial and figurative way of addressing unphilosophical minds with the effect of making them rational at least in conduct. To the end of his days, long after his reservations about certain elements in the Platonic tradition had become specific and explicit, Augustine would not fail to make handsome acknowledgement of his indebtedness to the Neoplatonic books. As he lay dying at Hippo during the long Vandal siege of his city, his last recorded words were a quotation from Plotinus.

Neoplatonic spirituality and the stress on interiority and on liberation from the distractions of the external world, sharpened Augustine's feeling of being pulled in two different directions with his sexual drive as a downward pull. As he read the letters of St Paul, he began to think his condition wholly understood by the apostle. He found himself in a whirlpool of inward conflict. The consciousness of his wretchedness was one day poignantly enhanced as he walked in a Milan street past a laughing beggar happy under the anaesthetic of liquor (C vi.9). He realized that his feeling on contemplating the man was not pity but envy. The professor of rhetoric found that his copy of the Pauline letters was becoming important to him.

At the end of July 386 in the garden of the house in Milan where he was living with his mother and with his former pupil Alypius (a competent lawyer who in 386 was still shedding Manichee beliefs, and later became bishop of Thagaste), Augustine finally came to the point of decision. His health had become poor with asthmatic trouble on his chest and loss of voice; whether this was a symptom of his malaise or a contributory cause of his decision cannot be determined. He decided to abandon his teaching post, and therewith ambitions for a secular career. The crux was the abandonment of all intention to marry. Could he bring himself to live without a woman? From an African friend working in the court bureaucracy he learnt of the existence of a community of ascetics living in Milan and of the renunciation of wealth by Antony, the Egyptian hermit, whose Life had been written by Athanasius, bishop of Alexandria, and was quickly translated into Latin for western readers. If they could achive continence, then he could also. Or was his will too weak?

According to the narrative in the eighth book of the *Confessions* written fourteen years later he picked up his copy of St Paul, opened it at random and, in the manner of those who sought guidance for the future from Virgil, took guidance from the first text he saw—the concluding words of Romans 13, contrasting sexual wantonness with the calling to 'put on Christ'. He described his decision in exquisite literary language, with echoes from the poet Persius, a striking phrase from Plotinus, and a symbolic allusion to fallen Adam in the garden of Eden. He recounted how he heard as it were a voice like a child's bidding him to 'pick up and read' (*tolle, lege*). How much of the narrative is plain prose and how much is literary or rhetorical decoration has been a matter of controversy. That there is a literary element is certain. It is also certain that in Milan at the end of July 386 he made a decision to abandon marriage and secular ambition and to be baptized. He resigned his city teaching post.

The conversion was no sudden flash, but the culminating point of many months of painful gestation. He himself was later to compare the process of conversion to pregnancy. The choice marked a shift more ethical than intellectual in content. The story told in the *Confessions* presupposes that in 386 he understood sexual passion as the one obstacle between his soul and union with eternal incorporeal truth. What Plotinus and Porphyry had taught him was now being made possible and actual with the help of a text from St Paul. Fifteen years later he would be writing of the 'illusion' some have that in this life it is possible for the human mind so to detach itself from the physical world as to grasp 'the unclouded light of unchanging truth' (CE iv.20). Nevertheless at the time he had the sensation of 'coming into harbour after a stormy passage'. Monica's prayers for his conversion and baptism were answered. The son of so many tears could not be lost.

A few months later he declared that, although old desires did not cease to disturb his dreams, nevertheless he was beginning to make progress, for he now regarded sexual union with revulsion as a 'bitter sweetness' (Sol. i.25). His ascetic aspirations did not make him wish to be a hermit. His longing was to be with a community of lay friends sharing his enthusiasm for Plato and St Paul with some Cicero (especially the *Tusculan Disputations*) thrown in. Eight months passed between his decision in the Milan garden and Easter 387 when he was baptized by Ambrose together with his natural son Adeodatus and his friend Alypius the lawyer. During these months he and Monica with a group of friends and pupils were lent a villa at Cassiciacum in the hills near Como. There he could recover his health and think out his position.

His conversion does not appear in his writings at the time as motivated by a desire to escape the painful uncertainties of philosophical scepticism by taking refuge in the dogmatic authority of the Church. The source of his misery and dissatisfaction lay in himself. Nevertheless the problem of authority was prominent in the controversies between Catholics and

Manichees, and he acknowledged that he was submitting to Christ and his community. A claim to self-determination he came to see as pride (C x.58). From the autumn of 386 onwards his writings would contain frequent allusions to the Bible and Christian doctrine. At Cassiciacum he wrote of authority and reason as parallel routes to the truth, authority being Christ, reason being represented by Plato. Authority can give directions which reason subsequently understands. Authority is prior in time, reason prior in the order of reality. The well educated prefer to follow the philosophic path of reason; but even there reason cannot be sufficient to provide all the guidance needed. On the other hand, an exclusive reliance on authority must be beset by great danger. Without reason how can one discriminate between competing claims to authority? How can one distinguish between authentically divine authority and that of inferior spirits venerated by pagans who claim to predict the future by divination and soothsaying? The divine authority of Christ, however, is demonstrated by being simultaneously the highest reason. He is the very Wisdom of God, identical with the Mind of Plotinus' supreme Triad (O ii.26–7).

Finally, one must ask what specific ideas about God and man were accepted by Augustine in consequence of his baptism and confession of faith. Reduced to its most basic and skeletal elements, the Christian faith invited him to make the following affirmations. First, the ordered world stems from the supreme Good who is also the supreme Power, not merely the best that happens to exist, but a perfection such that our minds cannot even frame the idea of any superior being. Therefore 'he' is the proper object of awe and worship. We should not think of God as involved in a process of struggling from lower to higher as human beings do (and as the Manichee Light power), but rather as having a consistent creative and redemptive purpose in relation to the universe in general and the rational creation in particular. The supreme level in the ladder of value is the love which is the very nature of God.

Secondly, human nature as now experienced fails to correspond to the Creator's intentions. Human misery is perpetuated by social and individual egotisms, so that man is haunted by ignorance, mortality and the brevity of life, weakness of will, above all by the arrogant and wilful rejection of his true good.

In short, humanity needs the remedy of eternal life and the forgiveness of sins, or restoration under the love of God.

Thirdly, the supreme God has acted within the time and history in which we live, and which 'he' transcends, bringing to us knowledge, life, strength, and (greatest gift of all) humility without which no one learns anything. This act has its culminating focus in Jesus, model to humanity by his life and wise teaching and by his unique filial relation to the supreme 'Father'. Jesus embodied the gift of God's love by the humility of his incarnation and death. Access to this movement of God to rescue fallen man is found through the assent of faith and through adhesion to the community of Jesus' followers, a structured community entrusted by him with the gospel and with sacramental covenant signs of water, bread, and wine. Thereby the Spirit of holiness unites man to God, to give hope for the life to come, of which Jesus' resurrection is the ultimate pledge, and to transform the individual's personal and moral life to be fit for the society of saints in the presence of God.

In these themes Christian preaching spoke to Augustine in strongly other-worldly terms which linked arms with Platonic morality and metaphysics. It was momentous that he brought together Plotinus' negative, impersonal language about the One or Absolute and the biblical concept of God as love, power, justice, and forgiveness. It is cardinal to theism that the mystery of God is known not only in the grandeur and glory of nature but also by a self-disclosure—on the analogy of a person making known to others what they could not find out for themselves. From 387 onwards Augustine took these ideas as first principles.

2 *Liberal arts*

Perhaps because Platonism contributed substantially to his conversion to Christianity, Augustine was at no time to draw sharp frontiers between philosophy and theology. He did not think of philosophic reason either as a mere handmaid to religion or as a dangerous whore out to seduce the mind into supposing that it could attain its supreme end without God's help and grace. The prime subject of philosophy he defined as 'the study of God and the human soul' (Sol. I.7)—one notices the exclusion of the physical world. The motive which led people to philosophize he described in Ciceronian terms as simply the quest for happiness.

Neoplatonic ontology, or doctrine of being and of how things are, described in the last chapter, is pervasive throughout his writings. Only there are respects in which he modified the detail of it, which leaves the impression that in so far as he accepted the Platonic arguments, he always turned them to conclusions defined by his faith. It would perhaps be truer to say that he saw little reason to dissent from the Platonic tradition unless it was incompatible with the implications of the catholic creed. Naturally, he regarded the pagan Platonists as mistaken in accepting polytheism, everlasting world-cycles and the transmigration of souls. The ancient belief in reincarnation was altogether too fatalistic to be compatible with the concept of God as uniquely creative power, acting in redemption to bring his rational creation to its true end of fellowship with himself.

There were other points of disagreement which were less obvious but not less important. Despite the prominence of the renunciation of sexual activity in his conversion, he did not agree with Plotinus in seeing matter and physicality as the prime root of evil. Again, unlike Plotinus (following Plato, *Republic* 509B), Augustine would not say that God should be described as the One 'beyond being'. The Platonic antithesis of the one and the many he could accept as an account of the relation between the transcendent Creator and the manifold diversity of creation. But the one God is never beyond being. Exodus 3: 14 assured him that God is being itself, *ipsum esse*: that which truly is is he. (Two excited and stirring sermons delivered at Hippo to his congregation of dockers and farm-workers developed this remarkable theme: P 134 and Jo 38.9).

Creation is 'participation' in being. This term implies derivation. It is characteristic of that which is derived, that what one has is then distinct from what one is. For creatures it is one thing to exist, another to be just and wise. But in God to exist and to be just, good, and wise are one and the same. Man can exist without being just, good, or wise; God cannot. God 'is what he has'. Plotinus had expressed the same point in Aristotelian terms: in the divine 'substance' (i.e. metaphysical essence) there can be no accidents. Plotinus and Augustine concurred that only the first of the ten categories, substance, is applicable to God's being (C iv.28).

Augustine found the prologue to St John's gospel (a piece of the New Testament that impressed Neoplatonic philosophers) a noble statement of the Platonic world-picture, and of the light of God shining into the darkness to turn the alienated world back towards the higher realms. But in finding Christianity to express the truth so nearly Platonic, Augustine noted one dramatic point of difference: 'the books of the Platonists' did not say the Word was made flesh. The concept of a unique revelation within a particular life was a Christian theme which Mani had had to alter radically. For a pagan Platonist its particularity seemed scandalously incompatible with divine immutability and with a universal operation of providence in the cosmos as a whole. Platonists did not think of a divine purpose being worked out in and through the mess of history, and their conceptions of time were cyclic, not linear, in other words, at immense intervals of time the configuration of the stars would come round to the same position, and then all things would start again on the same treadmill. The concept of a unique incarnation calling man to an existential decision with eternal consequences meant that Platonism was not something Augustine could leave unamended. On the other hand, he too felt it necessary to interpret the incarnation in terms of God's universal providence, as a momentous step towards the goal of history and a clue to its meaning.

At the time of his conversion Augustine was nearly 33, already established as a master of literature and rhetorical style. Had he gone on to the secular career of which he dreamed, little more than his name might have been known to posterity, perhaps only as a striking instance of social mobility on the part of a clever young man from a relatively impecunious provincial family in the Numidian countryside, who had worked hard, and had the luck to enjoy some useful patronage. Now he had renounced that. He had to work out the answers to pressing problems. His first literary undertaking was to inquire into the thorny questions about evil and providence once forced on his attention by the Manichees. He also had to settle accounts with the sceptical thinkers who, during a momentous period, had been deeply congenial to his mind.

During the months at Cassiciacum he composed a series of philosophical dialogues, often modelled on those by Cicero written in his retirement at Tusculum. The literary convention of the dialogue form enabled him to state difficulties with which he himself was still wrestling, and which he could discuss with a thoughtful élite. The atmosphere was that of a lecture-room, using dialectical dispute as a means of instruction, posing problems and seeking solutions. The subjects were, first, the nature of happiness (*De beata vita*), a critique of the sceptical theory of knowledge and the doctrine of suspense of judgement (*Contra Academicos*), and the affirmation that a personal or particular providence is possible within the consistent order of the universe and the chain of cause and effect (*De ordine*). In the last of these he included a defence of the study of the liberal arts as preparing the mind for higher truths, and suggested that they should be arranged in a ladder of ascent, with geometry and music particularly disclosing the mathematical order underlying the cosmos. Augustine borrowed an image from Plotinus and used the illustration of a mosaic pavement whose beauty is not seen by the eye that concentrates on one small piece, but only by the eye that tries to take in the whole. In one very Neoplatonic passage he declared that 'to see the One we must withdraw from plurality not only of men but from sense-perceptions; we seek as it were the centre of the circle which holds the whole together' (O i.3).

At Cassiciacum he also wrote *Soliloquies* (Augustine coined this word), a dialogue in which, in search of certitude especially on the immortality of the soul, he humbly submitted himself to instruction by Reason. A characteristically Neoplatonizing piece of dialectic led him to assert that because mathematical truth is timelessly true, the mind which knows it also shares in this transcendence of the space-time continuum—a view briefly adumbrated in Plato (*Meno* 86A) and then developed considerably by Plotinus (iv.7). In a rich medley of phrases borrowed from Cicero, the *Soliloquies* fuse biblical language with a potent mix of Neoplatonic ontology. Emphatic reference is made by name to both Plato and Plotinus, and the presence of themes derived from Porphyry is very probable. For Augustine here says that to attain the vision of God there is no single road; but at least one must flee everything physical; set aside the quest for fulfilment whether in sexual love 'even with a modest, well-educated wife', or in wealth and honour; train one's mind to invisible realities by a process analogous to geometrical abstraction, so that one thinks not of squares of varying sizes but of the principles by which all squares have squareness. Then one may begin to comprehend the mysterious transcendence of God, in whom the purified immortal soul finds its true end. The path of inner purification is by faith. The last proposition is the only one that would have puzzled Porphyry.

The Cassiciacum dialogues join confidence that a providential order exists with diffidence about human ability to discern it in all cases. Trust in providence is seen as more than an intellectual puzzle: 'Vision will be granted to him who lives well, prays well, and studies well' (O ii.51). But it is suggested that amid all the diversities and tensions of experience, there can be an ultimate harmony, a beauty found in antitheses and contrasts as in a painted picture where there is light and dark. So also unity of truth may lie beyond the various subjects of human knowledge with their different methods of investigation.

With this significant place assigned to the study of the liberal arts, it was natural for Augustine, in the early days following his baptism, to embark on a series of handbooks to the basic topics of the ancient educational syllabus. Of these textbooks only his books on logic and on music have certainly survived intact. His Grammar, a copy of which lay before Cassiodorus in the sixth century, was found so useful that the copy in his own library was stolen. Medieval manuscripts transmit two grammars under Augustine's name, and it is very possible that one of them (known as the *Ars Breviata*) is the 'lost' text. The conclusion is evident that conversion and baptism did nothing to crush the pedagogic and humanist instinct. The Neoplatonic influences set him on the way to seeing the liberal arts (especially dialectic, geometry, and music) as a highly desirable mental training in abstract thought preparatory to higher metaphysical explorations.

At the end of his life Augustine wrote a conscientious critique of his own life-work, the 'Revisions' or 'Reconsiderations' (*Retractationes*, not to be translated 'retractions', for the book is almost as much a positive defence as a withdrawal of indiscretions). In this book he felt that as a young man he had tended to exaggerate the value and importance of such liberal studies: 'Many holy people have not studied them at all, and many who have studied them are not holy' (R i.3.2).

Augustine's educational concern came to find different expression in his maturity, specially in one of his most influential books, the first to be printed in the fifteenth century. This was entitled *De doctrina christiana*, or 'On Christian culture'. He revised and added to it near the end of his life. One manuscript of the first edition, written during Augustine's lifetime, is preserved—now at Leningrad. The work is an examination of the skills needed to interpret the Bible correctly and persuasively. Augustine made use of the *Book of Rules* of the schismatic theologian Tyconius (below, p.242) to formulate canons of exegesis which would avoid subjectivity, e.g. in deciding what is literal, what allegorical and, if the latter, what the hidden meaning is. The Bible disclosed indeed the very wisdom of God; but human science was far from irrelevant to its discovery and elucidation. Vast and dangerous errors were made by interpreters of scripture confident of their own private inspiration. Augustine records with some astonishment that there were contemporary Christians in Africa who read no book other than the Bible, and who conversed in the often strange translationese of the old Latin Bible; an anticipation of Quaker English. He was sure that wider studies were necessary. A biblical scholar needed to know some history, geography, natural science, mathematics, logic and rhetoric (how to write and speak clearly and appropriately). There could be places where a little knowledge of technology might well help the interpreter. Certainly some knowledge of Greek was most valuable for checking translations and variant readings.

Hebrew Augustine never studied, though he understood words of Punic spoken by the peasants and well knew that it was a cognate Semitic language. He was relieved of the obligation to study Hebrew partly by the thoroughness with which his senior contemporary and pen-friend Jerome had mastered it, partly because he was convinced that the Greek translation of the Old Testament made by the Seventy (Septuagint) was no less inspired than the Hebrew original. Jerome's New Latin Bible (the Vulgate) distressed him when long-familiar words were needlessly altered. It upset the laity, always hostile to liturgical changes.

The tract on Christian culture reflected the special reverence with which Augustine regarded the Bible. He expressly denied that holy scripture represented the sole medium of divine revelation (S 12.4); but it represented the principle of authority which seemed central to Christian belief in a divinely given way of salvation for an ignorant and lost humanity. The authority of Bible and Church rested on reciprocal support. Usage in the churches had determined the limits of the canon. Bible texts established the divinely constituted nature of the Church.

Controversy against Manichee critics made Augustine insist on an inner spiritual meaning, especially of the Old Testament. 'The meaning of the New Testament lies hidden in the Old, the meaning of the Old Testament is revealed through the New' (CR iv.8). So Christ's coming fulfilled the aspiration of the Old Testament prophets. Manichees made him very conscious of the dividing line between the books accepted as canonical by the Church and the apocryphal Gospels and Acts to which Mani had often appealed, especially because these apocrypha were written to foster the view that marriage is out of the question for a believer. The Manichee contention that the New Testament text had been corrupted in transmission made him aware of the importance of variant readings among the manuscripts, or of errors in the Old Latin Bible. He did not understand the biblical text to bear only one sense intended at the time by the original author. The biblical writers themselves frequently used symbolism and allegory. To insist on a single literal and historical sense must mean failure to grasp the underlying message.

In a few places Augustine could write confidently of the clarity and perspicuity of the Bible. But there are other places where he had to allow that many texts are obscure, and that not everything necessary to salvation is obvious to any and every casual reader. This is reinforced by the observation that many heretics start from a mistaken or partisan interpretation of scripture and because they are both clever and proud, are reluctant to correct themselves. 'It is part of a catholic disposition to express the wish to accept correction if one is mistaken' (DEP ii.5).

3 Free choice

In the summer of 387, living with Monica at Rome during what was to be the last year of her life, Augustine began a substantial and complex treatise 'on the origin of evil and on free choice' (De libero arbitrio), a work which he finally completed six or seven years later. The critique of Manichee dualism and determinism led him to lay strong emphasis on the will. That it had a central position in every ethical action he demonstrated by appealing to the cardinal virtues of justice, prudence, self-control, and courage. Virtue depends on right and rational choices, and therefore happiness lies in loving goodness of will. By contrast, misery is the product of an evil will. And evil originated in a misused free choice which neglected eternal goodness, beauty, and truth.

We have seen that Augustine preferred to locate the root of evil in the soul's instability rather than, with Plotinus, in the body and in matter (CD xiv.3). The soul's weakness was for him the immediate, if not necessarily the all-sufficient, cause of sin. Yet he saw this instability of the soul as inherent in the very fact of being created out of nothing and therefore 'contingent', liable to be driven off course. Even its immortality it possesses not by its own inherent nature but by the gift and will of the Creator.

Creation out of nothing carried for Augustine the consequence that in everything so created there is an element of non-being and a 'tendency to non-existence', even though that ultimate stage is never actually reached. By using such language he sought to hold together a biblical concept of the createdness and dependence of the soul with a Platonic assertion of the soul's immortality. In an early essay on The Immortality of the Soul (a work containing numerous passages echoing Porphyry), he wrote that if even the matter of the body is not annihilated at death, so also the sinful soul retains for ever some trace of the divine image and form. In his maturity he would write that

'even the fallen soul remains God's image' (T xiv.4), 'capable of
knowing God' (*capax Dei*, xiv.11). For 'even irreligious people
think about eternity by implication, as when they make assertive
moral judgements on the behaviour of others ignoring the fact
that they behave none too well themselves (xiv.21). So even in
the worst cases, the soul retains the marks of rationality and
freedom which are the meaning of 'the image of God' bestowed
on man by creation. At the same time, being created out of
nothing, it is mutable, and the potentiality for the fall is therefore
given by creation. Even so the actual choice of the will to neglect
the good is causeless and inexplicable.

The dilemma here long troubled his mind. Why, he asked,
did some angels fall while others did not? In his maturity it
seemed to him inadequate to speak about random chance and
causelessness. To meet the difficulty he turned to a doctrine of
predestination.

Although Augustine dissented from Plotinus' opinion that evil
begins in matter, he agreed that the prime consequence of the
soul's mistaken choice is that it has become obsessively attached
to the body. Matter in itself is morally neutral; yet merely by the
fact of being created out of nothing, by being in itself formless,
it carries a profound metaphysical inferiority. Even so, the soul
is the real field of battle. The 'nature' with which humanity is
endowed by the Creator is good; Adam before the Fall and
Christ in his incarnation have 'pure nature' such as the rest of
humanity cannot have now. For the corruption of weak choice
results in a chain of habit being formed, which fetters the
character and becomes second nature, flawed or 'vitiated'
nature.

Experience in moral decisions shows that we are ignorant of
just what is right and moreover, when we do know, have great
difficulty in performing it. Augustine felt hesitation on the
question whether 'ignorance and difficulty' are part of God's
initial design for his creatures, to teach them as they mature
gradually to master their problems and stand on their own feet,
or whether the moral struggle is a permanent and penal consequence of the fallen estate of man since Adam's and Eve's first
disobedience. Augustine could afford to be hesitant at this point
since, for the argument of his treatise on freedom of choice, it
mattered relatively little. Later he became more inclined to the

penal view. But in the earlier work his objective was simply to refute the Manichee contention that the evils of human life prove the created world not to be the work of supreme goodness and unopposed power. He was aware that he was leaving a number of questions unresolved.

The treatise on free choice was later hailed by critics of Augustine who followed Pelagius (below, p. 288) in the conviction that the late Augustine failed to do justice to freedom and therefore took moral value out of acts of virtue. The critics liked to quote the treatise as containing arguments for free will unrefuted even by their author. He could reply with good reason that the attempt to play the young Augustine off against the old was ill founded. He admitted that there were some few sentences which he could have worded more precisely. He felt the book was better on sin than on grace. The argument of the treatise included an insistence on the transmission to posterity of Adam's guilt and penalty, on the impotence of sinful man to rescue himself by effort of will, and on the need for the humility of the Redeemer to conquer the pride and envy which constitute the most diabolical features of the Fall.

The second of the three parts of the treatise on free choice contains Augustine's most considerable and sustained statement of the argument for assenting to the existence of God. Characteristically he approached the problem as a central issue in the theory of knowledge. He did not undertake to prove God's existence as if he were demonstrating the existence of an object in the world of sense. His argument is not that the sum total of things includes God in the way in which it includes things perceived by the mind through the five physical senses. He understood God to be beyond time and space, for within time and space man cannot discover an ultimate happiness or perfection. Similarly God is presupposed by all thought about universals and by communication between minds. Mathematical, aesthetic, and moral reasoning takes it for granted that there is a realm of reality beyond the senses. (Physical objects can be perceived; physical theory cannot, and yet has to be formulated in language taken from the realm of sense-objects. A person who denied the truth of the fundamentals of physics would be thought strange; it is no serious objection that language about these fundamentals is largely analogical.)

Therefore if we question the wonderful order of nature with its noble objects, in reason's ear they declare 'The hand that made us is divine' (C ix.25; xi.6; quoting Plotinus iii.2.3,20). But the order, design, beauty, even the very mutability and flux of the world and the fact that its existence is not 'necessary', become no more than subordinate and supporting considerations in the argument. The essence of the matter appears in Augustine's conviction that God is not just someone or something who happens to exist; he is Being itself, and the source of all finite beings. As a good Platonist he finds this assured by the reality of the moral principles, justice, wisdom, truth. They stand supreme in the scale of value; yet they are realities no one has seen, touched, tasted, smelt, or heard.

Not that Augustine would disparage the importance of the senses. Their evidence is fundamental for all things that fall within their range. Questions of taste, colour, softness, size, shape, etc., we decide by the relevant senses. But the perceptions of the senses are a low form of apprehension. The sceptical philosophers rightly warned that the senses can be deceptive, as an oar in the water appears crooked. The information derived through the senses is checked and judged by the perceiving, knowing mind.

Augustine liked a formula which he found in Plotinus and which in turn Plotinus took from Plato's *Philebus*, namely that when the body receives sensation, the soul 'is not unaware' of the fact. The supremacy of the soul is implicit. There is, however, a gulf between the perpetual flux and change of the realm of the five senses and the timeless truths of mathematics and universals.

In Augustine's hands the argument about God's existence merges into the argument of the Platonists for the reality of universals as eternal and immutable truths, whether these be of mathematics or of transcendent values of justice and truth, in the light of which the mind judges whether a particular act or proposition is just or true. For him the crux is that there is a realm of reality, beyond and above the mind of man which is itself mutable and seldom continues long in one stay. We are again seeing the imprint of the conviction born of the mystical experience described in the seventh book of the *Confessions*, through which he was confronted by the antithesis between his own impermanence and the eternal changelessness of the God who is (above, p. 214).

Accordingly he saw the goal of his inferences in the notion of unchanging, eternal, necessary being. Naturally he was well aware that the goal was given for him by faith. No seeker after truth begins with no convictions about where and how it may be found. Faith is always prior in time to understanding. But the understanding remains a matter of reasoning and philosophical inference. 'Believe in order that you may understand', he liked to quote (from the Old Latin Bible version of Isaiah). But for Augustine the relationship between faith and reason is not what it later became for the medieval schoolmen. The propositions of faith which the understanding seeks to interpret turn out to be matters not of revelation, but of what medieval theologians would have called 'natural theology'; matters (that is) established by philosophical argument without accepting any claim to a specific revelation. In the treatise on free choice Augustine seeks to argue that it is reasonable to accept belief in God, immortality, freedom, and moral responsibility—beliefs which Platonic philosophers knew and shared without having a Bible to help them.

The treatises written by Augustine in his thirties have many references to the question of immortality, including the rather obscure essay in Neoplatonizing dialectic concerning *The Immortality of the Soul* (a work which he himself did not rate highly when he re-read it later in life). Death was often present to his consciousness, especially when friends or young people were carried off by sickness. Human life he described as a race towards death (CD 13.10); and 'one should begin each day not with complacency that one has survived another day but with compunction that one more day of one's alloted span has for ever passed'. Finally, his conviction that death is not the end rested not on Platonic dialectic but on faith in the risen Christ (T xiii.12).

4 A philosophical society

By the late autumn of 388, after Monica's requiem at Ostia, Augustine had returned to his native Africa (which he was never again to leave) and settled at his home town, Thagaste, to practise an experiment in ascetic retirement with Alypius and other friends. The lay community met regularly for daily prayers and the recitation of the Psalter. (It is hard to exaggerate the importance of the Psalter for Augustine's spirituality; psalm-quotations have been shown to be essential to the very structure of the *Confessions*.) In between their hours of devotion they discussed Cicero, St Paul, and Neoplatonic themes. The community was quietist, contemplative in spirit, and rather donnish, with Augustine as acknowledged leader providing answers to questions raised in the discussions. These answers circulated in writing and were later collected to make a notable book, *On 83 different questions*. The 46th contains an important statement about Plato's theory of Ideas, safeguarding biblical monotheism by holding that universals are 'thoughts in the mind of God'. The Thagaste community was not called a monastery. The 'society of brothers', as they were called, shared property, lived in frugal simplicity, but had no formal vows, no identical clothing, no fixed rule and requirement of obedience. They were far more intellectual than most later monasteries. Nevertheless the community had the thing, if not the name, and was in practice the first monastic community in Latin Africa.

In this lay community Augustine lived for two and a half years; it was a fruitful period for his writing. The gradual transition from teaching the liberal arts to serious engagement with theology was marked by his six books *On Music*. Five of the six books were devoted to a technical discussion of metre and rhythm. He intended later to continue his studies with a discussion of the theoretical aspects of pitch, but this was never written, and that field was left open for Boethius 120 years later.

(Practical music-making was no proper pursuit for an intellectual and a gentleman in antiquity; that was left to vulgar people and girls hired to entertain the gentlemen after dinner.)

The sixth book on Music is of a different character, and enjoyed some independent circulation. It was Augustine's restatement of Plato's belief that mathematical principles underlie everything in the universe and are the principal clues to its providential ordering. Especially in the *Timaeus* Plato had taught that the very structure of the soul is determined by ratios directly related to the ratios of intervals in music; e.g. an octave is 2 to 1, a fifth 3 to 2, a fourth 4 to 3, a whole tone 9 to 8. Indeed the same ratios governed the distances between the planets.

Augustine mentions more than once that he was vulnerable to being moved by the sound of music. At Milan, where at first he used to come to the cathedral to admire Ambrose's oratorical skill, he found himself not only impressed by the content of the discourses but also gripped by the psalm chants. He knew that fitting music is capable of bringing the meaning of words home to the heart. When he was a young man he found music indispensable to his life as a source of consolation. In his maturity there was little time for that anyway, but he remained persuaded by Plato's thesis that between music and the soul there is a 'hidden affinity', *occulta familiaritas* (C x.49). No other art is equally independent of at least four of the five senses, and so controlled by mathematical principles. What power of the mind is more astonishing than its ability to recall music without actually hearing any physical sounds? The observation seemed to Augustine a striking demonstration of the soul's transcendence in relation to the body.

The study of Plotinus' analysis of the nature of beauty (i.6) made a deep impact. Augustine was struck by the pervasiveness of mathematical order in the cosmos, and this had been a prominent theme in the Cassiciacum dialogues. There his vindication of providence is in substance aesthetic and Plotinian: i.e. the chiaroscuro of light and dark contribute to the beauty of the whole. But this beauty is not merely a subjective feeling; it is grounded in numbers. There is precision not only in the inanimate environment, but also in the processes of human life, as is obvious from the study of embryology which shows how the embryo reaches each successive stage of development at constant and exact intervals of time. Moreover, Augustine added, the beauty of a building depends on its mathematical proportions. Symmetry of fenestration depends on measurements. So beauty has an objective ground. Things please the eye because they are beautiful, not merely vice versa. (This was a judgement he would qualify only in part when speaking of a man's love for a woman. While the symmetry and proportion of the human body were indeed measurable in mathematical terms, Augustine added, with what may seem to the modern reader extraordinary romanticism, 'Adam did not love Eve because she was beautiful; it was his love which made her beautiful': P 132.10).

In some texts we meet the normal Neoplatonic view that mathematics is a halfway house in the ascent from the physical world to metaphysics and theology. He had to warn his readers against taking him to mean that pure mathematics is metaphysics without qualification. One should not suppose that geometry is a particularly obscure way of talking theology (Sol. i.11). In any event, he drily remarks, not more than a handful of the clever mathematicians known to him could actually be called 'wise' (LA ii.30).

Augustine wanted to ask not merely why the world is there at all, but also how our minds can know things both through the five senses and through words which are 'signs'. Analytical questions about the function of language need first to be asked if one is to go on to the existential questions which lie beyond them. This concern for words and meanings and their relation to reality was stimulated by his growing role as a lay theologian interpreting a divine self-disclosure through 'the word of God'. He was highly sensitive to the fact that much religious language is figurative and indirect: what unreflecting people, whether believers or unbelievers, may take as plain matter-of-fact prose is often a pile of imaginative metaphors enshrining profound intuition and insight rather than representing the conclusion of reasoned inference. He was aware that religious aspiration can have, at least for many, a close affinity with music. During his lifetime the Catholic churches of North Africa were increasingly coming to terms with pictorial art and were installing murals portraying Christ, Mary, Peter and Paul, or Old Testament saints—Adam and Eve (decently covered), the sacrifice of Isaac, and others. The Platonist in him felt reserve towards the power of art to come between the soul and God rather than always to act as a bridge from sense to spirit. But he defended church music against puritans who wanted to exclude it altogether, and acknowledged that, dangerous as music may be, it is a natural medium for emotions of exaltation and awed abasement.

As a layman at Thagaste Augustine also wrote two of his most effective works, 'The Teacher' (*de magistro*) and 'True Religion' (*de vera religione*).

'The Teacher' was written as a memorial to his clever natural son Adeodatus, in conversation with whom the ideas were worked out. It concerns how human beings can communicate truth. The discussion begins with the simple answer that we do this by words. But then that naïve answer is brought increasingly under the fire of criticism. Words are sounds significant by convention, but convey meaning only in an ambivalent and limited degree. The meaning of an utterance is at least as much determined by the tone of voice or the context or gestures as by the syllables pronounced. The facial expression of the speaker will disclose to members of his own circle if he is being ironical. Some idiomatic phrases can bear a sense which is the opposite of what the words appear to say. To describe a man as an honest lawyer indeed may not mean just what it says. Moreover, words can be used as a smokescreen, to conceal or to deceive, to impart disinformation. In any event, words are mere physical sounds. It is mind that gives them significance.

Certainly Augustine was the last person to deny that words are useful. So great a master of their employment was unlikely to think they played no part. Moreover, the Bible uses words; and sacraments are 'visible words' (F 19.16), for it is the Word and Spirit which impart power and inward meaning to what would otherwise be only an external ceremonial act (Jo 80.3). But it does not follow that words can in themselves be effective or adequate for conveying full meaning in matters of great weight. Truth is ultimately communicated through an intangible, inaudible, indescribable experience of the interaction of mind with mind. For mind can be known only by mind.

This thesis led Augustine to reflect on the nature of prayer. Minds of close friends can communicate with one another without a word being uttered, perhaps with not even a gesture.

The God who is incomprehensible and transcendent is also more 'interior' than anything we can express. 'When we pray, often we can hardly know the meaning of the words we are using' (Sol. i.9). This inadequacy is partly inherent in the fact that our terms and categories belong to discourse taken from this world of space, time, and successiveness. They therefore blur and distort the truth about the immutable and eternal. Partly it is a mark of all matters involving deep feeling (and no word became more characteristic of Augustine than 'longing', *desiderium*) that they lie too deep for words. 'Man can say nothing of what he is incapable of feeling, but he can feel what he is incapable of putting into words' (S 117.7f.; P 99.5).

The ultimate power of mutual understanding between friends, he believed, rested on a common participation in the divine Reason. This belief cohered with his exalted, sometimes emotional language about the gift of friendship. To share in the light radiating from Christ the Teacher is to be enabled to recognize the identical faith in others. Augustine sometimes spoke of the religious community as having a capacity, through an indefinable intuition, to discern authentic and inauthentic forms of the faith. 'Catholic ears', he thought, did not normally need formal decisions by synods to tell them the fundamentals of their faith (DEP iv.36). This illumination of the mind, then, is a power or sense of discretion rather than information about the facts. It penetrates the profounder levels of the personality. Introspection taught Augustine the existence of the sub-conscious: 'You can know something which you are not aware that you know' (T xiv.9).

Admittedly, there is another series of texts in which he wrote of the impenetrable depths of the human heart, of the 'abyss' of man. 'Every heart is closed to every heart' (P 55.9). To God every motive is known, but not to man (134.16). Man himself is an ocean depth, *grande profundum* (C iv.22), and the individual cannot even comprehend his own character and heart (P 41.13).

He had a more than ordinary interest in logical tangles. But his interest in what a modern reader would think of as depth psychology helped to make him sceptical of ingenious language-games played by clever dialecticians. Their doctrine 'lacked heart' (C ix.1 and elsewhere). Valuable as a training in logic was in his view (for theologians he thought it indispensable), religion engaged yet deeper levels of the personality. Religious truth he spoke of as an inner illumination from 'God the sun of souls'. He never suggested that true ideas are inherent or innate within the soul. They always appear as the Creator's gift.

By the term 'soul' (*anima*) Augustine meant the highest immaterial element in man, the part of man to which the mind (*mens*, more rarely *animus*) is but a function. Exactly what 'soul' is and how God creates souls he regarded as beyond human knowledge. It would make for simplicity, he once remarked apropos of infant baptism (GL x.19), if all Adam's posterity derived souls as well as bodies from their first parent by heredity. But this doctrine (traducianism) that souls are acquired by heredity carried more physical implications than at least some Platonists could feel at ease with. Perhaps it would be preferable to say that God expressly creates a soul for each individual as conceived. (Augustine ignored as silly the objection that the Creator should be spared endless fuss.) Or, more platonically, all souls exist in God from the first, and are either sent or even choose to come and inhabit bodies on earth. Neoplatonic philosophers were disagreed among themselves on the correct answer, and the Bible offered no guidance. In Augustine's mind none of these options could be finally excluded. His refusal to give a decision incurred sharp criticism from some who felt that such a question simply could not be left in the limbo of indecision. He remained unmoved.

Diffidence about the capacity of finite minds to comprehend the infinite and eternal led him to use strongly relativist language about the God who is beyond our knowing. Commenting on the prologue to St John's Gospel he wrote that 'Because John was inspired he was able to say something. Had he not been inspired, he would have said nothing at all.' Even the acceptance of a divine revelation mediated through the Bible left unqualified the proposition that this is accommodated to the modest capacity of the recipient and expressed in images (C xiii.18–19). In one stark sentence he declared that the concept must be less than adequate to God 'if you can comprehend it' (S 117.5), or, in a paradox, 'it is better to find God by not finding him [i.e. by learning that he is beyond your grasp] than by finding not to find him'. (C i.10). The causality of grace is always beyond human grasp (SL 7). Nevertheless the massive agnosticism of such sayings did not decline into scepticism, and he knew that there are degrees of inadequacy.

Augustine confronted the Academics sceptical of the possibility of certainty as a man who had once been one of them. They liked to say that one could never attain truth, only probability or an approximation, something like the truth. He thought that if a proposition could be said to resemble the truth, there must be truth which one is judging it to resemble. He also attached emphatic weight to an argument which he often repeated and which, in another context, became important to Descartes in the seventeenth century: 'I think, therefore I am; even if I am mistaken, nevertheless I am.' A person who doubts must at least be utterly confident of his own existence, or he would not be in a position to doubt. Suspense of judgement is therefore not a watertight or rational position.

In passing, we may notice that, unlike Descartes, Augustine did not argue that certitude is found exclusively in the subjective state of the doubting mind. He did not need, as Descartes did, to make his *Cogito* the sole foundation of knowledge. But it is true that he regarded the pure truths of mathematics as incomparably more certain than any perceptions of the five senses.

Augustine pushed the argument further, in a Platonic direction, to imply that there is a capacity in the mind to know truths in a way far more significant than the stream of sensations and perceptions coming through the body. If something, then, is indubitable, there really are truths to be known. The mind hungers for truth; no one can bear to be deceived (C x.34; S 306.9; DDC i.40). None can be happy if he greatly desires but cannot attain the truth. But this last proposition is modified by Augustine under the pressure of a religious consideration: in religious truth, knowledge is not a static possession of the knower, but an ever-growing relationship to God. Every person who seeks truth has God beside him to help, and that suffices for happiness even without the full grasp of the truth sought (BV 20). The enjoyment of God is an 'insatiable satisfaction' (S 362.28). In a number of texts Augustine constructs a ladder of ascent with seven stages of the soul's progress in maturity of comphrension (VR 49; QA 70–6; DDC ii.7).

He did not think there is knowledge in which the knowing

mind does not play a large role. On the one hand, nothing is known unless there is an inward desire of the mind moving it to desire understanding. We cannot love that of which nothing is known. But that axiom presupposes that one already has an inkling about the subject arousing one's curiosity. 'It is an important element in discovery to ask the right question and to know what it is you wish to find out' (QH prol.). He used Platonic language about the educational process; it is an evoking of a capacity, in some sense a knowledge, which is already present.

He shared Plotinus' dislike of the notion that the object known is so wholly distinct from and external to the knowing subject that in the act of knowing there is no significant personal element. An element of self-consciousness attaches to our know-ledge of the external world, and the personal subject is not to be eliminated. If you know something, you also know that it is you who knows. So the theme that understanding requires love to attain its end merges by this route into theology. He put it in this way: all inquiry about how we can know God comes back to the question 'what do we understand by love?' (T viii.10). The Creator's love is immanent within the mind and will of his rational creatures (T viii.12). 'We move towards God not by walking but by loving' (*non ambulando, sed amando*). 'Not our feet but our moral character carries us nearer to him. Moral character is assessed not by what a man knows but by what he loves' (E 155.13).

Hence the negative path, which surrounds the idea of God with exclusively negative epithets, is not the only way. Certainly we can more easily say what God is not than what he is (P 85.23). But at least our ignorance is informed, *docta ignorantia* (E 130.28). The believer's language oscillates between confidence and diffid-ence. Here Augustine made his own a paradox he found in Porphyry. The contemplation of God is an experience beyond intellection, and 'somehow such things are known by a not knowing, and so by this kind of knowing their mysteriousness is realized' (CD xii.7; C xii.5).

'On True Religion' was composed for Romanianus, the wealthy landowner of Thagaste who had once financed his education, and had been converted to Manicheism by the clever young

Augustine. Augustine had to unconvert him and bring him to Catholicism. The treatise has an anti-Manichee thrust, but is chiefly remarkable for the presence of Neoplatonic themes within a strongly Christian and Catholic framework. His appeal was to the uniqueness of the one Church, the 'catholica' which even rival sects would recognize as such ('ask them where the Catholic church is in a town, and even they will not have the nerve to direct you to their own conventicle'). The title-deeds of this one church lie in a sacred history recorded in holy scripture. Its doctrines are then vindicated by their coherence with reason (meaning Platonism).

The coherence of faith and reason Augustine saw in the fact that if concessions to polytheistic rites were removed from Platonism, this philosophy came so close to Christianity that 'with the change of a few words and opinions many Platonists have become Christians' (VR 7). The Neoplatonists' notion of the hierarchy of being and their vindication of providence could be given systematic integration into a Christian framework, and the aspiration of the Platonic tradition was that which Christ had made possible. The content of salvation is then defined as happiness, the inner security which comes as the soul turns away from pride, passion, and the multiplicity of distractions, and ascends towards the One, towards pure reason, to the God who is met in the humility of Christ. Augustine saw Christ as able to bring redemption because in one person he is both God and man. The God-Man is the way and the ladder by which God enables us to rise from the temporal to the eternal. He is both road and goal, Jacob's ladder. By knowing the Son of Man in history, we may come to discern the eternal wisdom of God (T xiii.24). He is both example and gift, our pattern and our expiation; the Mediator for whom Porphyry had no room, though he fitted in a large number of other inferior mediators. At first believers begin with the example of Christ the man, who is 'the milk of babes', but Christ raises to his own true level all who obey and trust in him (C vii.20). Several texts of Augustine boldly describe salvation as 'deification', language commoner in the Greek than in the Latin theologians of antiquity. But the language is often qualified: 'it is one thing to be God, another to participate in God' (CD xxii.30,3). We cannot be sure that 'in the next life we shall be changed into God's substance and become what he is, as some say' (N 37). What is meant is that we are 'united to God by love' (M i.20).

Some contemporaries of Augustine who had lost all belief in the old gods sought no replacement by looking towards Christianity. He described them as dismissing all religion as enslaving superstition. They wished to assert the freedom and sovereignty of the individual as master of his own soul in sailing the sea of faith. Augustine's comment (more unkind than untrue perhaps) was that the assertion of splendid autonomy would be more impressive if those who claimed to have shuffled off the fetters of all religion were not found to end up in bondage. Their egocentric enslavement might be to bodily pleasure and comfort, or to naked ambition for power and wealth or, in the case of the intelligentsia, to an endless quest for a this-worldly knowledge which could never hope to be more than relative and tended to dilettantism. (Platonism, which did not much encourage Augustine to be interested in natural science, also influenced him against the Aristotelian notion that knowledge may be sought for its own sake. He took it to be self-evident that the prime tasks of philosophy lie in logic and ethics.) 'Man is slave to that by which he wishes to find happiness' (VR 69). The longing for authentic happiness is the point at which man discovers God within. (One notes here the fusion of the *Hortensius* with Porphyry.) 'Do not go outside yourself', even by looking at the external world with its mathematical perfection; but return into your own personality. The mind is a mirror reflecting divine truth; but it is mutable. Therefore 'transcend yourself' and seek the unchanging and eternal ground of all being. Then you will find that 'the service of God is perfect freedom' (VR 87).

The tract's appeal to what is universal in nature and in reason is crossed by a very different theme, namely the affirmation of a divine purpose in history. This is summed up in the biblical antitheses between the wheat and the tares, the old man and the new, outward and inward. There are 'two kinds of people'. This duality speaks of the mysterious presence, in an alienated and secular society, of a hidden people of God. In this way the Platonic contrast between sense and mind become fused with a major theme taken ultimately from biblical Apocalyptic. This passage (VR 49–50) is the earliest occurrence of a theme which he would later come to orchestrate for full brass. Ten years later the two kinds of people have become 'two loves', two cities, Babylon and Jerusalem. More than twenty years later the doctrine of the two cities became the foundation of one of his greatest works, the *City of God*.

There has been scholarly controversy about the source or impetus which made this notion important to Augustine. Was it a residuum of Manichee dualism with its cosmic conflict of Light and Dark, of God and the prince of darkness? An alternative which has seemed much more plausible to most scholars is the deep impression made on Augustine by Tyconius, a theologian of the schismatic Donatists who dissented from his colleagues in holding that the true Church must be universal. His opinions brought him so close to the hated Catholics that he was excommunicated. He did not join the Catholic community for reasons that can only be conjectured—e.g. that a shift of individual allegiance could hinder corporate *rapprochement*. Tyconius' wrote an extant *Book of Rules* for interpreting scripture, and a commentary on the Apocalypse of John, the surviving fragments of which show that the contrast of the two cities of Babylon and Jerusalem was important to him.

A strong interest in the Apocalypse of John was not, however, confined to the Donatist schismatics. It was common to African Christians generally.

5 *Vocation*

In the lay society at Thagaste Augustine did not find that he had solved his problems. At one stage he seriously considered withdrawal to desert solitude. But that was never to be. Early in 391, on a visit to the port of Hippo Regius 45 miles from Thagaste, he was forcibly ordained presbyter for the small Catholic congregation. (Most Christians at Hippo were then of the Donatist persuasion.) His contemplative endeavours were abruptly ended, but he could not refuse. He sat down with his Bible to equip himself for a calling to which he felt unfitted by temperament, inclination, and physical health. He wanted to be a monk, not a busy town parson continually beset by unreasonable people. The old bishop who had ordained him allowed a compromise. In a garden by the Hippo church he built a monastery. There came to live with him a few elderly and retired clergy, but in the main the community consisted of lay brothers who maintained the house either by manual labour or by working as clerks for the merchants on the waterfront. Much less well educated than the lay society at Thagaste, which broke up on Augustine's departure, the Hippo brothers daily chanted the Psalter and biblical canticles. (Hymns with words not in scripture were only sparingly admitted to Catholic practice in Africa—they were a Donatist custom.) Though no formal vow of poverty was required, all surrendered property on entering the house; for most of them it represented greater economic security than they might get outside the walls. Wine was allowed for the sick, meat when guests came. On entry they were formally vested in a monastic habit, and wore a distinctive cap so that they were at once identifiable in the street. They had to become accustomed to being pitied by the crowd who were returning from the music hall or the amphitheatre; Augustine pin-pointed the essence of the matter in the remark that their life could be significant only in the light of otherworldly values

(S 46.10). 'He who does not think of the world to come, he who is a Christian for any reason other than that he may receive God's ultimate promises, is not yet a Christian' (S 9.4). Soon there was also a house for nuns of which Augustine's widowed sister became 'mother'.

He found that people brought their old problems with them when they entered the monastery. Experience quickly showed that those with defects of character, with a weakness for drink, with a propensity to avarice or other negative traits, did not leave them behind on making their solemn profession and statement of ascetic resolve. This evoked from Augustine the sad observation that there are crooks in every profession (P 99.13). He had intended his monastery as a battle-school for Christ's front-line soldiers; and many of his monks did go out to serve as bishops. But the Hippo house was also a hospital for some of the more striking misfits and casualties of life.

He composed a Rule for his monastery (E 211) which survives in two distinct lines of transmission, one the edition intended for the sisters in the nunnery, the other a masculine version for the men's house. From the mid eleventh century the latter was taken as a basis for the communities of Austin or Regular Canons, an order which continues to this day. The Rule is remarkably brief, and also noteworthy for its lack of emphasis on penitential motivation. But Augustine was much opposed to excess in mortifications. His ideal for 'Christ's Poor' was contemplative tranquillity with frugality and self-discipline, but not self-hatred, not the suppression of all natural feeling, and never the risking of health.

The rules of discipline were not casually administered. We (once only) hear of corporal punishment being administered to a young monk found chatting with the nuns at an 'unfitting hour'. Augustine's central message was that since we have here no continuing city, let us travel very light. Nevertheless his ideal, like his own personal practice (of which we have an eye-witness description from his contemporary biographer Possidius, who lived with him at Hippo before becoming bishop of the next town, Calama, nearby), has the stamp of deep austerity. He was continually suspicious of the senses as a hindrance to the ascent of the spirit to God, and thought the believer must be continually vigilant against all insidious laxity. Many passages of Augustine warn his readers of the fact that the corrupting and corroding effect of sinful habit begins with 'little things'. In the *Confessions* (ix.18) he even instanced the way in which his mother Monica, when young, had developed a habit of sipping wine in the family cellar until she became almost addicted. Moreover, one sin may lead to another. A serious lie is told to cover a minor peccadillo. A murderer whose crime has been seen by another will have to murder the witness too if he is to escape being found out (P 57.4). Little grains of sand can weigh as much as lead (S 56.12).

The ascetic movement and institutions of the fourth century sprang from one of those profound longings of human aspiration which are much easier to describe than to account for. The ascetic principle is as old as Christianity (Matt. 19: 12; 1 Cor. 7). Moreover, serious philosophers of the classical world spoke with one voice against self-indulgence as a generator of misery, none more eloquently than the theoretical hedonist Epicurus. Stoics had powerfully urged the need to suppress the passions, the desire for wealth and honour and indeed for all transient goods which someone may take away from the holder. In the Platonic tradition the powerful contrast between soul and body as belonging to essentially different worlds encouraged a disparagement of worldly things. Pagan Neoplatonists were hardly less given to austerity than their Christian contemporaries, and had their own holy men, inspired charismatics with powers of moral discernment enhanced by their frugal simplicity of outlook and by their renunciation of marriage.

In comparison with Plotinus and Porphyry, Augustine spoke more positively about the concrete merits of a lay vocation in the world. Lay Christians, he said in his *Questions on the Gospels* (ii.44), can do the things of the secular world and 'keep the wheel of the world's business turning in ways that can be put to the service of God.' He emphatically affirmed that a Christian who had the opportunity to become a magistrate had a duty to do so (CD xix.6).

Nevertheless the rigorism of his ascetic resolve was never relaxed. People who became monks or nuns and then left the monastery for the life over the wall were more than a deep disappointment to him. Ex-monks he thought very unsuitable candidates for holy orders. One widow vowed that if her daughter recovered from her sickbed, the girl would take the veil as a nun. When the girl recovered, the mother asked if her daughter could now be released from any obligation, and if the vow of her own widowhood could be accepted in lieu. Augustine thought that what she had promised should be carried out; i.e. the mother's duty was to persuade her daughter to become a nun. For if the girl did not do so, while she would not thereby exclude herself from the kingdom of heaven, her reward hereafter would certainly be diminished.

Penitence of heart Augustine regarded as part of the regular pattern of all authentic spiritual life. Austere frugality should be voluntarily accepted by believers as a self-imposed discipline (Augustine did not speak of such austerities as imposed formally by the clergy). Intervention by authority was necessary for very serious sins such as adultery, murder, and sacrilege. Of these adultery was far the commonest problem in his flock. It would entail suspension from eucharistic communion and taking one's seat in a special part of the church building reserved for penitents. The absolution and remission of sins is the gift of Christ alone, he taught (T xiii.26); it is Christ who has entrusted to his Church the power of the keys whereby on condition of faith believers may be absolved (DDC i.17). Penitents were solemnly restored in Holy Week, in the presence of the assembled faithful, in preparation for Easter communion. Augustine mentions pastoral counselling and private rebukes of individual sinners, but no regular system of auricular confession and private absolution which was not pastoral practice in his time. Restored sinners were welcomed back to communion by laying on of hands, and the line of penitents in Holy Week might be 'extremely long' (S 232.8). But these were special cases of serious lapses.

Even the best and holiest of believers, he once declared (CD xix.27), knows that in this life 'our righteousness consists more in the remission of sins than in perfection of virtues'. The baptized believer is both just and a sinner (P 140.14f.; E 185.40). For Augustine this confession of the believer's continual need for pardon was enhanced by his strong sense of the nothingness of the creature before the sublimity of God. Here was language to fire Martin Luther.

Coherent with this spiritual ideal is his ascetic longing to purge the empirical Church of compromises with the world. Some of his most alarming utterances in sermons and letters were addressed to delinquent or weak clergy who fiddled the accounts of the church chest, or who found that their duty of hospitality disclosed in them a fatal weakness for the bottle, or who gave an imprudent hug of consolation to a woman in spiritual distress and found that the relationship did not quite stop there. The duty of administering rebuke cost him much inward pain and strain. But he was sure that those who praised a bishop for being easygoing could only be wicked people (P 128.4). To be approved of for broadmindedness was a sure sign of treachery to one's calling. Augustine spoke with a hesitant voice about secularity within the church community. On the one hand, he freely acknowledged that no believer attains perfection in his life, and that many are beset by weaknesses and failures. On the other hand, when speaking of 'nominal Christians', baptized perhaps but not visibly admitting the grace of God into their lives, Augustine wrote that they are not authentic believers and should not be counted among God's elect. Similarly the episcopate included very worldly and mediocre men, ambitious for the secular standing and temporal honours, but essentially numbered among the tares to be left until the harvest and then burnt as worthless and injurious.

Dedicated without reservation to the ascetic life, Augustine longed to diffuse it throughout the African churches. He wanted town clergy to live not with their families but together in a clergy house. Naturally he did not expect all Christians to become monks. But he certainly asked 'ordinary' Christians to live highly disciplined lives touched by stern renunciation. Christ had given precepts essential to all followers, but there were also in the gospels 'counsels' or recommendations given to those who would be perfect and aspire to higher things. Missionaries in the African churches, and probably elsewhere, were normally unmarried ascetics living in the utmost simplicity. In a striking phrase Augustine speaks of them as 'fires of holiness and glory' (C xiii.25). But he was much opposed to a contemporary tendency for monks to think of themselves as having a quite separate calling apart from the Church as a whole, as if they were called out of the Church rather than out of the world. He strongly felt that they should never refuse the call to serve as bishops or parish priests where that was what the Church needed them to do. The nuns had a special social role in care for the sick and in rescuing foundlings. In antiquity exposure was a fate to which baby girls were peculiarly liable. But there were also many desperately poor families for whom the arrival of any additional child beyond two or three spelt economic disaster, and who could not be sure of being able to sell off to slave-traders children they could not afford to feed. Foundlings and orphans were a special object of care to bishops, and the church chest provided the only welfare service—inadequate, always a source of anxiety to Augustine, but at least better than nothing. His sisters had a vital practical part to play.

The growing expectation during the second half of the fourth century that clergy would be unmarried or at least would not cohabit with their wives is illustrated by several texts in Augustine's writings. The motive was mainly ascetic, but was in part connected with the greater authority which, in antiquity, attached to such renunciation.

The novelty of the monastic community as an institutional ingredient in African Catholicism and fear of Augustine's past made many suspicious that he was propogating crypto-Manicheism, an accusation which he was to meet throughout his life in various shapes and forms. During the first five or perhaps six years that he served as a priest at Hippo, his main literary efforts were devoted to anti-Manichee polemic. He set out to vindicate first the authority of the book of Genesis, then that of the Church.

Delicate ethical questions were also raised by the Manichees. They complained of the polygamy and vindictive morality of the Israelite patriarchs. In reply Augustine granted that at different times and places what is morally appropriate can vary. Ethical precepts did not need to be as absolute as people often supposed. The Golden Rule (Do not do to others as you would not wish them to do to you) was absolute; its application in different circumstances might produce varying answers. Moreover, what imparts value to an ethical action is the motive with which it is done and the moral consequences of the act. As an external, overt event, an act may be neutral in itself. Sexual intercourse is good and right, indeed a positive duty, in one context; very wrong in another. Yet Augustine allowed that he could envisage very exceptional and rare circumstances in which, with the motive of rescuing her beloved husband from death, a Fidelio-like wife might even go so far as to sleep with his oppressor; and that would be an act of loyalty to her spouse and a means of winning his release. Roman law, public opinion, and the Bible were against men wearing feminine clothing. But no objection would be raised if one used it as a disguise for passing through enemy lines in war, or just because the weather suddenly turned bitterly cold and there was nothing else available. The situation is relevant to judging what is right. Naturally enough, Augustine did not suppose that one could draw up a practical moral code on the basis of the exceptional and unusual.

The distinction between means and ends seemed to him of cardinal importance. Injustice would result as soon as means were treated as ends and vice versa (F 22.78). The distinction was one he could apply to his concept of time and history as a staircase by which we should seek to ascend to the eternal. To seek only goods in time and to neglect eternal good, worse still to treat the eternal good as a tool for obtaining a this-worldly end, is to act unethically. Even one's fellow men may become mere tools for one's self-advancement if they are not respected as deserving to be 'loved in God'. The supreme end of man is to enjoy God for ever. Accordingly Augustine translated the distinction between ends and means into 'enjoyment and use'.

In Augustine's ethics and psychology the will was a central concept and theme. Its operations are indeed hard to account for; but without the will's decision or assent to direct attention to a given matter, one can neither perceive with any understanding, nor acquire scientific knowledge, nor come to faith. The will lies at the heart of an individual's personality. It is directed to whatever is the object of love; and love is like the pull of a weight, dragging the soul wherever it is carried (C xiii.10). Love is both search and delight in its object (S 159.3). The grand moral question to humanity therefore concerns the object(s) of our love, or, in other words, what is supremely important, whether to an individual or to society. Most of Augustine's ethical criticisms of Roman society and government concern either the criminal code's more ferocious enactments or the way in which people spent their money. There the moral values or 'loves' of a society lie naked and open to view.

Plotinus before him had already seen one cause of evil in the perversity of the will rejecting 'interior' (i.e. non-physical) goods and preferring external and inferior goods. For Augustine, man's dilemma is that when he has seen what he ought to do, his will is too weak to do it. The will is indeed in working order for making choices, but the preferred choices are for whatever is comfortable and pleasurable. Hence the problem of the very nature of man, ever restless, ever seeking happiness in places where it cannot be found, knowing not only that he is sick at heart but that he is the very cause of his own sickness (C x.50).

6 Confessions

The old bishop of Hippo who had ordained Augustine presbyter feared lest some other church might carry him off to be their bishop. He therefore persuaded the primate of Numidia to consecrate Augustine to be coadjutor bishop of Hippo. The appointment (irregular in canon law) became surrounded by some controversy. The combination of Augustine's Manichee past and his extreme cleverness helped to make him distrusted. Hippo was not a city where people read books. Numidia was not a province where congregations expected to have a prodigy of intelligence on the episcopal bench. (Augustine noted that illiterate bishops were a favourite butt for the mockery of the half-educated: CR 13). Augustine's presence induced apprehension. He was known to be a terror for demolishing opponents in public disputations. Some did not quite believe in the sincerity of his conversion at Milan.

During his first three years as a bishop Augustine composed his masterpiece, the *Confessions* (a word carrying the double sense of praise and penitence). The work is a prose-poem in thirteen books, in the form of an address to God—a profound modification of the very Neoplatonic *Soliloquies* where Augustine was in dialogue with Reason. In so far as the work had a polemical target, it was directed against the Manichees. There are also dark allusions to stern critics of Augustine's biblical exegesis who stand within the Catholic church, but are never identified. The schismatic Donatists have not so much as a walk-on part in the play.

He wrote the first nine books in the form of an autobiography down to the time of Monica's death; the ninth book in particular is almost as much about her and his relation to her as about the development of his own mind. The last four books were to describe not the past but the present concerns of his mind as a bishop and expositor of holy scripture. They consist of Neoplatonic analyses of memory, time, creation, and lastly a *tour de force* of subtle exegesis of Genesis 1, interpreted as an allegory about the nature of the Church, the Bible, and the sacraments. The autobiographical sections illustrate a thesis restated in more theological dress by the last four books: the rational creature has turned away from God by neglect, preferring external things and the illusion that happiness consists in bodily satisfaction. Therefore the soul falls below its own level and disintegrates like the prodigal son reduced to feeding on pigswill. But at the deepest abyss of the ego ('memory' is Augustine's word for everything not at the top of the mind) the soul retains a longing for reintegration and completeness. This is realized in the love of God, and the example and expiation of Christ as the mediator and proclaimer of that love. God has made us for himself, and the heart is ever unquiet until it finds rest in him.

The *Confessions* narrate Augustine's conversion, and the scene in the Milan garden is told with a rich mosaic of literary echoes. Critical comparison with the Cassiciacum dialogues written soon afterwards shows that in essentials the later retrospect of the *Confessions* gives a reliable story, though clothed in quasi-poetic dress. At first sight there is a contrast between the stormy and passionate *Confessions* and the serene inquiring atmosphere of the Cassiciacum dialogues. Augustine himself first drew attention to the difference of mood, remarking that he found the urbane tone of Cassiciacum too secular and scholastic in spirit. It is nonsense to say that the Cassiciacum texts are more Platonizing than the *Confessions*, where the influence of Plotinus and Porphyry is demonstrably no less ubiquitous. But thirteen years have passed, and Augustine was now responsible for ministering the word and sacraments to his people. The *Confessions* show a profounder engagement with St Paul.

Augustine became persuaded that the inner moral conflict described in Romans 7 was not just a personified portrait of man not yet under grace, but a self-portrait of Paul with a divided mind uncommonly like his own. Man, noblest of God's earthly creation, gifted with extraordinary intelligence and capacities for social cooperation, has become antisocial by inner corrosion (CD xii.28), by a perversion of the will and by consequent imprisonment in evil habit. In a cosmos of supreme order and beauty humanity and its egotism sound the jarring note. The morbidity of the human heart is illustrated by that split second of shaming secret pleasure when one learns of someone else's misfortune, or by the desire to do something forbidden not because it is enjoyable in itself but merely because it is forbidden—a truth which Augustine underlined with the story of his teenage delinquency in stealing pears, not because he had any taste for them, but because it was a lawless escapade, a re-enactment of the fruit taken by Eve and Adam. He saw his own story as that of Everyman.

At first sight the structure of the *Confessions* is puzzling. After nine books of autobiography culminating in a deeply touching description of his mother's death and requiem, it baffles the uninitiated that he goes on to speak of memory, time, and creation. The last four books actually carry the clue to the whole. Augustine understood his own story as a microcosm of the entire story of the creation, the fall into the abyss of chaos and formlessness, the 'conversion' of the creaturely order to the love of God as it experiences griping pains of homesickness. What the first nine books illustrate in his personal exploration of the experience of the prodigal son is given its cosmic dimension in the concluding parts of the work. The autobiographical sections are related as an accidental exemplification of the wandering homelessness of man's soul in 'the region of dissimilarity' (Plato's phrase for the material realm far removed from the divine). The wanderer is like a dehydrated traveller in a waterless desert, or a lover longing to see the distant beloved (P 37.14).

Throughout his life he was peculiarly interested in the study of infant behaviour as a special source of understanding for the student of human nature. In the *Confessions* he set out to show that human beings do not begin their lives in innocence, trailing clouds of glory, which then become darkened by the adult environment. No creature is more selfish, he thought, than the baby in the cot: 'If infants do no injury, it is for lack of strength, not for lack of will' (C i.11). To comprehend the antics of adults negotiating a hard-nosed commercial transaction one need only watch tiny children at play. And then there is the misery of school. The acquisition of mental skills is a toil no less awful than the back-breaking labour to which Adam's fall condemned him. Augustine remarked that the intellectual worker's toil is worse, for at least the manual worker sleeps well.

Friendship is a God-given solace in a tough world (CD xix.8). To Augustine Monica was the supreme friend. He recognized that her love and ambition and possessiveness included a worldly element. Though a citizen of Zion, 'she still lived in the suburbs of Babylon'. But the exalted language of grateful affection towards his mother sometimes passes into the sort of thing he would say of mother Church. A climax of the *Confessions* occurs in book 9 where Augustine described a mystical experience shared by Monica and himself at Ostia when her death was approaching. They spoke together of the transience of all earthly things with their beauty and glory, in contrast with the eternal wisdom of God. For a moment they felt as if their conversation had caught them up into a timeless world. Augustine expressly noted that he was using language in his book which they did not actually use at the time. The passage is rich in phrases drawn from Plotinus, and illustrates how the Neoplatonists provided a language for talking about his experience (C ix.24–5).

Some of the profoundest analyses in the *Confessions* appear in the treatment of memory in the tenth book. The discussion is independent of both Aristotle and Plotinus. The identity and continuity of the self is seen as rooted in memory. It is a level of the mind which imparts unity to a multiplicity of disconnected experiences in the stream of time. Lying deeper than knowing and willing, memory is 'the stomach of the mind' (C x.21), a storehouse only potentially in the consciousness. Through the universal quest of humanity for happiness, it is also the medium through which the person becomes responsive to grace (C x.29). Augustine did not say that the natural man apart from grace already has God in his subconscious, even when denying or ignoring him with the conscious levels of his personality. To remember God is a conscious act of will, a decision. The love of God is 'no indeterminate feeling, but a certitude of the consciousness' (C x.8).

Yet he did not think God is found by humanity other than in the deepest abyss of the 'memory', present to the mind of the person who wills to order his life in obedience (C x.37). This reflection evokes one of the most famous texts of the confessions: 'At long last I came to love you, beauty so ancient, yet ever new.' There follows the declaration 'You command continence;

give what you command, and command what you will' (below, p. 288).

The tenth book continues with an examination of the extent to which, now a bishop, Augustine had come to self-mastery in face of the attractions bombarding his mind through the five senses. The passage closely resembles an extant text of Porphyry. In the *Confessions* the problem lay not so much in what the senses perceive as in the mind's consenting. 'I have become my own problem' (C x.50). The tenth book ends with a confession of self-surrender to the forgiving grace of God, pledged in the sacrament of the eucharist—a very un-Platonic theme. This leads, however, into an elaborate inquiry into the nature of time.

Time was a major topic on the agenda of Neoplatonic philosophers, partly because of Plato's remarks in the *Timaeus* about eternity, partly because of the paradoxes in the fourth book of Aristotle's *Physics* showing that time is unreal. Aristotle bequeathed a potent awareness of the complexity of the question. Augustine remarked 'I know what time is until somebody asks me' (C xi.17). Plotinus had said much the same, only less trenchantly. Augustine differed from Plotinus in that he did not hold that the self is timeless. The soul is created out of nothing. It is involved from the start in the process of successiveness. But then there is the question whether salvation can be deliverance out of time, a question acute for a Christian theologian who believed that God, himself changeless and transcending both time and place, had acted in time for the redemption of humanity. Augustine was evidently familiar with Aristotle's paradoxes, especially with his argument that the past exists no longer, the future not yet, while the present is an instant without that extension which our notions of time appear to require.

Plato has spoken of past, present, and future as forms of time which seek to imitate the simultaneity of eternity. Most Platonists spoke of time as defined in terms of the movements of the heavenly bodies. Plotinus defined time in psychological terms as the experience of the soul in moving from one state of life to another.

Augustine was of course aware that we ordinarily reckon time by the sun and moon—'a year being 365¼ days, the ¼ requiring an intercalary day to be inserted every four years' (GL ii.29). But in the *Confessions* the analysis of time is set in the context of mysticism as a timeless awareness of the eternal. So he did not want to define time in astronomical terms, nor as the movement of any physical object. Successiveness and multiplicity are simply the experience of the soul in the flux of history. Because multiplicity is a mark of inferiority in a Platonic structure, the transience and mortality of our condition must be in one sense painful. Time presupposes change (C xi.9), and 'change is a kind of death' (Jo 38.10). But in its nature time is a dimension of the mind, a psychological condition attaching to being creaturely. Indeed even the angels, themselves also created, are somehow halfway between time and eternity. But of God we must say that he is unchanging and therefore timeless. He knows past and future, but not as we do in a psychological experience of successiveness. Strictly speaking, therefore, it is a misnomer to speak of divine *fore*knowledge. God knows past and future but not, as we do, in a procession of events.

On this basis Augustine met the questions, Why did God create when he did? Why not sooner? What was he doing before he decided to create? It was a serious matter. Augustine deplored the frivolity of the witty answer that before creation God was preparing hell for curious questioners. The correct reply he thought to be that before creation there can be no time; time and creation are made simultaneously. (To put creation earlier by a finite number of years does nothing to change the question; to say it could have happened an infinite period earlier is to use words with no clear meaning.)

Pagan intellectuals attacked Christianity for supposing that whether in creation or in incarnation, or indeed in answering petitionary prayer, God would be changing his mind, or doing something new. They regarded it as axiomatic that only the everlasting cycle of the cosmic process, into which no particularity can possibly intrude, can be reconciled with the rationality of God. In Augustine's eyes this position locked the world into a finite system. The pagan cosmos had no room for infinity, but only for what is limited and relative. In the twelfth book of the *City of God* Augustine mounted a full-scale assault on the dogma of the eternal cosmic cycle. It had no room for creativity, uniqueness, the absoluteness of divine grace.

On the other hand many sermons of Augustine warned that prayer is neither informing God nor cajoling him into a change of mind, but is the way to conform our wills to his. For God's will and purpose are 'sempiternal'. Not only God but indeed man can will a change without changing his will, without being inconsistent overall with long-term designs. Moreover, Augustine was deeply aware of the dangers of disappointment in petitionary prayer. In such expreriences one ought to reflect that we often love the wrong things, and that if our prayers were then answered positively it could be a manifestation of divine wrath. Answers to some egocentric prayers could be punishments (P 26.ii.7). He knew well enough the hazard of excessive anthropomorphism. Of the unchanging presence of God to his world, he wrote confidently: 'The Creator maintains the created order from the innermost and supreme hinge-point of causation' (T iii.16). Among the things the pagan philosophers did not see he numbered the fact that time and the historical process have critical turning-points in the hidden wisdom of God (CD ix.22).

Augustine perceived the problem of God's relation to his world to turn on the question whether (a) creation issues from the sole goodness of God by spontaneous outflow, as an inevitable almost physical emanation, or (b) if the creation results from the omnipotent will of a wholly self-sufficient First Cause which does not in any sense need the created order. The former model tends to use physical analogies like the diffusion of light or the growth of a plant. The latter model sounds like a glorification of autocratic arbitrariness as a divine characteristic. Is the creation caused by an overflowing of divine goodness, or by an inexplicable decision of the divine will? Augustine did everything in his power to avoid this dilemma of nature or will. He warmed to a proposition found in Plotinus that in God substance and will are inseparable.

What then of miracles? Augustine saw order as the supreme manifestation of providence. But the omnipotent Creator may surely have an order and design which include not merely the natural environment but the special case of his free rational creation. Unusual events can occur as part of the providential purpose of giving an erring mankind admonition and instruction; that we call a miracle. But the spiritual Christian does not look for physical miracles. There is no greater miracle than the inner transformation of repentance and faith. For the post-apostolic age the counterpart of New Testament miracles, the

swaddling clothes of an infant Church (PM ii.52), should be
sought in the sacraments of baptism and eucharist (B iii.21). In
old age Augustine came to modify this position. Cures were
taking place at the shrines of some African martyrs. Popular
devotion prized relics (hawked by charlatans), soil brought from
the Holy Land, holy oil from St Stephen's shrine when some
bones reached Africa. Nevertheless, the more mature a believer
was in the faith, the less he would look for visible wonders
(PM ii.52). He did not encourage his flock to seek special
providences: the sacraments were enough.

Augustine regarded neither petitionary prayer nor miracle as
involving a change in the mind and purpose of God. Requests
to God for the necessaries of life, for physical health, for the
fertility of one's spouse, he did not think the highest form of
prayer; but they did not rank as unworthy petitions, like a
prayer for the death of a relative so that one might inherit a
legacy. They constituted an acknowledgement that all good
things are the gift of the one God, not of inferior pagan deities
(P 66.2). But except for sudden moments of arrow-like aspiration, prayer needed silence and solitude (QS ii.4.4). Augustine
did not follow Porphyry's argument that petitionary prayer
entails the (Aristotelian) conclusion that in God's providence
there remain contingent events and coincidences which are not
predetermined. On Augustine's assumption God has determined both effects and causes, but the prayers which God hears
are among the secondary causes that God uses to bring about
his will (O ii.51).

7 Unity and division

The aftermath of the Great Persecution under Diocletian (303) left the African churches divided. They did not agree on the point at which one could or could not compromise with the secular power; African Christians held strongly apocalyptic beliefs. They read the Revelation of St John to mean that Christ would literally return to earth and reign with his saints for a thousand years, a doctrine shared by Augustine himself at first—until he came to interpret the millennium allegorically of heaven. Apocalyptic beliefs commonly went hand in hand with a highly negative view of the imperial government as an agent of virtue, and pessimistic opinions were easily spread among the agrarian small-holders and tenant farmers of Numidia. The edicts of the pagan emperor forbidding Christians to meet for worship and requiring the surrender of sacred books and vessels moved enthusiastic Christians to study the heroic story of the Maccabees and their fierce resistance to Antiochus Epiphanes more than four centuries earlier. But there was a sharp division of ethical judgement between the hawks and the doves. Christian hawks absolutely refused to cooperate with the secular authorities. The doves wanted no confrontations, but only to live quiet lives of modest virtue. Among the doves were the bishop of Carthage and his archdeacon, who regarded the zealots as provocative and undeserving of the title of martyr or 'confessor' (the early Christian term for one who confessed the faith before the governor and suffered torture and imprisonment, but was not granted the supreme gift of martyrdom). Even before the persecution broke out, there was deep disagreement among the Christians of Africa about whether it was right for acts of vandalism to be committed against pagan shrines as citadels of demonic corruption, or whether such acts merely generated hatred of the Church among pagan worshippers, and failed to respect the sincerity of the pagan intention.

In 311 the bishop of Carthage died and the doves' party acted
fast. They hastily gathered three bishops to lay hands on th
archdeacon as his successor. It was widely believed that th
principal consecrator was one of those bishops who eight year
before had surrendered sacred books or vessels to the confiscat
ing authorities. The hawks brought in the old primate of Numi
dia with a very large body of supporting bishops, and a riva
bishop was consecrated. After some uneasy negotiations, th
Numidian candidate was recognized neither by the churche
north of the Mediterranean nor by the emperor Constantine th
Great. From thenceforth until the Muslim invasion of Africa tw
rival groups existed, each with its own episcopate, each recitin
the same creed, each with identical sacramental forms an
liturgical structures. Altar was erected against altar in every cit
and village.

The Numidian faction came to be led by Donatus, their bisho
in Carthage. The Donatists rejected the Catholic community
which in Numidia was a minority group both in town an
countryside, and despised it as the puppet of the secula
government, an instrument of political ends, polluted by
consistent record of compromise with worldliness. Donatist
refused to acknowledge the validity and purity of Catholi
sacraments of any kind, so that in their eyes Augustine was
schismatic and heretical layman. Group distrust and rancou
became inveterate. Both sides discouraged mixed marriages an
made canonical enactments against them. It was very commo
for families to be divided. Augustine himself had a Donatis
cousin.

The Donatists held with deep passion that they alone wer
safeguarding the authentic holiness and ritual purity of God'
temple, the Church. To defend their refusal to recognize sacra
ments given outside the pure Church they could appeal, witl
reason, to the writings of Roman Africa's greatest Christian
hero, St Cyprian bishop of Carthage, martyred in 258. Th
claims of the Catholic Church to be the one true communior
seemed to the Donatists utterly invalidated by their toleration o
the catastrophic sin of apostasy. The Catholic bishop of Car
thage, and indeed the bishop of Rome himself if he supportec
the African Catholics (as indeed he did), were agents of Anti
christ sitting where he ought not in the very sanctuary of God

Some Donatists even said that, instead of being some sort of holy communion service, a Catholic mass was a corrupt ceremony at which nameless blasphemy was enacted. Donatist tradesmen would not deal with Catholic clergy if they could avoid it.

To the critical contention that God could hardly have intended his universal Church to be reduced to one small region of the empire, the Donatists replied that particularity was the very principle of the incarnation; that on moral issues minorities are generally right, the silent majority being another name for spineless compromisers; and above all that the holiness of the Church is prior to and the ground of its unity and unicity. Both Donatist and Catholic agreed that Noah's Ark prefigured redemption through the one Church of Christ. It gave the Donatists satisfaction to think the Ark contained only eight persons.

When Augustine became a bishop, he found the two communities numbly resigned to eighty-five years of mutual hostility and absolute distrust. The rancour was well sustained on the Donatist side by acts of fearful violence against Catholic buildings and clergy. The zealots who had once assaulted pagan shrines now found a new target in Catholic basilicas, where they would smash the wooden altar over the head of the poor Catholic bishop if he were so unwise as to be available. The list of Catholic clergy who suffered maiming, or blinding when lime and vinegar were thrown into their eyes, or outright death, was not short. Augustine himself once escaped a Donatist ambush intended to silence him for ever, only because his guide mistook the road. Donatist bishops publicly deplored the violence, which was mainly organized by the rural clergy.

Augustine saw that it was essential to provide the Catholic community with an effective arsenal of the theological argument. He moved the Catholic bishops to hold a series of synods at which they could form a united front and common policy. The primate of Carthage, a humble man who much depended on Augustine to write his sermons for him, was very ready to give a lead if Augustine would advise him what to do. Augustine argued from biblical prophecies about the extension of God's rule over all the earth, not merely in Africa. Moreover, the parables of the kingdom (Matt. 13) taught that in the Lord's field both wheat and tares should be left until the harvest of the last judgement. Therefore no scandal could ever be sufficient ground to introduce division and to leave the one Church. Noah's Ark was a sign that it is indispensable to stay in the Church if one is not to perish in the Flood. For Augustine the eight persons in the Ark symbolized the Church's inner core of spiritually minded faithful, who had to endure the stink of less rational company but much preferred that to drowning. As for the Donatist claim that the rest of the Christian world had become guilty of apostasy by association, 'the whole world judges that without the least anxiety': *securus judicat orbis terrarum* (EP iii.24). Indeed 'it is a characteristic mark of all heretics that they are unable to see what is perfectly obvious to everyone else' (ii.5).

Among the marks of a true believer Augustine specified that he would always love the Church, warts and all. He did not deny that at the time of the Great Persecution some bishops had improperly compromised with the government. He too admired the Maccabees and their fervent zeal for God. But the errors of individual bishops could not bring pollution on a community or upon an episcopal succession. The grace of God did not depend for its efficacy on the personal sanctity of the individual minister, but on whether he did what God commanded to be done and thereby showed himself aware that in his sacramental action the whole Church is acting. For every act of the Church is catholic, universal. The sacrament is Christ's, not the minister's personal property, and salvation is always and throughout the work of God, not of man. Therefore a sacrament of baptism bestowed by an orthodox but schismatic priest must on no account be repeated. Baptism has stamped the soul with a decisive once-for-all seal, just as Christ died once-for-all to redeem. Admittedly, baptism given in schism could not be fully a means of grace until the recipient had been reconciled to the Church. On the same principles, Augustine flatly denied that, even when a line of ordinations stemmed from a bishop guilty of mortal sin, there could be transmission of defilement.

Donatist atrocities by the zealots of Numidia finally moved the imperial government to adopt a stronger policy of state coercion against the schismatics. Initially Augustine had the strongest reservations about the deployment of force by the government, and his doubts were shared by many Catholic bishops in Africa.

He did not deny the coercion to restrain acts of criminal violence was legitimate, but to put pressure on the Donatists to join the Catholic Church under threat of fines or of being deprived of the right to bequeath property seemed to Augustine highly inexpedient. It would produce either hypocritical conversions or a great increase in unstoppable acts of terror, or even Donatist suicides. Under strong government pressure, the Numidian zealots used to throw themselves over cliffs, and their deaths hugely increased the odium with which Donatists regarded the Catholic community who were held responsible.

Augustine hated violence. He sternly rebuked fellow-Catholics who spoke uncharitably of the Donatists (E 61.1; 65.5). Argument did not comfortably lie with coercion. Augustine's theology included the doctrine, surprising to many of his contemporaries, that all Donatist sacraments, including ordination, were valid. He saw that this would remove a major barrier to corporate reunion and perhaps, simultaneously, solve a problem for the Catholic community which was extremely short of clergy to staff its parishes. Moreover, the Donatists included many Christians of honest and good heart, among whom he felt sure that God numbered some of his elect. They would show themselves to be truly elect if they came to adhere to God's true Church.

In practice, the government policy of coercion had astonishing success, especially among property owners and traders in the towns, less so at first among the Punic-speaking peasants of the countryside; but many of them also came over in time, and Augustine then had the difficult task of finding fluent Punic speakers for rural bishoprics. Many lay people in Africa frankly regarded it as a matter of ultimate indifference for salvation which communion one belonged to. Among the peasants there were rice-Christians ready to go along with whichever faction better cared for their material interests. The misery and torment of the schism made many revert to their old paganism. In Numidia intimidation played a substantial part in maintaining Donatist loyalty, and converts from Donatism to Catholicism were peculiarly liable to be mugged.

The process of reconciliation occupied a very large proportion of Augustine's time and energy over a great number of years. Reunion was accelerated after a large conference at Carthage in

411 where Donatist and Catholic bishops confronted one another under the presiding hand of a (Catholic) imperial commissioner entrusted with giving a verdict between the contending parties. Augustine was principal spokesman for the Catholic cause. He persuaded the Catholic bishops to begin by publicly declaring that if the Donatists would take communion with them and unite, they would then invite their Donatist opposite numbers to share in the pastorate of each diocese. The generous offer cost nothing. The mutual rancour was too great for the proposal to have any chance of acceptance.

The government's intention in summoning the conference, with a predetermined verdict in favour of the Catholics, was to justify a subsequent policy of steady pressure on the Donatist laity. Could coercion be justified on any grounds other than practical success? Unfortunately Augustine saw how much good the government pressure was doing. In his own city of Hippo a Catholic minority was converted into a majority. He decided to offer a theoretical defence which would meet the anxieties of Catholic bishops who felt that no force or social pressure should be used to unite anyone to the Church, and that the Church had enough hypocrites of its own already without welcoming to its bosom a large body of alienated and explicitly insincere adherents. Augustine soon discovered that among the Donatist converts there were many devout and virtuous people he was glad to have. The process of conversion was in any event a lifelong affair, never a matter of a sudden flash. Even the sullen and alienated would surely come to see in time that the pressure to reunite with the Church was for their own good, since it was for their salvation now and hereafter. The lord in the gospel parable of the wedding feast told his servants to fill his table by compelling people to come in. A greater Lord ejected traders from the Temple with a scourge of small cords. To spare chastisement is not always the act of wise and loving parents. A surgeon cannot cure without causing pain, but his purpose is remedial.

Select quotations from Augustine's anti-Donatist writings enabled some medieval canonists to make him look as if he were justifying the stern measures against heretics adopted in the later middle ages. Augustine would have been horrified by the burning of heretics, by the belief, found not only among sixteenth-century Protestants and medieval Catholics but even in the medieval world of Byzantine Orthodoxy, that heretical ideas are of so insidious and diabolical a nature that the only available way of stopping them is to exterminate the propagators. In late medieval times people came to think of heretics in the way some today regard murdering hijackers or pushers of hard drugs, in practice difficult to eliminate without killing. They appealed to texts picked out of Augustine's works to justify severity, and ignored the numerous places where he wholly opposed torture and capital punishment or any discipline that went beyond what a truly loving father might administer to an erring son. Especially after the revocation of the edict of Nantes in France, the apologists for the repression of the Huguenots looked to Augustine for help. When he wrote 'Love and do as you like' (EJo 7.8 and elsewhere), the context shows that he regarded this epigrammatic formula as providing both a justification for the discipline of the erring and also a principle of great restraint in the manner of that discipline.

The Donatists protested that the actions of the imperial government against them did not feel like love; that it was in principle wrong for the Catholic Church to make use of force provided by the secular arm; that a body which resorted to persecution *ipso facto* discredited itself from ability to represent the word of Christ. Augustine did not think such protests entirely plausible in the mouths of a party responsible for an immense catalogue of violent acts against Catholics in Africa. Nor did he think 'paternal rebuke' of criminal dissidence amounted to persecution.

To Augustine it finally seemed axiomatic that action bringing one into the authentic fold, even if a little uncomfortable, is love. But of course the means used to achieve that end had to be carefully watched, and should not go beyond the imposition of mild disabilities on property owners or, in the case of rustic labourers, a moderate flogging.

One major difference between Augustine and the Donatists lay in the doctrine of the perfection of the Church militant here in earth. Donatists quoted St Paul's saying that the Church is 'without spot or blemish'. They granted that, even among their own number, there were individuals who received the sacraments and then turned out to remain as unreconstructed as before. But the failures of individuals, clergy and laity, were not at all the same thing as the pollution of the Church. This they affirmed to be the very body of Christ, the locus of holiness, the society of saints, guaranteed by the unquestioned apostolic succession of their bishops.

Apostolic succession mattered to the African Catholics too, for it was the external form that helped to safeguard the sacred tradition of apostolic teaching and sacraments. But it was not stressed except when they were speaking of the succession to St Peter in the Roman see with which they enjoyed communion while the Donatists (since 313) did not. Augustine thought that the Donatists could not plausibly claim to be the one true Catholic Church when they were in communion with 'neither Rome nor Jerusalem'. He did not think Peter personally was the rock on which the Church was built, though at the end of his life he noted that some interpreters took the text in St Matthew that way, and allowed that it was very possible. Normally he understood the 'rock' to be Peter's confession of faith in Christ the Son of God; and 'we Christians believe not in Peter but in him in whom Peter believed' (CD 18.54). Peter is frequently presented by him as a symbol of the universality and unity of the one Church. When he speaks of 'apostolic sees' he often used the plural (DDC ii.12).

However, like all other African bishops of the Catholic community, Augustine was very conscious of the fact that the Catholic *raison d'être* in largely Donatist provinces like Numidia depended on communion with Rome. He took it for granted that the Roman see could exercise a dispensing power if the rigorous operation of conciliar canon law was producing great awkwardness. He assumed that on African church affairs the African bishops could give an independent synodical judgement; but they were glad when Roman authority reinforced their verdict. Where that had happened, it was surely the end of the matter under debate—*causa finita est* (S 131 and elsewhere). On the other hand, the African bishops cordially hated it when clergy disciplined in Africa appealed directly to the Roman see, and when the Popes did not fully inform themselves about the cases in question. In the year 418 there was a notorious instance of a delinquent presbyter named Apiarius, suspended by his bishop; he appealed to the Pope (Zosimus) and received so benevolent a hearing that the African bishops were much offended by the slight to their autonomy and asked pertinent questions about the canon law under which the Pope alleged his authority to decide. Finally they themselves enacted a formal canon 'that none may dare to appeal to the Roman Church'.

Augustine much regretted the Pope's imprudence over Apiarius, and the same Pope's willingness to listen to other heretics, but significantly did his best to whitewash these affairs. He felt sure than no bishop of Rome would make the mistake of reaching a verdict contrary to the general mind of the episcopate.

Of the Church as the body of Christ Augustine used lyrical language. The word and sacraments entrusted to the Church were the very means and instruments of salvation. So the Church is the Dove or the beloved Bride of the Song of Songs; the society of all faithful people; the body of which Christ is so inseparably head that 'the whole Christ' is the Lord and his Church indissolubly together; the body of which the Holy Spirit is the soul. The Church militant and the Church triumphant were symbolized by Martha and Mary (Luke 10), symbols of the active and the contemplative. But in this life the empirical Catholic community is not without spot. Individual lapses and mistakes are many and great.

Augustine did not share the pessimistic view of his friend Jerome that the contemporary Church was prefigured by the Israel of the Old Testament, denounced by the prophets as having a unique propensity to apostasy. His portrait of the clergy of his time shows that both quantity and quality were low, and that scandals were not infrequent. He knew that among the laity some of the baptized fell into mortal sins, and then had to be told that they could not come to the eucharist until absolved. But mortal sins were grave matters such as flagrant adultery or theft. Venial sins were to be cleansed by daily use of the Lord's Prayer and by almsgiving.

Donatist language about the ordained ministry as the supreme guarantee of their sacraments seemed to Augustine to presuppose a much too clericalized notion of the Church. The ministry had a very necessary service to perform. Ordination was a sanctification by the Holy Spirit. It was self-evident that the presidency at the eucharist should be given to those commissioned by ordination for this work. No one (except in heretical sects) dreamt of lay presidency. But Augustine never thought of the Church as consisting in the clergy. The ministry was subordinate, a service. The continuity of the Church in the apostolic faith had its instrument and sign in ministerial order, but when in his refutation of Mani's so-called *Fundamental Letter*, Augustine looked for authentication of the truth of the gospel he looked to the faith of the universal church: 'I would not have believed the gospel if the authority of the universal Church had not constrained me to do so.' The converse of this sentence is not one that he would have denied.

Augustine did not think that God spoke to man exclusively through appointed means of grace, through Bible and sacraments, but these were certainly the central and normal media. In themselves both the human words of scripture and the water, bread, and wine of baptism and eucharist are frail earthly elements. But God makes them his own instruments, and to the believing heart they convey truth and grace. Without faith the sacraments do not profit the soul. Therefore 'believe and you have eaten' (Jo 25.12). Sacraments are signs; but 'scripture speaks of signs as being the reality signified' (Jo 63.2). Augustine's eucharistic language employs both the symbolist language congenial to a Platonist, inclined to be embarrassed by the externality of the sacramental sign, and the realist language characteristic of the Bible and closely linked with the eschatological theme of the actualization of the kingdom of God here and now. So we find a distinction drawn between the sacrament and the *res* or reality (Augustine did not mean anything material) which is conveyed thereby (Jo 26.15; CD x.20; xxi.25.4). Controversy with the Donatists led him to lay emphasis on the interior reception by the soul, while controversy with the Manichees prevented him from supposing that the elements of the eucharist are too earthy to be used by God.

8 Creation and the Trinity

About the time Augustine completed the *Confessions*, his mind was already turning towards two topics which, in the intervals of Donatist affairs, occupied his few leisure moments for the next fifteen and more years. These topics were, first, the exegesis of the first three chapters of Genesis, and, secondly, the doctrine of the Trinity. Both were areas in which pagan intellectuals were much inclined to mock. As an account of God creating the world, Genesis 1 seemed to suggest creation was all at once and instantaneous. Philosophers (or at least some of them) thought of it as a process in which the divine Artist did the best he could with formless matter. The story of Adam and Eve and the Serpent seemed a naïve myth. Most Platonists admitted the language of 'creation' in speaking of God's relation to the cosmos; Plato had used the word in the *Timaeus*. But they thought this figurative language for a timeless dependence; in reality the cosmos was eternal, and had neither beginning nor end.

Augustine composed five expositions of Genesis, including *Confessions* 11–12 and *City of God* 11. His first was an allegorical commentary in refutation of Manichee criticism. But allegory was vulnerable to the charge of being a sophistical device to avoid embarrassing difficulties. Augustine began a literal commentary, but that was never completed. About 401 he began a massive commentary on the literal sense of the book, which ranks as one of his major achievements. The twelve books of his *Exposition of the Literal Meaning of Genesis* begin from the assumption that, if he was not here treating Genesis 1–3 as an allegory about the Church and sacraments, sin and grace, nor could he regard the opening of Genesis as a piece of 'Creation Science'. It was awkward when Christians talked as if the Bible offered an alternative explanation of the world in rivalry to that of astronomers and other natural scientists. It made them and their faith look foolish, and obscured the really important matters which Christians had to say.

Galileo warmly approved of Augustine's remarks on this subject. Augustine's commentary betrays a strong interest in questions we would classify as scientific, but at the same time refuses to impose a decision in obscure matters merely on the ground that the sacred text was being taken by some as a handbook of natural science.

'Literal' in Augustine's understanding did not mean that the sacred author was giving a matter-of-fact account. Nevertheless Genesis did mean the world was actually created. Both the existence of humanity and that of the cosmos are dependent on the will and goodness of God. In this sense of the term 'literal', Augustine understood Genesis to be telling us what is the case, and not to be a complicated way of talking about the eternity of the world and an inherent immortality of the soul. He did not suppose that to speak of God's existence as First Cause is a way of saying that the universe came to be at the start of a finite period of time. Whereas most Platonists thought the creator should be understood on the analogy of an artist or craftsman doing his best with the recalcitrant sludge of matter, since the second century Christian theologians had been assertive that the creator also made matter, and the world is 'out of nothing'. Porphyry's commentary on the *Timaeus* of Plato helped Augustine here; Porphyry had there said that while matter is in the order of being prior to the form the Creator has given it, nevertheless there was never a moment in time when it lacked form. Augustine made this language his own, and (as Porphyry himself observed) it met the strictest demands of monotheism.

The notion of an instantaneous act of creation suggested to the philosophers a kind of conjuring trick. Augustine saw that the world was a developing process. Not everything in the world now was created so in the beginning. God, he thought, had created 'seminal principles' or causal reasons for everything that subsequently came to be, and this language allowed him to envisage new genera appearing later. Neoplatonic language about the evolutionary development of the grades in the hierarchy of being may have provided him here with a vocabulary. Plotinus' language about 'emanation' may also have influenced him. It was a Neoplatonic axiom that all effects are contained in potentiality in their causes. He did not think chance or randomness played a part in the amazing order and design of the world. 'Chance' is a term used when we do not happen to know the cause (Ac. I.1). Nothing occurs without a cause of some sort (CD v.9). Augustine was confident of the rationality of the universe; only the quirks of free choices introduced apparent irrationalities.

Augustine has a reputation for disparaging the feminine sex. This can be supported by selective quotation; but some utterances are very positive. He opposed the current exposition of St Paul's words (1 Cor. 11:7) according to which the male, not the female, is made in God's image. He held that men and women are differentiated in body, not in soul or powers of mind. On the other hand, he took it to be self-evident that the prime function of woman is biological. 'Had Adam needed a helpmeet in the sense of a partner in really intelligent conversation and companionship, God would surely have provided another man; in providing Eve his intention was to ensure the continuance of the race' (GL ix.9). He assumed that in marriage the wife's role is to be domestic and supportive, like Monica tolerating and tranquillizing even a hot-tempered and none too faithful partner. The partners were to 'walk side by side' (BC i.1)—perhaps regretting the custom, still common in parts of the world today, by which the husband walked in front with the wife carrying babies and baggage behind. Unequal in public life, husband and wife were absolutely equal in conjugal rights (F 22.31; QH iv.59).

A number of Augustine's sayings illustrate the commonplace that generalized attitudes to women are often determined by attitudes to sexuality. The man who had once adhered to the ascetic Manichees and simultaneously lived with a woman to meet his erotic need could be expected to be inconsistent. His conversion to Catholic Christianity enforced a positive evaluation of the body which was potentially at odds with the fact that renunciation of sex lay at the nerve-centre of his decision. One sermon proclaims the lawfulness of delight in the wonders of nature, music, flowers and scents, good food, 'and conjugal embraces' (S 159.2). In the *City of God* (xxii.17) he vehemently rejects the notion of some that in the world to come the resurrection will bring both men and women into male bodies, as if femininity had been a regrettable error by the Creator. On the other hand, he feared sexuality (not least in himself) as passing easily out of rational control. Even the sisters in the Hippo nunnery were warned that a woman can unconsciously and unintentionally throw a man off balance merely by a flashing eye (E 211).

The *Literal Exposition of Genesis* is not pervaded by polemical passages, but offers many discussions of problems concerning the idea of creation and the nature of man. The tension between Platonism and the Bible is apparent throughout, and it is possible to read the commentary as marking a stronger awareness that he had to put more distance between the two than he had once thought in his Cassiciacum days. Porphyry, not mentioned by name in the text, was a major figure in the background of the commentary. Because the book has relatively little polemic, its character is markedly exploratory and tentative. When in the *Revisions* of his old age Augustine looked back on the work, he felt that it was all too conjectural and provisional to be a useful book. The modern reader is most unlikely to agree with this adverse verdict.

An engagement with Neoplatonism appears even more strikingly in many parts of the fifteen books *On the Trinity*, a work he finally completed when he was sixty-five. The first seven books examine the tradition of the Church, first in scripture, then in the orthodox commentators and theologians. The masterful work written a generation earlier by Hilary of Poitiers on the same subject greatly impressed him. One of the central questions addressed by both Hilary and Augustine was one especially associated with Arius, an Alexandrian parish priest early in the fourth century. Arius had precipitated a major controversy by his thesis that the doctrine of the divine Triad could be reconciled with monotheism by conceding, or indeed insisting on, the metaphysical and moral subordination of the Son to the Father. Augustine felt, with some reason, that the anti-Arian arguments of orthodox writers, including even the best Greek theologians of the fourth century, had been less effective and forceful than they should have been. They had made too many concessions of principle to Arius' way of thinking. The last eight books explore the possibility of understanding 'three in one' by a series of analogies drawn from human psychology. The two halves of the work therefore corresponded to his antithesis between faith and understanding.

The orthodox tradition rejected not only Arius but also the rival notion, associated with an obscure third-century heretic named Sabellius, that Father, Son, and Spirit are adjectival terms expressing attributes of the one God. In short, it rejected the idea that Father, Son, and Spirit are either merely adjectives or full substantives. To philosophical inquirers among thoughtful non-Christians of the age, this made it look as if the doctrine of the Trinity defied rational understanding. Granted that 'God' is a sublime mystery, yet this way of talking seemed like an unintelligible formula, almost a liturgical incantation impervious to reason. When the subject was mentioned, pagan intellectuals laughed.

Augustine showed effortlessly that the concept of being both one and three is so far from being gobbledygook that simple reflection on the nature of human personality offers an immediate example. Introspection shows a triad of being, knowing, and willing. These three operations are mutually interconnected and of equal significance. Similarly there are other triads, such as memory, intelligence, will; or mind, knowledge, and love; or the lover, the beloved, and the love that binds them. None of these, however, offered for Augustine a simple ladder up to God, whose image in man is found not in body but in the mind, in freedom, reason, and self-consciousness. The analogies crushingly answered the critics who thought 'three in one' ludicrous nonsense. But their flexibility and multiplicity of meaning are too great to enable our minds to make a transfer of these concepts to God. The nearest and best analogy is reached in the fifteenth and last book, in the intimate unity of thinking, speaking, and willing, and in the affinity between knowing and loving.

'Analogy' was a term which, for Augustine and his contemporaries, did not mean a vague resemblance, but rather something exact and mathematical. In one place he uttered warnings that for talk about God analogy could be too precise, and end in being anthropomorphic (S 52). The unity of the mind and its operations he took for granted. He did not speak of the mind possessing independent faculties or non-communicating departments. Nevertheless, under the pressure of his search for 'vestiges' or 'footprints' of the Holy Trinity in the soul of man, his language could sometimes be taken to suggest quasi-independent parts of the psyche. The fact betrayed his theological difficulty. He could find no terms to explain clearly the distinction between Father, Son, and Holy Spirit. In their works in relation to the world they are undivided. Since Tertullian at the end of the second century Latin theology had spoken of 'three *personae* in one substance' (this last term carried no necessarily material connotation). 'Persona' had come into use because Tertullian found in the Old Testament, e.g. Psalm 2, passages which he expounded as dialogue between *dramatis personae*.

'Substance' was a word which Augustine thought acceptable with qualifications as a term for transcendent metaphysical Being, as long as it had no implication that in God there are both substance and accidents. But 'three persons' disturbed him greatly. God transcends all number, and cannot be counted. Perhaps one could say 'three' without answering the question 'three what?' 'Three persons' had long been hallowed community tradition in the Church, and Augustine was respectful of usage in both philosophy and theology.

Using Aristotelian language Augustine saw the terms Father and Son to be words expressing relation. So he proposed: The Trinity is one of relations, but not of substances. The Father is the fount or principle of Godhead, the Son 'begotten' (i.e. his relation to the Father is internal to the divine unity and has no analogy to the dependence of the contingent created order). The Holy Spirit 'proceeds'—the word came from St John's Gospel.

Latin theology of the generation before Augustine (Hilary of Poitiers and Ambrose of Milan) had already spoken of the Holy Spirit as proceeding from the Father and the Son. A Greek creed accepted at the Council of Constantinople (381) had said 'proceeding from the Father'; that Council had no western representation, and made canonical decisions uncongenial to the West. That it had sanctioned a creed was unknown to the West until more than twenty years after Augustine's death. There was therefore no reason why Augustine should hesitate to affirm that the spirit proceeds from the Father *and the Son*. He felt that this way of speaking protected the Trinity from being understood as an unequal graded Triad; it gave altogether more emphasis to the unity of God than the Greek formula did. Very gradually Augustine's formula entered the liturgical creed in the

West. Four centuries later this point became an issue widening the gap between the Greek East and Western Christendom. The medieval West defended the insertion of 'and the Son' (*Filioque*) into the Creed as resting on papal authority. Even in the sixteenth century the Western Christians who were taken out of communion with Rome kept the Augustinian formula against the original conciliar text. Catholic monasteries in South Italy, on the other hand, did not make the Augustinian addition.

Augustine's work on the Trinity had profound influence on subsequent western concepts of personality. Porphyry had thought that all souls had a share in the 'world-soul', source of all energy and vitality in the physical universe. The early Augustine used the notion of a world-soul. The late Augustine never said there was no such entity, but thought the young Augustine rash to assume that there was: 'For us God is not this world, whether or not there is a world-soul. If there is, God created it. If not, the world cannot be anyone's god, *a fortiori* not ours. But even if there is not a world-soul there is a life-force obeying God working through the angels.' (R i.11.3).

Making the world a god was not the only problem. Porphyry's language tended to locate individuation not in souls but in physical differentiation. To Augustine each soul is distinct, with his or her own personal destiny in the purpose of God. Moreover, the biblical concept of God he saw to stand apart from the Platonic tradition because of the stress on will, on what is creative, original, unique. So the term personality came to mean not only the non-material, interior character of a human being, but also what is distinctive and unshared. Boethius' classical definition of person as 'the individual substance of the rational being' spelt out in detail what was already implicit in Augustine.

The concept of a supreme Triad at the apex of the hierarchy of being was not a notion which could long be mocked by Neoplatonist minds without falling into hopeless inconsistency. Plotinus and Porphyry had worked with such a scheme, with their metaphysic of the One, Mind, and the World-Soul. This helps to explain why in *True Religion* Augustine regarded the doctrine that God is Trinity as being a truth readily accessible to philosophic reason, whereas the incarnation could be apprehended only in the humility of faith. The point reflects Augustine's tenacious hold on the Christian presupposition that the untidy flux of history is the stage of divine self-disclosure: God's saving word to man was embodied, at its nodal and focal point, in a personal historical life, and is witnessed through and in a historical visible community. Platonist though Augustine was, he did not think salvation lay in timeless abstractions. He needed therefore a view of history arising out of and expressing his central religious conviction, an interpretation which would simultaneously offer a vindication of faith in providence despite all the catastrophes of historical experience, and despite the impossibility of adopting anything but a sombre estimate of the present condition of human nature.

History he regarded as the object of a this-worldly knowledge (*scientia*) quite distinct from higher wisdom (*sapientia*). But the Platonic disjunction of the two worlds of sense and mind could be overcome by applying the Christian concept of history as being like a sacramental ladder which God can use, elevating the soul from the active life to the contemplative, from temporal to eternal, through the Jesus of history who becomes the Christ of faith (F 12.26; T 13.24). We are to pass by him on the path to the vision of unchanging eternity (S 88).

9 City of God

The conflict of argument between ancient pagan intellectuals and Christianity is as early as the first century (see Acts 17). The pagan Celsus' attack in the second century was answered by Origen in the third. Porphyry in turn attacked Origen. From Constantine onwards the emperors other than the excitable, shortlived Julian, professed Christianity. But most of the aristocrats and rich landowners, with the peasants on their estates, remained conservative, attached to polytheistic cult. Not that the intellectuals believed the old myths. The gods adored in the temples had long been mocked in the theatres and more politely demolished in lecture-rooms. But the rites were received ways of keeping unseen powers propitious. Neglect surely produced famine, drought, plague, military defeat. To abandon them was to assume one had reason to follow a superior way. On the question of temple cult Neoplatonists were divided. To many what most mattered was the inward purification of the soul; sacrifices, images, and external ceremonies of any kind were a distraction, at best symbols. To others the old rites were important, and became the more so as the Christians attacked them. Fourth-century Neoplatonists could be much given to an obsessive ritualism, in some cases with miraculous phenomena to vindicate their beliefs. They acted in a way that seemed to confirm the Christian identification of pagan cult with sorcery and the occult.

On the question of cult (as we saw earlier) Porphyry wrote with two voices. On the one hand he conceded that the old rites had the weight of immemorial tradition behind them, and no doubt propitiated malevolent spirits. On the other hand, he abhorred animal sacrifices.

About the time Augustine was ordained, imperial policy set in train a series of edicts closing temples and forbidding pagan sacrifices. The effect was to engender sullen hatred of the

Church. More than one anti-Christian riot occurred with substantial loss to life and property. At Rome in 410 pagan aristocrats held special sacrifices to avert Alaric's Goths, while the Christian clergy were begging the intercessions of Peter, Paul, Laurence, and other patron saints of the city. Alaric sacked the city, but his soldiers showed respect for Christian basilicas. Christians thought the catastrophe caused by the existence of too many pagans. The pagans blamed Christian neglect of the old gods, and asked why in Christian times disasters were more numerous. The fall of the eternal city on 24 August 410, which was of greater symbolic than political importance, provoked a discussion of divine providence in history, and debate whether Christianity was about to bring about the collapse of the Roman empire. Against this ferment of argument Augustine began to write 'a large and arduous work', *magnum opus et arduum*, the *City of God*, developing themes which had already appeared in *True Religion* which he wrote as a layman, but now set in an altogether grander perspective.

The title came from the Psalter, and was chosen to offer a conscious contrast to the *Republics* of Plato and Cicero, with whom parts of the work were a running combat. The writing of the twenty-two books of this work occupied thirteen years. He began at the age of fifty-nine and completed it when he was seventy-two.

The first five books replied to polytheists who saw the old gods as uniquely protecting Roman interests. But were not the gods merely deified men? Augustine made much use of an archaic study of Roman religion by the famous scholar Varro, replete with exhausting erudition on the most trivial aspects of pagan cult. One wonders why Augustine compiled his description of polytheism from a book written five centuries previously instead of describing what was going on in Africa until only a few years previously. The contemporary pagan intellectuals, perhaps in self-defence, developed strongly antiquarian interests, as one can see in Macrobius' *Commentary on Scipio's Dream* or his *Saturnalia*. Their argument against Christianity said that it was not the pristine tradition. Augustine set out to show, from unimpeachable authority, just how uninspiring and embarrassing the pristine stuff was.

Books 6–10 were directed to Neoplatonic minds who were

reinterpreting the polytheistic tradition as a path of purification, the gods being mediators between humanity and the highest realms. The Platonic writings of his fellow-African Apuleius offered many texts for debate.

Augustine was aware that his friendly but critical discussion of Platonism would shock the contemporary enthusiasts who treated Plato as a sacred authority in whose writings nothing should ever be modified. But in Porphyry he found a modernist reinterpreting the Platonic tradition in radical ways, and thereby bringing it remarkably close to the Christianity Porphyry hated.

Augustine rejected Roman imperialism, Stoic self-sufficiency and (for all his deep admiration and personal debt) Neoplatonic self-purgation as a variety of expressions of pride. The ultimate tension for humanity he saw as being not that between passion and reason, both of which can be equally vehicles of self-assertion. In the fourteenth book of the *City of God* he defended the emotions as good constituents of human nature by the creator's intention, and attacked the Stoic notion that emotion must be suppressed. Loving was a basic human drive; it should be rightly directed, that is to God and our neighbour. The old humanist ideal was to elevate human dignity to equality with the divine. It was to achieve that end that Porphyry's book *On the Return of the Soul* recommended flight from everything bodily. Augustine refused to identify the body with the root of evil. On the other hand he thought it illusion to suppose that man's highest good is attainable in this life and may be found in his magnificent social or cultural or technological achievements. Man's highest good lies in eternal life in and with God. This does not entail a rejection of this life's values; but it does make them relative.

Some passages in the *City of God* give the impression of wholly discarding the Roman Empire and all political institutions as power-hungry organizations for wicked domination and oppression by the powerful. Sallust's austere pages on the internecine struggles of Roman republican history certainly influenced Augustine, and he quotes with assent Sallust's mordant dictum that Roman society was characterized by private affluence and public squalor. Cicero (a casualty of those internecine struggles) saw that any coherent society must have a system of law, and would be held together by bonds of mutual interest and interdependence. Yet Roman history had never ceased to be a catalogue of aggressive conquests. How could a polytheistic society be one in which justice could prevail? 'Take away justice, and what are governments but brigandage on a grand scale?' (CD 4.4).

But now Christian times had come. Could justice now be established by an emperor acknowledging the true worship of the one God manifested in Christ? The young Augustine from time to time wrote as if the answer to that question was or could be Yes—as if conversion to Christianity was bringing regeneration to a tired and sick society and was making possible 'a just empire' (E 138.14); as if by imperial legislation supporting the Catholic Church against pagan cult and schismatic dissidence such as Donatism, the empire would become 'a Christian empire' (GC ii.18). (This last phrase occurs only once in Augustine's voluminous writings, but the thought is implicit in several places and he liked to speak of 'the Christian world'.) If so, it was not inherent in all government as such that it must seek a monopoly of power and loyalty and try to annihilate the Church as a threat to its own sovereignty. Moreover, St Paul (Romans 13) had given authoritative support to a positive evaluation of government as a providential instrument of order—if not getting one to heaven, at least hedging the road to hell.

The mature Augustine of the *City of God* no longer used such optimistic words about political structures. Constantine's conversion had been very welcome, but had not introduced the millennium. The nineteenth book analyses the overlap of values between the earthly and heavenly cities. Certainly they are utterly distinct, the secular from the sacred, Babylon from Jerusalem. The earthly city which is organized for power and wealth, comfort and pleasure, is poles apart from the heavenly city. The values of the city of God are sought even in this life by the Church which, to that degree, is identifiable (Matt. 13) with the kingdom of God. But though the difference is on a truly apocalyptic scale, nevertheless both cities are concerned with two things which they have in common, justice and peace, though by these words they do not always mean exactly the same things.

In regard to justice, the city of God had an obvious bias to the poor. Augustine noticed that the most vocal defenders of paganism were in general defenders of the old social order in which the poor fawned on the rich, and the rich exploited their dependent clients (CD 2.20). He realized how inadequate was private almsgiving and the Church chest with its register of paupers daily fed from the soup kitchen. The dimensions of destitution were too great to be met except by redistributive taxation (CD 5.17).

When a pagan intellectual contended that the Sermon on the Mount could not be put into practice without bringing the empire to an end, Augustine replied unabashed that retaliation for injuries was no way to make any society work, so that Christ's principles were far from irrelevant to the happiness and tranquillity of the secular world. An affluent society obsessed with wealth and power suffered the anxieties and all the diabolical pride and envy which haunted very rich individuals. With remarkable prescience of what was to come in the West within a generation after his death, Augustine suggested that the world would be a happier place if the great and proud empire were succeeded by a number of smaller states (CD iv.15). The kingdom of God had as much room for Goths as for Romans.

Augustine's language angered imperialist patriots. He was aware that empires come and go. He did not think the Roman Empire was doomed, as some contemporary pessimists were saying. Rome would collapse only if the Romans did. People cursed the times they lived in; 'but whether times are good or bad depends on the moral quality of individual and social life, and is up to us' (S 80.8). Each generation, he remarked, thinks its own times uniquely awful (S 25); that morality and religion have never been at so low an ebb as in their generation, and civilized values have never been more threatened. He thought it his duty to attack fatalism and to arouse people to a sense of being responsible if things went wrong. They could have a say in what was going to happen next.

Augustine did not define the 'peace', for which both Church and Empire strove, in merely political or civil terms as if it were merely the result of some fragile and transitory compromise in the unending struggle for power. He granted that only a strong government could assure people of peace and enable them to live without fear of social disorder. Roman law, which he knew quite a lot about, he treated with deep respect as indispensable for the coherence of society. One should not, for example, simply take the law into one's own hands when confronted by a bandit. Law and government are necessary because of the distortion, greed, and anti-social corruption in the human heart. At the same time this corruption goes so deep that there can be no true peace without the healing grace of God. The foundation of peace is a justice which gives each his due. True peace and true justice lie beyond this world as it is and will be, and belong to a higher order of God's purpose. Admittedly, the number of citizens whose lives are touched by grace is not more than a very substantial minority, but that minority can be of crucial importance. He well understood that government is more effective in suppressing vice than in stimulating virtue. Governors had a prime responsibility to provide for defence, public order, the physical comfort and prosperity, perhaps even the entertainment of the people. But it was not without a responsibility for civic virtue. If a proconsul or a magistrate were a Christian, then he had a religious and public duty to support goodness and truth and those concerned to disseminate them.

Augustine never wrote about political problems without an awareness that the system has to be established on the assumption that human cupidity will produce vast disorder unless there are restraints and penalties. Yet he still thought the world to belong to God; his world was not as ferocious as that of Thomas Hobbes, and he could speak of good government and legislation as dependent for its authority not on mere force, but on being recognized to possess a moral basis, and therefore a shadow or image of true justice, 'the eternal law'. Government was for him an exemplification of the providential principle of order imposed on the disruptive forces let loose by the Fall. In this respect order may not abolish what is wrong so much as adapt the evil to unintended and good purposes; e.g. slavery and private property.

The domination of one man over another may be abused, but it is the lesser of two evils where the alternative is anarchy and every man for himself. Augustine hated the slave trade. Whenever feasible, he used the church chest to emancipate slaves oppressed in bad households. On one occasion his people took direct action to liberate slaves from a ship in Hippo harbour, and the chest was used to reimburse the aggrieved owners. It was hard to stop destitute parents selling their children. Augustine was once nonplussed by a reasonably well-to-do tenant farmer who sold his wife and, when Augustine expostulated, declared that he preferred the money. Yet slavery was not an unmitigated evil when slaves in good homes were better clothed, fed, and housed than the free wage labourers who were the great majority of the labour force.

Order was so important that a malevolent if legitimate emperor had a right to obedience. The follower of Christ would render to Caesar the obedience of his body, and to God that of his mind and soul. Though 'like a traveller in a foreign land' (CD xix.17), his participation in political life, if qualified by his talents, should not be a passive acquiescence but a positive duty. Society needs people of integrity in the public service, as in commerce; people with the courage to withstand the Mafia-like bribery and threats of the powerful and rich. Augustine's remarks show that such people were rare.

For the Christian conscience, criminal justice and military service created the most problematic areas of moral decision. Augustine shared the almost universal view of the early Church that torture and capital punishment were unacceptable in a commonwealth informed by a Christian estimate of man. One must say 'almost universal' since there also existed an opinion, advocated by a solitary unnamed Christian jurist late in the fourth century, that the criminal code of the Christian empire should embody the retaliation principle of the Old Testament and be altogether stricter than traditional Roman law; in medieval times his little book became quite widely read. Augustine was much opposed to torture, which was regular in criminal procedure and especially treason trials; it made innocent people confess to acts they had not committed and left them maimed. Capital punishment he judged incompatible with a remedial intention; moreover, mistakes were sometimes made. On military service, however, he was less rigorous. He accepted that in self-defence or for the recovery of stolen property, force could be legitimate. Had not Cicero himself contended that wars should be fought only in self-defence or for upholding honour? For Augustine war was not a fitting way of settling disputes, and he shared the hope that in Christian times it might be checked. But he recognized that there would continue to be

unjust aggression which had to be resisted for the sake of values
that Christians held dear. When Sahara tribesmen attacked
Roman settlements, he wrote to the Christian military com-
mander exhorting him to consider it a religious duty to suppress
the marauders.

Nevertheless Augustine believed it to be both a religious and
a political necessity to maximize restraint in hostilities. The
humanity demanded by religion was also politically correct.
Wars, granted that they were sometimes necessary, must be
conducted with such respect for humanity as to leave the
opponent without the sense of being humiliated and resentful,
thereby sowing the seeds of future conflict. Prisoners should
never be killed (as was common in ancient warfare). If, however,
a soldier found himself fighting in a war the justice of which
seemed questionable, it was a sufficient acquittal of his conscience that he had to obey orders. But the general principles of
the internal criminal code of a just empire were equally applicable to conflicts between States.

Like Plato and Aristotle, Augustine did not see the business
of politics as divorced from all ethical issues, even though he did
not think the secular world capable of establishing a truly just
society.

In the *City of God* there are places where Rome is symbolic
head of the earthly community in the grip of satanic forces,
while the Church is at least an anticipation of God's city. The
old apocalyptic antithesis is being given its full force, thereby
creating the presuppositions of 'secularization' in the sense of
the assumption that religion is a realm of concern irrelevant to
the world's principal business of power, honour, wealth, and
sex. But there are also texts where Rome is given a positive
significance in God's purpose for his world, whereas the empirical Church is seen as failing to realize divine intentions because
of compromises with the secular world. Augustine was certain
that conversion to Christianity would alleviate some social and
political problems but not provide instant solutions. The anti-
Donatist writings show that he did not see 'Church and State' as
independent powers. Although he believed a Christian ruler
should support the Church and be known to be against sin, he
would have been greatly astonished by the medieval canonists
who interpreted him to imply that the empire ought to be run

by bishops with the pope at their head. He passionately loved the Church, but the failures of its members, both clerical and lay, gave him moments of dark gloom.

At the conclusion of the *City of God* he came to state the Christian doctrine of the Last Things: the earthly and the heavenly city have their respective culminations in hell and heaven. The absoluteness of this black-and-white choice gave him misgivings. The Church on earth certainly included individuals of dedicated, if often inconspicuous, devotion and goodness, who realized the angelic condition in this life. It also included people whose conversion, at least initially, had had a very secular motivation: they feared annoying a powerful patron, or aspired to a lady's hand, or hoped it might bring them luck in commerce. Some came in quest of physical health, and Augustine was never slighting about those who did so, though the catechists should teach them that religion had higher ends. A majority of Augustine's church members were 'average sensual people'. On the foundation of faith, their moral record was more like combustible wood, hay, and stubble than gold or silver capable of surviving the purging fire of God's judgement (1 Cor.3). They prayed God would forgive their faults and, for their hopes hereafter, they relied on God's mercy pleaded in the eucharistic memorial of Christ's redemption and on the intercession of the Church both living and departed. Augustine was never a man to suggest that the ethical demands on Christians are less than rigorous or that destiny hereafter is unrelated to conduct now; but he recognized that in the pilgrimage of the soul now and in the age to come the physical death of the body is but an incident along the road. In this life none is free of sin except Christ; and if, 'as piety demands', we add that Mary was free of actual sin (N 42), Augustine assumed that she was not born free of original sin, and is redeemed by her Son (P 34.3). Otherwise, the daily soiling of life in this world leaves everyone stained (CD xx.6.1).

Sanctification, therefore, was a long process which continued. After death there would be those whose 'sleep' would be disturbed by such dreams as would give them pause (S 328.5). 'Hell' Augustine thought not so much a physical place as a condition of the soul in blindness and alienation from God. Pagans mocked the notion as a bogy to frighten people into

Church. But the Platonic philosophers themselves thought no sins pass unpunished, and that there is remedial correction and discipline. Augustine agreed that for all who so receive it divine punishment is remedial.

The *City of God* is treated incorrectly if it is regarded as a statement about political theory or as containing a philosophy of history intended to discern a divine pattern in the course of events. In fact, at many points in the work the argument is designed to show how hard it is to discern such a pattern. Great powers rise and fall in world history, and the reason why is anything but clear. The unpredictability both of death and of decisions by human wills means that much is uncertain. The believer holds that what is incoherent to the mind of man is coherent to God. Disasters may move one to tears, but should on no account provoke astonishment (E 111.2). Augustine offers much more hope to the individual than to the institutions of human society, peculiarly liable to be vehicles of group egotism. In any event, no Platonist could easily have a feeling for history in the sense of a self-sufficient, self-contained process with its own observable causes and effects and with goals that are immanent within the movement of causation.

10 *Nature and grace*

In his thirties, in reaction against Manicheism Augustine stressed both church authority and individual freedom. But even when writing on free choice he had declared that without God's grace to rescue fallen man, one cannot be set on the right path. This acknowledgement of weakness was not a disparagement of reason. Cicero's *Hortensius* always made him ask about the application of reason to the identification of happiness. In his maturity, aged sixty-six, he wrote a crushing rebuke to a self-taught and opinionated theologian who adopted a wholly fideist position and thought reason irrelevant to faith. 'Greatly cherish intellect', he told him (E 120.13 *intellectum valde ama*). Nevertheless, he was also sure that sin warps the judgement, weakens the will's determination. For sin impels the mind towards external things, away from the contemplation of transcendent realities. Hence the need for authority to implant the 'beginning of faith', which is then developed and consolidated by reason.

After Augustine had become a bishop, the theme of man's absolute need for grace rose to a crescendo. The anti-Manichee *Confessions* have at their heart a sense that sinful man, hamstrung by selfishness from the earliest moments of infancy, is the prisoner of habits which are second nature. Only grace can restore authentic freedom. Therefore, 'when God rewards our merits, he crowns his own gifts' (C ix.34—a formula he often repeated later, gratefully borrowed by the Council of Trent in 1547).

The *Confessions* became an immediate best-seller, which won Augustine many friends and gave critics additional grounds for being critical. Among the opulent aristocrats of Rome, now beginning to think it need not be un-Roman to turn to Christianity, the exquisite rhetoric was admired. But the book was also taken to presuppose that moral compromises were pardonable. If, as Augustine repeatedly declared, continence could be had only as God's gift, could one not be tolerantly compassionate towards would-be believers who found such austere discipleship very costly?

At Rome by 400 there was a lay ascetic of British origin named Pelagius, popular as a spiritual counsellor in high society. After travels in the East he settled in Rome and wrote a commentary on St Paul's letters, partly designed to avert Manichee appeals to them. The east Christian theological tradition which helped to form Pelagius' mind was much more positive about human nature than was the Augustinian estimate. He feared both despair of human power to do what God commands, and also cheap grace. He felt it must be unthinkable that God would ever command the impossible. If man so chose, he had the power to keep the commandments, even that awkward one forbidding adultery. The substance of Christian worship lay in moral action rather than in the self-indulgent cultivation of mystical feelings. Did it not strike at the roots of endeavour if one held that from Adam each has inherited a flawed nature? To tell people that their will was corroded to the point of almost total incapacity seemed to Pelagius fatally enervating. No act could be counted as a sin unless deliberately chosen. Sin's universality Pelagius explained as the result of social habit after Adam had set a disastrous example. Certainly without the help of grace the sinner could not do all that he ought, and his duty is the imitation of Christ's example. But grace is assisting, not all-controlling. Oarsmen can get their craft to their destination without wind and sail, though sail makes it easier. There must be some moment when man actually resolves, really makes an effort, truly does something which is all his own. The doctrine that everything is the gift of grace, including the very will itself, seemed to Pelagius debilitating to the point of catastrophe.

The train of events which brought Augustine and Pelagius into open controversy was very gradual. The two men were agreed on far more than that on which they disagreed. Both saw humanity as locked into a corporately sinful social tradition. Pelagius insisted that sin is not physically hereditary, and therefore by free choice one can escape. God (he said) had given moral laws for the conscience; free will; remission of sins in baptism and penance to rebuild resolve; above all, grace to help wherever there was truly good will. The grace of God would

ve illumination to know what was right, and extra assistance,
1ort of doing absolutely everything. Augustine on the other
and was sure that if there was any point in the process of
scape at which humanity was on its own, there egotism and
erversity would take charge. For Pelagius sin and evil were a
ontingent, non-necessary fact. Augustine thought that, since
1e Fall, that had ceased to be the case, and pointed to the
atural will's recoil from pure goodness and failure to take
leasure in it.

Both men saw the human condition as misery ending in
eath. Pelagius thought death a biological necessity. Augustine
1ought the fear of death could not be so universal or profound
nless it were a penalty for sin.

Inherent in Augustine's lifelong concern to vindicate provi-
ence was his belief that no pain or loss is undeserved. This
xiom, if applied with Pelagius in wholly individualist terms,
1ust end by seeming to make God an arbitrary tyrant; or why
re some people deformed or otherwise defective, often from
irth? Augustine could never accept that inference. Therefore
1e said) to be a member of the 'mass of perdition' it was enough
• be one of Adam's posterity, as such excluded from access to
liss except by the merciful but inexplicable intervention of
race. Those who receive mercy can only be grateful for grace
1ey had done nothing to deserve. Those who do not receive
1ercy can have no ground to complain of a justice which all in
dam deserve. Even they can bless God for the natural delights
f this life. Though it is never said that the non-elect are
redestinated to damnation, Augustine was inclined to dis-
nguish his view from Manichee dualism by stressing freedom
1 God, not freedom in man (DP 19). God allowed but had not
ctually decreed the loss of the reprobate.

He thought it self-evident that human nature as now consti-
1ted could not be normal, could not be as the Creator originally
1tended. Before the Fall man had the power by free choice not
• sin, and no weakness of will hindered him from doing what
as good. Had he not sinned, Adam would have lived with Eve
or ever in immortality. But even in paradise Adam needed grace
:D xiv.27), not only as a helpful adjunct to his will but as an
1dispensable means. In his early exposition of Genesis in
efutation of the Manichees, Augustine once explained in pass-

ing the two accounts of the creation of man, suggesting that th
ensouled man may have received a divine inbreathing to rais
his soul to the level of spirit. That would imply that supernatur
grace was an addition to natural humanity even in paradise, an
that this was what was lost at the Fall.

Pelagius seemed to Augustine to be advocating a half-Sto
humanism, asserting splendid ideals but quite failing to pene
trate the abyss of the human heart. Moreover, though Pelagiu
had no such intention, his language was heard by Augustine t
imply that for redemption the human example of Jesus
sufficient, and indeed that the sacraments of the Church ma
not really be necessary. But Augustine replied that Christian
hastened to bring their infants to baptism for the remission c
sins. The universal practice of infant baptism required n
defence at all on an Augustinian view; it was the suprem
illustration of the sovereignty of God's electing grace prior t
any movement on the part of the individual's will, in no sense
reward for virtuous aspiration or action.

The question at issue in this last exchange of argument bring
out the major point that Augustine's doctrine of the corruptio
of man's moral being required a balancing emphasis on th
power and necessity of the objective means of grace ministere
in the sacraments of the Church. Grace had its focus in th
remission of sins pledged and communicated through baptism
and in the new life renewed in the eucharist. The implication
for the authority of the Church were considerable.

When writing on free choice before he became a bishop
Augustine had speculated that infants dying unbaptized woul
find their destiny in neither heaven nor hell. The Pelagian
accused the older Augustine of abandoning this wise suggestion
and of believing that a merciful and just God was capable c
consigning babies to hell when their parents failed to get then
to the font in time. Augustine agreed that such events wer
painful, but they were neither fate nor chance because in God'
world nothing is (DP 31). From John 3 he felt certain that no on
deliberately refusing baptism could get to heaven. If unbaptize
babies are condemned, that was not because of any persona
choice, but only because Adam's posterity shared in a collectiv
alienation. The admitted necessity of baptism proved origina
sin, and the flaw in human nature proved the necessity of fait

nd baptism. It is clear that Augustine's view fused biological
ideas of heredity with the idea of the juridical liability of
humanity. He quickly found that he had sailed into a storm.

The Pelagian controversy drove him to occupy positions which
critics, at the time and later, felt to be regrettable.

Among Augustine's critics the Pelagian Julian, bishop of
Eclanum (near Benevento in south Italy), stands out as having a
stature within range of Augustine's own. African pessimism
was not, he felt, the natural air of the Italian churches. The last
years of Augustine's life were devoted to sharp exchanges with
him, in which fair comment was mingled with vulgar abuse.
Julian picked on Augustine's language about the role of sexuality
in the transmission of sinfulness. To Julian Augustine seemed to
stand revealed as an impenitent Manichee, more influenced than
he himself realized by his decade under Mani's spell, hating the
Creator's handiwork, and denying that in giving man free will
God 'emancipated' humanity to stand on its own feet.

Augustine defended himself with intensity. He was vindicated, he felt, by the way in which all human beings regard sex
as a source of personal and social difficulty. In animals the
mating instinct operates only at certain times of the year; in man
the impulse puts him continually in trouble (S Frangip. i.8).
Shame is a universal phenomenon. Within marriage itself, where
sexual union is honourable beyond question, the act normally
takes place in privacy and darkness. Cynic philosophers so
outraged public opinion by copulating in the streets that they
had long stopped doing that by Augustine's time. Outside
marriage sex attracted fascinated gossip. The gulf between
dignity and animality made the subject central to much comedy.
Why are tabu words coined except to express humanity's combination of fascination and revulsion? Town brothels are in
special areas, not the main street. There is an intuitive sense that
sexuality can come into tension with higher aspirations.

Augustine repeatedly made capital out of an argument that
seems bizarre to the modern reader. The physiological changes
that make sexual union practicable are uncontrolled by reason
or will. Body and reason can often be at loggerheads, the body
stirred when the will and reason do not want it, or vice versa.
Moreover, 'sexual ecstasy swamps the mind', obliterating
rational thought (J 4.7). In this irrational and involuntary char-

acter of the impulse Augustine saw the ultimate demonstration of the truth of his view. He did not understand anything about reflexes. He therefore constructed an imaginative picture of the sex-life of Adam and Eve before the Fall (if indeed the Fall did not occur very soon after the creation of Eve). Their union must have been tranquil and under the control of the will, just as we can move our hands and feet whenever we wish. Their union in paradise was a source of 'supreme pleasure'. Augustine did not accept the old notions, popular among gnostic sects of the second century, that the Fall consisted in the serpent's seduction of Eve or that Adam and Eve fell by having sexual union before the proper time. He vehemently disavowed the view (which he had once held) that sexual intercourse was a result of the Fall But the Fall had affected it.

His considerable discussions of sexuality are conspicuously free from prudery, so frank that he feared being read by people whose minds were unequal to the seriousness of the subject Medicine was a department of science on which he made himself informed. His library included clinical textbooks and, while composing his replies to Julian of Eclanum, he studied the best guide to gynaecology. In any event, no one could accuse him of being a remote celibate who did not know what he was talking about. As a bishop he felt he had a duty and a right to tell married Christians what they might or, in Lent, might not do in bed.

As we have seen, his estimate of sexuality was marked by tension between his personal renunciation and a positive Catholic evaluation of the beauty of bodily form given by the Creator (e.g. R ii.15). But the most positive estimate could not eliminate the truth of experience that even for married couples sex can have its problems. The body can be disobedient to both will and reason, and (adopting an idea from Porphyry) Augustine saw that fact as a penalty for the soul's resistance to the divine goodness. So the physical act was, he urged, the vehicle for the transmission of the flawed human nature subsequent to the Fall. Were that not the case, the New Testament would not have regarded married life as surpassed by the greater good of celibacy—again a view shared by Porphyry. Hence 'the very root of sin lies in carnal generation' (PM ii.15).

Augustine boldly suggested that this hypothesis explained

why Jesus' was born of a Virgin (a miracle which, like the Resurrection, evoked much pagan criticism): from Mary Jesus took 'the likeness of sinful flesh' (St Paul's phrase), not a flesh flawed by original sin. Thereby Augustine injected a powerful and toxic theme into medieval theology, namely that the Virgin Birth presupposes that even within marriage the sexual act cannot be done without some taint of cupidity. In the twelfth century the presuppositions latent in this view were exposed and vigorously attacked by Peter Abelard and Robert of Melun.

Nevertheless, Augustine was aware that he needed to safeguard his ascetic stance against overstatement. When about 390 a critic of asceticism named Jovinian (himself a monk) denied that virginity as such is morally superior to marriage, Jerome's onslaught upon him became such a hymn of hate against sex and marriage that the charges of Manicheism came to look uncommonly plausible. To avert the consequence of Jerome's grosser indiscretions, Augustine wrote in 401 a treatise *On the Good of Marriage*. The book was addressed to nuns warning them that, while they had indeed chosen a higher life, they must not disparage Christian marriage. The physical delight inevitably accompanying the sexual act ought to be distinguished from the libido which is a wrong use of the impulse. He defined three good constituents of marriage in terms which did not include mutual delight. They were procreation, mutual fidelity, and the 'sacrament' or rule of indissolubility (i.e. the ban on remarriage after divorce or separation). This last point of indissolubility was one concerning which, in the light of Matt. 5: 32 and 1 Cor. 7: 10–11, he long felt hesitations, gradually moving to a strict and rigorist position in the later stages of the Pelagian controversy.

Marriage, Augustine taught, was constituted by the consent of the couple rather than by physical consummation. (He accepted the view dominant in Roman law.) And while the sexual act was primarily intended for procreation, Augustine judged it 'pardonable' if married people enjoyed conjugal union without the intention to procreate. Like Aristotle and St Paul, he laid stress on the mutual obligations of the partners (above, p. 271). He recommended the maximum restraint to serious and highminded Christian couples, and thought nothing more beautiful than the sexless friendship of the elderly. But he readily conceded, indeed insisted, that in Christian marriage the carnal impulse is put to

'a good and right use'. What he could not bring himself to say is
that what is being used is in itself morally indifferent or a most
natural act for the divinely created animal nature of man. But
then the Platonic tradition made him want to define the essence
of man in terms which almost omitted the physical nature of the
creature. He could cite Aristotle's familiar definition of man as a
rational mortal animal, but certainly preferred to speak of man
as a soul united to a body, or using a body.

Another major point at which controversy impelled Augustine
into the use of tougher language than many found congenial
was the doctrine of predestination with the related question of
perseverance, subjects felt to be so complex that eleven centuries
later the council of Trent wore kid gloves to deal with them and
gave verdicts which removed none of the serious ambiguities.
(Thereby it opened the door to the Jansenist controversy).
Augustine understood the priority of grace to entail the conclusion that God could not finally allow his elect to fall away from
grace. Predestination must imply that the intended destination
would be reached. So while human foreknowledge is not causative, God's foreknowledge is. Augustine could not abide the
notion, found almost universally in the Greek theologians of his
age, that the divine decree of predestination is based on foreseen
merits. Nothing in man, past, present, or future, can be the
moving or meritorious cause of God's election. The acute difficulty, that this treats God as a wholly inscrutable arbitrary
autocrat, Augustine had to meet with his dictum that God not
only predestinates but also imparts merits. And he saw in Jesus
himself the best illustration of his point. As being one with God,
his goodness could not be contingent or in any sense precarious.
He could not sin, we can. But if we are among the elect, surely
we shall rise from sin to fulfil God's predetermined purpose.
'The whole Christ' (above, p. 267) is predestinate.

Augustine granted, indeed insisted, that the elect can never
know for certain whether or not they are elect, unless it be most
exceptionally by private revelation. There could be only one
empirical test of election, and that a necessary but not a sufficient
test, namely perseverance to one's last breath, dying in a state
of grace. But God alone knows who are his own. Perseverance
is an unmerited gift of grace, just as is also the initial turning of
the will to God in faith and penitence.

Augustine's doctrines elicited vehement criticism among monks in North Africa and most notably in Southern Gaul at Marseille and Lérins. From Aquitaine he received staunch support. (Over many centuries a high proportion of the controversies about the Augustinian doctrine of predestination have taken place on French soil.)

Augustine's critics fastened on the evident fact that his doctrine of predestination appealed to a partial selection of texts in scripture and had to use force on other texts which did not fit his thesis. The New Testament text that 'God wills all to be saved' had to be interpreted to mean that the elect include representatives of every race of mankind (CG 44). The critics' case against him is almost reducible to the weighty charge that he had (inconsistently) strayed into 'curiosity'—claiming to inquire into matters God has not revealed and which lie beyond human knowledge. But behind the anxieties there was the reasonable apprehension that the Augustinian doctrine would produce moral carelessness. Many of his critics in southern Gaul supported his opposition to Pelagius and Julian, but were embarrassed by the arguments he deployed.

From time to time high Augustinian doctrines of election have been advocated in Christian history, as by Gottschalk in the ninth century, by John Calvin in the sixteenth, by Jansenius in the seventeenth. They have invariably provoked opposition which has sought to avoid the Pelagian alternative, but at the same time to preserve the freedom of the will and human responsibility. Augustine's own verdict on the discussion of grace and free will in a book he wrote for Simplicianus of Milan (above, p. 209) may stand for a summary of the problem as his opponents, themselves anti-Pelagian too, saw the matter: 'In trying to solve this question I made strenuous efforts on behalf of the preservation of the free choice of the human will, but the grace of God defeated me' (R ii.1).

Augustine came to enjoy far-reaching influence during his lifetime as a result of his writings, which circulated wherever Latin was read. Correspondents unknown to him used to write asking him to unravel their puzzles or hoping (usually vainly) that he would smile on their own theological efforts. Even Jerome during the last year of his life sent a most flattering letter from Bethlehem to tell him that by his books he had virtually 'refounded the old faith', and that the bitter attacks on him by heretics were sufficient testimony to his achievement (E 195). Augustine himself was never less than embarrassed to be treated as an 'authority' in the sense of not being expected to give reasons. Only holy scripture and, where that was silent or ambiguous, ecumenical consensus had such authority for believers. Moreover, his ideal was to continue correcting and improving his understanding to his dying day. In general he was not a man out to defend a position merely because he had himself once adopted it. His method with his critics was often to point out the difficulties in their position and to suggest that he preferred to live with his own. His work always reflected the critical independence of his mind, and perhaps his supreme forte was a rare ability to get to the heart of a complicated question. Without being a technical philosopher in a professional sense, his mind was well equipped, and his writing remains of considerable interest to the philosophically-minded concerned with the Platonic tradition. Much of Plotinus got into his blood stream, but he remained pre-eminently a master of persuasive speech. Despite his conversion from rhetoric to philosophy in 386, the effect of ordination five years afterwards was to put him back into a situation where oratory again became important to him, with the fresh conviction that he was advocate not of some human interest but of the very truth of God. A fascination with words never left him.

Edward Gibbon scornfully wrote of Augustine: 'His learning is too often borrowed and his arguments are too often his own.' A modern scholar would take out the scorn and invert the judgement. His learning was largely his own. He always had a fine library to hand, both in classical and in Christian literature (including Greek theologians), and his mind was richly stocked with classical literature. He knew how to use his books. As for his arguments, many are in fact often borrowed, especially from Porphyry and Cicero, whose *Hortensius* he could never forget. The borrowing from the Neoplatonists did not mean that his debt was not coupled with critical dissent.

Gibbon's scorn articulated the general hostility towards Augustinianism characteristic of the eighteenth-century Enlightenment. For that hostility there were reasons. The bitter wrangles of the Reformation and Counter-Reformation, producing long wars that inflicted vast damage, had largely been disputes between different interpretations of Augustine's doctrine of the Church and of grace. The sixteenth century controversy about justification by grace alone on condition of faith alone (a controversy which seemed boring and irrelevant to the eighteenth-century men of reason) was conducted within an Augustinian and medieval framework of ideas, and was a further chapter in the dispute about the relation between nature and grace. In the sixteenth century both sides made great appeal to Augustine. The Council of Trent's decree on justification (1547) was a mosaic of Augustinian phrases, so anti-Pelagian that the Protestants could not bring themselves to believe in its sincerity. Above all, the Augustinian denial of human capacity for perfectibility had, especially among Jansenists and Calvinists, representatives against whom the Enlightenment was in sharp reaction.

Again, Augustine stood for the ascetic ideal. The Protestant Reformation enlisted widespread lay support by its politically motivated aversion to the monastic ideal, which lay anticlericals opposed as absorbing too much wealth in support of its institutions. Although there is no fundamental tension between ascetic discipline in community and the doctrine of justification by grace on condition of faith, Luther had tried to argue that monastic vows are inconsistent with New Testament Christianity. The Enlightenment shared the aversion, but accepted the Counter-Reformation's Augustinian conviction that ascetic renunciation of natural goods was taught in the New Testament. Voltaire and Gibbon saw this inherent asceticism of Christianity as a ground for rejecting it: the gospel of grace and peace did nothing to make the world materially richer, and discouraged military grandeur.

Augustine certainly thought authentic Christianity otherworldly. It derived its reference-points and criteria from considerations beyond the process of time and history. Though convinced that this world is God's world, he did not believe that human life can belong wholly to the secular and material order, or that the primary values can be power, honour, wealth, and sex. Cicero had indelibly printed on his mind that they can be no road to happiness, either for the individual or for society.

Index

Short reading list

The edition of Augustine by the Benedictines of St Maur (Paris, 1679–1700), often reprinted, is in J. P. Migne, *Patrologia Latina* (Paris, 1841–2). Further sermons in G. Morin, *Sermones post Maurinos reperti* (Rome, 1930) and C. Lambot, *Sermones Selecti* (Utrecht, 1950). A guide to these in P. P. Verbraken, *Études critiques sur les sermons authentiques de S. Augustin* (Steenbrugge, 1976).

Many principal works have modern editions in the two series, Corpus Scriptorum Ecclesiasticorum Latinorum and Corpus Christianorum.

For a high proportion English translations exist, such as in the Oxford Library of the Fathers (1838–81), a series edited by M. Dods (T. & T. Clark, and Eerdmans), and three recent series, Library of Christian Classics, Fathers of the Church, and Ancient Christian Writers. Penguin translations of *Confessions* (R. Pine-Coffin, London, 1961) and *the City of God* (H. Bettenson, London, 1972, new ed. 1984). The best edition of the *Confessions* is by A. Solignac (Paris, 1962).

For biography without the theology see the excellent Life by Peter Brown (London, 1967). On the ideas see E. Gilson, *The Philosophy of St Augustine* (Eng. tr., London, 1960); J. Burnaby, *Amor Dei* (London, 1938); G. Bonner, *Augustine, Life and Controversies* (London, 1964, new ed. Norwich, 1986); E. TeSelle, *Augustine the Theologian* (New York, 1970); R. A. Markus (ed.), *Augustine: A Collection of Critical Essays* (New York, 1972); on the Church, R. F. Evans, *One and Holy* (London, 1972); on ethics, H. A. Deane, *The Political and Social Ideas of St Augustine* (Columbia, paperback 1963). On the Donatist schism: W. H. C. Frend, *The Donatist Church* (Oxford, 1952, reprinted 1985). Neoplatonism: J. J. O'Meara, *The Young Augustine* (London, 1954, paperback 1980); G. R. Evans, *Augustine on Evil* (Cambridge, 1982); R. Sorabji, *Time, Creation and the Continuum* (London, 1983); Paul Henry, *The Path to Transcendence* (Eng. Tr. Pittsburgh, 1981); P. Courcelle, *Late Latin Writers and their Greek Sources* (Eng. Tr., Harvard, 1969). H. Hagendahl, *Augustine and the Latin Classics* (Gothenburg, 1967).

Plotinus is edited and translated by A. H. Armstrong, Loeb Classical Library. An annual survey of literature on Augustine appears in *Revue des études augustiniennes* (Paris).